T0323791

THE CIVIL WAR INCOME TAX AND THE REPUBLICAN PARTY 1861–1872

THE CIVIL WAR INCOME TAX AND THE REPUBLICAN PARTY 1861–1872

Christopher Shepard

Algora Publishing
New York

Library of Congress Cataloging-in-Publication Data —

Shepard, Christopher Michael.
  The Civil War income tax and the Republican Party, 1861-1872 / Christopher Shepard.
    p. cm.
  Includes bibliographical references and index.
    ISBN 978-0-87586-786-1 (trade paper: alk. paper) — ISBN 978-0-87586-787-8
(case laminate: alk. paper) 978-0-87586-788-5 — ISBN 1. Income tax—United States—
History—19th century. 2. Republican Party (U.S.: 1854-)—History. 3. United States—
History—Civil War, 1861-1865—Finance. I. Title.
  HJ4651.S54 2010
  336.240973'09034—dc22
                          2010000099

Printed in the United States

I dedicate this work to my wife Joanna, for loving and believing in me.

Table of Contents

Preface and Acknowledgments

I became interested in the subject of the Republican Party and the Civil War income tax when I was a graduate student at the College of Charleston/Citadel Joint Program in History. I had a long-standing deep interest in the two main political parties and the changes that have occurred in them throughout time. Having been told repeatedly that the Republican Party of today is completely different from its original nature, I certainly saw evidence that it was true, due in large part to the "conservative" takeover by the Barry Goldwater, Ronald Reagan and Newt Gingrich forces. That was until I ran across a book by Edwin Robert Anderson Seligman called *The Income Tax*; I was stunned to discover that Radical Republicans of the Civil War and Reconstruction period — such honorable men as Thaddeus Stevens, Justin Morrill, Noah Davis, Charles Sumner and James Garfield — advocated the same principles that are promoted religiously today by Grand Old Party members. I began to research the topic more thoroughly, but soon realized how little research had been published on this topic, fascinating as it is.

During the debate over the Civil War income tax in its later stages, the Republican Party split into factions: the Northeastern and Western wing, which mostly opposed the measure, and the Midwestern and Southern wing, which mostly supported the income tax. Each side strongly pushed a viewpoint that was based upon the make-up of their constituencies. For instances, many Northeastern Republicans represented wealthy industrial capitalists that were paying the majority of the income tax bill, so understandably they were vehemently opposed to it. On the other hand, Midwestern Party members were from mainly poor agricultural states that were taxed little, if at all. This deep divide led to contentious debates in the halls of Congress that continued for almost an entire decade.

Upon the completion of my research, I ultimately concluded that, in many respects, there has not been much alteration in philosophy throughout the history of the Republican Party. Without question, numerous Republicans have championed an income tax, but, for the most part, an anti-income tax ideology permeates the party faithful. I argue in this work that the conservative economic wing of the party, which despises tax, has not simply had control of the party for the past half-century; it has held a strong place and shaped the principles of the Party of Lincoln for all of its history.

I would first like to thank my parents, Michael and Bettye Jean Shepard, for giving me the foundation to write this work. I would also like to thank my history professors at the College of Charleston, especially Dr. George Hopkins, my thesis director, Dr. Stuart Knee and Dr. Bernard Powers.

My colleagues and students at James Island Christian School offered inspiration and in many ways lifted my spirit.

"Sir, the income tax must go. It must not be continued. It has already lived too long for the good of the country."[1]

"I think the principle of taxing a man who is worth twenty thousand dollars more in proportion to his wealth is an unjust one."[2]

"In a republican form of government the true theory is to make no distinctions as to persons in the rates of taxation. Recognizing no class for special favors, we ought not create a class for special burdens."[3]

These quotes may sound like something out of a recent right-wing Republican campaign rally. Certainly, numerous members of the Grand Old Party in the last half-century have articulated such scorching rhetoric against the income tax. These words conjure images of anti-income tax Republicans such as Ronald Reagan, Newt Gingrich, Tom Delay or George W. Bush giving firebrand speeches to the core of their party's base. The Republican Party consistently presents itself as the party of lower taxes, and, in some cases, sponsors the elimination of the income tax in favor of other forms of taxation — for example, a national sales tax. Was it always this way? When did this opposition to taxes begin in the Party? Obviously, this principle of the G.O.P. started somewhere, and surprisingly that

---

[1] *The Congressional Globe: Official Proceedings of Congress, 41st Congress, 2nd Session* (Washington, D.C.: John C. Rives, 1870), 4709.

[2] *The Congressional Globe: Official Proceedings of Congress, 38th Congress, 1st Session* (Washington, D.C.: John C. Rives, 1864), 1876.

[3] *The Congressional Globe: Official Proceedings of Congress, 39th Congress, 1st Session* (Washington, D.C.: John C. Rives, 1866), 2437.

somewhere was early in the history of the party, in the Civil War and Reconstruction eras.

No Republican in the last ten, twenty, fifty or even one hundred years, said
the lines quotes above. Antislavery activists spoke those words on the House and
Senate floors as they debated the future of the Civil War income tax first implemented in 1861. The first quote was by Massachusetts Senator Charles Sumner,
who infamously was beaten on the Senate floor for speaking out against the institution of slavery. Republican House Majority Leader Thaddeus Stevens of Pennsylvania is credited with the second quote, and the third is from Justin Morrill of
Vermont. Although the Republicans of this period have been identified as "liberal"
(chiefly because of their actions on equal rights and ending slavery), their views
on economic issues can be deemed quite conservative, especially with reference
to the income tax. Indeed, these Grand Old Party members gave arguments that
have been repeated by current and recently elected Republican officials — lower
taxes, flat tax rates, and even total annihilation of the income tax. Members like
Sumner, Stevens and Morrill shaped the economic views of the Republican Party
that would remain a strong portion of its platform for the next one hundred and
forty years.

Few works have investigated the topic of the Civil War income tax and the
Republican Party, mostly due to the fact that the Republicans were concerned
with other pressing issues at that time. The income tax was a minor issue compared to winning a war, ending slavery, and finding ways to promote equality and
help the newly-freed blacks. Historians mostly have focused on addressing those
integral subjects rather than the income tax. For the historians who attempted to
explain why scores of Republicans, mainly in the Northeast, chose to oppose the
income tax fall into two major categories: Republicans always despised internal
taxes, or Republicans supported the interests of industrial and wealthy areas.

Several historians have asserted the Republicans, in general, disputed the income tax for the reason that it was counterproductive to their view of how best
to advance the growth of the American economy. To these scholars, the Republicans represented the old ideologies of the Whig Party and the American System,
which preferred tariffs to internal taxation. In *The Greatest Nation of the Earth: Republican Economic Policies During the Civil War*, Heather Cox Richardson pointed out
that, although Republicans initially created the income tax to support the government during the Civil War, apprehension grew steadily as the war ended and
the nation moved into Reconstruction. "National taxation did not play a part in

the initial Republican program to build the country," Richardson noted. "Republicans feared and hated internal taxation, for they believed that unfettered accumulation of private property enriched the nation by creating a strong incentive to labor."[1] Alexander Harris added to that reasoning in his work, *A Review of Political Conflict in America, From the Commencement of the Anti-Slavery Agitation to the Close of Reconstruction.* Harris contended that since Republicans were opposed to producing a federal income tax, they "steadily resisted the enactment of a sufficient internal revenue law as long as possible." To Harris, the mounting debt of the Civil War forced Republicans to accept the tax as part of the overall revenue stream for the United States government.[2] In *Refinancing America: The Republican Antitax Agenda,* author Sheldon Pollack acknowledged that Republicans, although foes of internal taxes, eventually backed an income tax "purely for instrumental purposes, willing to accept the known evil rather than face that which they truly dreaded further down the line." Remarking that what the Republicans actually feared was high progressive tax rates that would radically redistribute the wealth of the nation, Pollack showed that in order to avoid this disaster, Republicans reluctantly supported a small income tax even if they found it morally repugnant; anyway, they could rescind it when it was no longer necessary.[3]

Other historians, however, presented a different argument as to why Republicans began to oppose the income tax. It was not because Republicans had always abhorred internal taxation; they believed that, as the Civil War came to a close, Republicans who had primarily concentrated on the slavery issue now preoccupied themselves with moving the United States economy forward. They were more receptive to the needs of the industrial and wealthy classes who wanted the tax repealed since they were the only ones footing the bill.

In his essay, "The Income Tax," Edwin Robert Anderson Seligman said that Republican opposition to the tax did not have to do with party philosophy, but that they "represented the great industrial centers." In fact, Seligman indicated that western Republicans enthusiastically defended the tax, even as the Northeastern Republicans opposed it. Seligman explained that the G.O.P. did

---

[1] Heather Cox Richardson, *The Greatest Nation of the Earth: Republican Economic Policies During the Civil War* (Cambridge: Harvard University Press, 1997), 112.

[2] Alexander Harris, *A Review of Political Conflict in America, From the Commencement of the Anti-Slavery Agitation to the Close of the Southern Reconstruction: Comprising Also a Resume of the Career of Thaddeus Stevens, Being a Survey of the Struggle of Parties, Which Destroyed the Republic and Virtually Monarchized Its Government* (New York: T.H. Pollock Publishers, 1876), 296.

[3] Sheldon D. Pollack, *Refinancing America: The Republican Antitax Agenda* (New York: State University of New York Press, 2003), 24.

not combat the tax in general, but members of the party who represented more industrious and rich areas did disagree with it.[1] Elmer Ellis alluded to this same argument in his essay, "Public Opinion and the Income Tax, 1860–1900." In it, he revealed that the Republicans became "the most consistent defender of those economic interests which would gain by having no income tax."[2] Making a similar judgment was W. Elliot Brownlee. "Congressional Republicans," he wrote in his book, *Federal Taxation in America: A Short History*, "generally wanted to respond to the demands of the extremely affluent citizens, who had accepted the income tax only as an emergency measure and now lobbied vigorously to ensure first the reduction of the tax and then it discontinuance at its sunset date of 1870."[3] John F. Witte stated in his work, *The Politics and Development of the Federal Income Tax*, that the Republicans represented wealthier areas in the New England region, and many of their constituents bellowed for the income tax to cease because they were the ones paying most of the tax. The elected officials of the Grand Old Party had to either sink or swim, and most chose to swim with their more prosperous citizenry.[4]

In *The Great Tax Wars Lincoln to Wilson: The Fierce Battles Over Money and Power that Transformed the Nation*, Steven R. Weisman observed that Republicans were "more sensitive instead to the demands of the growing number of wealthy entrepreneurs, investors and tycoons, who were at their moment of maximum influence."[5] These historians felt that the Republicans only opposed the income tax because of the interests they represented, and not because they were philosophically against the tax, as others have argued. Instead, they pointed to the fact that Republicans not only had created the income tax in the first place and backed it throughout the war, but that when the Civil War was over, Western Republicans still championed it. In order to remain politically relevant in the Northeast, they reasoned, the Republicans had to respond to the cries of the people they represented, and the wealthy classes and businesses contributed to campaigns

---

[1] Edwin Robert Anderson Seligman, "The Income Tax," *Political Science Quarterly* 9 no. 4 (December 1894): 620.

[2] Elmer Ellis, "Public Opinion and the Income Tax, 1860-1900," *The Mississippi Valley Historical Review* 27 no. 2 (September 1940): 225-226.

[3] W. Elliot Brownlee, *Federal Taxation in America: A Short History* (New York: Cambridge University Press, 1996), 29.

[4] John F. Witte, *The Politics and Development of the Federal Income Tax* (Madison: The University of Wisconsin Press, 1985), 70.

[5] Steven R. Weisman, *The Great Tax wars Lincoln to Wilson: The Fierce Battles Over Money and Power that Transformed the Nation* (New York: Simon and Schuster, 2002), 100.

and voted in elections. Northern Republicans had no other option but to support the repeal of the income tax.

Both groups made compelling arguments as to why Republicans opposed the income tax in the aftermath of the Civil War. Although historians have attempted to explain their rationale, none has really delved into the effects of it on the party's future. This book will show that, at the end of the debate over the income tax, the anti-income tax forces in the Republican Party dominated and shaped the policies of the party for most of its history. The great majority of Republicans today offer the same arguments that Republicans during the war and Reconstruction utilized in opposition to the income tax.

Chapter 1. The American System

"It might be demonstrated that the most productive system of finance will always be the least burdensome." — Alexander Hamilton

"By the direct tax system, none can escape... he is to be perpetually haunted and harassed by the tax-gatherer." — Whig Campaign Circular, 1843.

To understand why the Republicans eventually combated the Civil War income tax, it is important to mention how they cultivated their concepts on economic policies. The Republicans did not develop this hatred overnight; far from it, their detestation for the income tax, and all internal tax, can be traced back to Alexander Hamilton's economic vision for the United States, which found favor with many Whigs, and, in turn, became part of the Republican Party's principles. When the income tax was debated in Congress, countless Grand Old Party members merely adopted the economic ideals of Hamilton that they felt were vital to the growth of real wealth for the country.

Alexander Hamilton, the first US Secretary of the Treasury, strongly fought for the capitalist system, establishing many economic policies that enabled the nation to grow in wealth and industrialization. His ideas on debt, a national bank, and tariffs protected American entrepreneurship from faltering during the early years of the republic. He explained his theories on economic policy in *The Federalist Papers*, a volume of essays written by him, James Madison and John Jay to drum up support for the US Constitution in 1787. In most of his essays, Hamilton concentrated on finance and how best to sculpt the nation into an industrialized powerhouse. Throughout his writings, however, internal taxation did not play any prominent role as he insisted that it would actually stunt growth and place monetary burdens on a government that would receive less revenue because of a stagnant economy. "If the duties are too high, they lessen consumption," Hamilton wrote in "Federalist 21." In essence, he felt that if taxes were excessive, people naturally reduced their expenditures, thus limiting the valuable revenue needed by the government to perform its proper functions. He continued by saying that "the product to the treasury is not so great as when they are confined within proper and moderate bounds. This forms a complete barrier against any material oppression of the citizens, by taxes of this class, and is itself a natural limitation of the power of imposing them." Hamilton showed reluctance to have high tax rates directly placed on citizens, as he believed that it only impeded true economic progress.[1]

Hamilton also contested the notion of progressive tax rates. Remarking that unequal taxation was unjust, Hamilton described a good politician or leader as one who "will be least likely to resort to oppressive expedients, or to sacrifice any particular class of citizens to the procurement of revenue. It might be demonstrated that the most productive system of finance will always be the least burdensome." To him, it was foolish to fix a tax system so that all of the financial burdens of the nation fall on the backs of a few people, mainly the wealthy, even though they could best afford it. It made more sense to Hamilton to tax each person equally, and to keep the tax as low as possible so that an individual could enjoy the fruits of his or her labor. Republicans in Congress later utilized many of Hamilton's views as arguments against the Civil War income tax.[2]

Instead of having a large system of taxation, Hamilton preferred to design the system so that the government received most of its revenue through tariffs, which were paid by foreign companies on their goods sold in the United States, and excise taxes, which were paid by those who purchased luxury items and not the basic necessities of life. Arguing that these taxes were the least burdensome on the people, Hamilton maintained that this idea was the best alternative to internal taxation and a reliable source of government revenue. Hamilton also believed that the wealthy would most likely pay this tax because it only placed a levy on consumption and not directly upon the money they earned from hard

---

[1] Alexander Hamilton, James Madison and John Jay, *The Federalist Papers* (Cutchogue: Buccaneer Books, 1992), 102.

[2] Ibid., 168-169.

work. The affluent classes would always be guaranteed to pay for luxury items because "luxuries of every kind lay the strongest hold on the attachments of mankind." Other parts of Hamilton's plan to industrialize America were internal improvements such as roads and bridges and the formation of a national bank to collect the duties for the government.[1]

Hamilton died in 1804 in a duel with former Vice President Aaron Burr, but his economic philosophy did not die with him. When the Federalist Party declined in the early 1800s, the Whigs, a remnant of the Federalists, later adopted many of Hamilton's plans for the country. Formed in the early 1830s as a response to the Jacksonian Democrats, the Whig Party made its views evident when it came to economic issues, as the 1831 platform put into plain words that they wanted "adequate protection for American industry,... a uniform system of internal improvements sustained and supported by the general government," and a national bank.[2] These were Hamiltonian concepts. As Malcolm Moos indicated in his work, *The Republicans: A History of Their Party*, "By and large this program conformed to the tenets of the early Federalist party, which had taken so much from the policies of Alexander Hamilton."[3]

Indeed, one of the Whigs' founding members, Henry Clay of Kentucky, initiated the "American System" that detailed his economic ideas for the United States; it called for tariffs to protect US businesses, a national bank, and internal improvements; it was, in essence, Hamilton's program. Clay, along with numerous Whigs, also displayed a disdain for taxation on the citizens of the country.[4] For instance, during the War of 1812, President James Madison and Congress enacted new taxes on land and other direct taxes to finance the government. Secretary of the Treasury Alexander Dallas even considered implementing an income tax, citing the fact that "an income tax may be easily made to produce three millions." They did not, however, create an income tax.[5] After the war ended, Clay vocalized his sheer contempt for these duties, while at the same time working to remove all them in favor of revenue through excise taxes and tariffs. As Maurice Baxter noted in his book, *Henry Clay and the American System*, Clay "was pleased that

---

[1] Ron Chernow, *Alexander Hamilton* (New York: The Penguin Press, 2004), 300.

[2] Malcolm Moos, *The Republicans: A History of Their Party* (New York: Random House, 1956), 22.

[3] Ibid., 23.

[4] Lewis L. Gould, *Grand Old Party: A History of the Republicans* (New York: Random House, 2003), 11.

[5] Edwin Robert Anderson Seligman, *The Income Tax Part 2* (New York: The Macmillan Company, 1911), 430n.

the direct levy on land would be phased out the following year and that reliance on other taxes would diminish in comparison with proceeds from public-land sales and especially from the tariff." Clay, like his idol Hamilton, chose to oppose internal taxation unless it was the absolute last resort, and, once a tax was no longer needed, he desired to see it gone.[1]

Clay nevertheless was not the only prominent Whig to disagree with internal taxes. Daniel Webster, the famed Secretary of State and Senator from Massachusetts, made it known on several occasions that he despised taxing the people directly. In the famous court case of *McCulloch v. Maryland*, the state government of Maryland attempted to tax the United States national bank out of existence in favor of local banks. The state placed a special high tax on the national bank in hopes that it would force the bank to shut its doors as it would not be able to compete with the local state banks. The actions by the Maryland state government forced the U.S. government to take the issue to the courts. In his final decision, Chief Justice of the Supreme Court John Marshall ruled against Maryland, stating that the taxes were not equal upon every bank. Webster applauded the decision, as he did not support taxing businesses or people to death, affirming the concept that the power to tax was "the power to destroy."[2] In another instance, President Andrew Jackson vetoed the Bank Bill of 1832 that would have extended the life of the National Bank, leading to sharp criticism from his opponents in the Whig Party. During the debate, Webster made several derogatory comments about government and its taxing authority. "Congress has not undertaken," remarked Webster, "either to take away, or to confer, a taxing power; nor to enlarge or restrain it; if it were to do either, I hardly know which of the two would be the least excusable." The Massachusetts senator understood that it was dangerous to allow the government the unlimited ability to tax the people; in that instance, the government would, in his view, overstep its boundaries unless some rules were enacted to restrain them from doing so.[3]

Even a former Whig and future president would find faults with internal taxation. Abraham Lincoln was a disciple of Henry Clay, referring to him as an "ideal

---

[1] Maurice G. Baxter, *Henry Clay and the American System* (Lexington: University Press of Kentucky, 1995), 19.

[2] Richard N. Current, *Daniel Webster and the Rise of National Conservatism* (Boston: Little, Brown and Company, 1955), 32.

[3] Charles M. Wiltse and Alan R. Berolzheimer, eds., *The Papers of Daniel Webster: Speeches and Formal Writings, Volume 2 1834-1852* (Hanover: University Press of New England, 1988), 527.

of a statesman," and embracing many aspects of his "American System."[1] Since he supported the "American System," Lincoln also took the same view as Clay on taxes. In 1843, Lincoln helped to write and publish the "Campaign Circular of Whig Meeting." Lincoln promoted the common principles of the "American System," such as funding railroads for internal improvements and reinstating the National Bank. Because it was cheaper to collect tariffs imposed on foreign goods, he preferred them rather than imposing internal taxes on the citizenry. "The tariff," stated the circular, "is the cheaper system, because the duties, being collected in large parcels at a few commercial points, will require comparatively few officers in their collection." He argued that with direct taxes, "the land must be literally covered with assessors and collectors." In the circular, Lincoln also explained that tariffs were almost exclusively paid by the wealthy class "while the substantial and laboring many who live at home, and upon home products, go entirely free." He believed that this was a much better system to raise money for the government compared to internal taxes that fall on all classes of society. At the conclusion of the circular's economic points, it stated,

> By the direct tax system, none can escape. However strictly the citizen may exclude from his premise, all foreign luxuries — fine clothes, fine silks, rich wines, golden chains, and diamond rings; still, for the possession of his house, his barn, and his homespun, he is to be perpetually haunted and harassed by the tax-gatherer.

Lincoln thought, like many other Whigs and Hamilton, that it was best to let foreign nations and the wealthy pay the revenue for the government, so long as it did not put a direct tax on their income, but rather had them pay the tax on luxury items. In this way, the people would be able to enjoy the fruits of their labor without the government directly seizing their wealth; instead, with a tariff, people could choose if they wanted to spend money on items whose price would partially be used to fund the government.[2]

These are but a few of the many examples of Whigs opposing the implementation of internal, also called direct, taxation. Stating that tariffs and excise taxes were more suitable, Clay, Webster, Lincoln and other members of the doomed political party made it clear that they disliked intrusive taxation upon the labor of the American public. As will be explained in the next chapter, the deaths of

---

[1] Merrill D. Peterson, *The Great Triumvirate: Webster, Clay and Calhoun* (New York: Oxford University Press, 1987), 434.

[2] Roy P. Basler, ed., *The Collected Works of Abraham Lincoln Volume I* (New Brunswick: Rutgers University Press, 1953), 311-312.

Clay and Webster left a deep void in the Whig Party that was never filled, which culminated into the party's downfall. Members like Lincoln had to find or create a new vehicle through which they could express their views; that vehicle became known as the Republican Party. This new party promoted the same ideas as its predecessor, especially on economic issues and taxation.

CHAPTER 2. FORMATION OF THE REPUBLICAN PARTY

"I mean the name 'Republican.' It is the only one that that will serve all purposes, present and future — the only one that will live and last." — Alvin Bovay, founder of the Republican Party

"'A house divided against itself cannot stand'. I believe this government cannot endure, permanently, half slave and half free." — Abraham Lincoln (Republican — Illinois)

The formation and rise of the Republican Party coincided with downfall of the Democratic Party's opposition at that time — the Whigs. As antislavery activism grew stronger, especially in the Northeastern United States, a rift emerged between the Northern and Southern wings of the Whig Party. Southern Whigs tended to be agricultural land owners and slave owners who supported tariffs on imports that competed with their own products, such as cheap sugar from the islands in the Caribbean. Northern Whigs, on the other hand, subscribed to the ideals of Hamilton and Clay which tended to be more geared to the needs of the manufacturing and financial industries. They also gingerly opposed "the peculiar institution," slavery. These problems became of greater concern with the end of the Mexican War and the subsequent election of 1848.[1]

The Whigs could not truly be considered a successful party. The Party had won the election of 1840 by nominating military hero William Henry Harrison, utilizing the famous slogan, "Tippecanoe, and Tyler Too." The victor of the Battle

---

[1]   Allen C. Guelzo, *The Crisis of the American Republic: A History of the Civil War and Reconstruction Era* (New York: St. Martin's Press, 1995), 48-49.

of Tippecanoe utilized his image as a war hero to display his unique qualifications for occupying the White House. Harrison, however, did not remain in office long. After giving his inaugural speech in freezing, rainy weather, the sixty-nine year old Harrison caught a deadly strain of pneumonia and died less than a month into his presidency. His successor, John Tyler, turned out to be more of a Democrat than a Whig. He vetoed many of the bills that were popular among the Whigs, such as the reinstitution of the National Bank, causing the Party eventually to abandon him along with most of his cabinet members. He later joined the party where he felt most at home — the Democratic Party. Needless to say, the Whigs had not made a good first impression on the nation, and what occurred the second time around for them was almost an exact replica of the Harrison-Tyler years.[1]

In 1848, the Whigs quarreled over who the Party's nominee for president would be for that year. The frontrunner was General Zachary Taylor, the hero of the Mexican War. Northern Whigs, though, were alarmed by this choice because Taylor owned a plantation with slaves in Louisiana. Some argued that the best course of action would be to nominate either a moderate candidate or an all-out radical opposed to slavery. These objections to Taylor did not faze the Party faithful as he successful received the nomination. Many Northern Whigs, fearing that Taylor would ignore their cries against slavery, bolted and formed the Free Soil Party. They nominated Martin Van Buren, the former president and friend of Andrew Jackson, who ran on the platform, "There must be no more compromises with slavery; if made, they must be repealed." Indeed, these Free Soilers were adamant about their opposition to the unjust and unequal institution that was vibrant in the South.[2] The Democrats put forth Lewis Cass, the man who created the concept of popular sovereignty — the people's inherent right in each state to determine if it was going to be "free" or allow slavery. The Democratic president at the time, James Knox Polk, decided against running for a second term even though he had won the Mexican War and gained new territory for the United States. Taylor won the election but was soon faced with a controversy that only the Great Compromiser could solve for the nation — and at that, only for a short time.[3]

[1] Ibid., 47-48.
[2] William S. Myers, *The Republican Party: A History* (New York: Johnson Reprint Corporation, 1968), 24-25.
[3] Ibid., 48-49.

One year into his presidency, Taylor was confronted with the problem of whether the new territories gained during the Mexican War should be slave, free, or allowed to choose their own destiny. During the war, some legislators had attempted to pass the Wilmot Proviso, which declared,

> [A]s an express and fundamental condition to the acquisition of any territory from the Republic of Mexico by the United States, by virtue of any treaty which may be negotiated between them, and to the use by the Executive of the moneys herein appropriated, neither slavery nor involuntary servitude shall ever exist in any part of said territory, except for crime, whereof the party shall first be duly convicted.[1]

It ultimately failed to receive congressional approval. The issue of slavery in the new territories obtained through the Treaty of Guadalupe-Hidalgo remained heated as the war ended. As the Southern members of Congress promoted state choice and Northern members argued against slavery's expansion, Henry Clay came forth with what became known as the Compromise of 1850.

Consisting of five separate bills, the compromise stated that California would enter the union as a free state; New Mexico and Utah could decided whether to be slave or free states by popular vote; the border between Texas and New Mexico was finalized; the slave trade in Washington, D.C. was abolished; and the federal government enacted a new fugitive slave law. The Compromise was meant to appease both abolitionists and slavery supporters by giving them each something that supported their principles without giving them everything they wanted.[2]

Of course, aspects of Clay's compromise also irked individuals on both sides of the debate. Many strong abolitionists resisted any form of compromise on the issue of slavery. "There is another aspect of the principle of compromise, which deserves consideration," argued William Seward, the future Secretary of State who was currently a senator from New York. "It assumes that slavery, if not the only institution in a slave State, is at least a ruling institution, and that this characteristic is recognized by the Constitution. But slavery is only one of many, institutions there — freedom is equally an institution there. Slavery is only a temporary, perpetual, organic, universal one, in harmony with the Constitution of the United States."[3]

---

[1] Guelzo, *The Crisis of the American Republic*, 45.

[2] Ibid., 48-49.

[3] William Seward, "Higher Law," 22 August 2009, http://history.furman.edu/~benson/docs/seward.htm.

Most Southerners, in contrast, denounced the compromise because they believed it did not guarantee adequate rights for the slaveholding states in the country. Although they found the new fugitive slave law helpful to their interests, they were angered that not one of the new states created was assured to be a slave state. One of those who deeply opposed the compromise was the dying John C. Calhoun of South Carolina. In one of his last speeches, he told his Senate colleagues about his contempt for the way California was being admitted into the United States:

> You admit her under all the difficulties that oppose her admission, you compel us to infer that you intend to exclude us from the whole of the acquired Territories, with the intention of destroying irretrievably the equilibrium between the two sections. We should be blind not to perceive in that case that your real objects are power and aggrandizement, and infatuated, not to act accordingly.[1]

Unquestionably, Utah and New Mexico could choose, but there was no promise that they would be slave states; as Calhoun expressed in his remarks, most Southerners feared that the balance of power in Congress would shift, giving influence to the radical abolitionists whose plans would destroy the South's agricultural economy that depended significantly on slave labor and with it, their landowner lifestyle. Southerner legislators attempted to sway Taylor to their position and support slavery in the new territories by meeting with him and pleading their case. However, Taylor refused to back them on the issue. Taylor, although a slave owner himself, did not wish to see slavery expanded any further.[2]

The President would not live to see the accomplishment of the Compromise of 1850. After spending a few hours outside on a hot and humid day in Washington, D.C., Taylor returned to the White House to enjoy a midday snack, but was soon stricken with a deadly case of food poisoning. His vice president, Millard Fillmore, took the reins of power, and many abolitionists hoped that they had finally received support of their cause. Fillmore was from New York, a northern state, and had previously expressed sympathy toward the anti-slavery cause. But abolitionists were soon shocked and saddened by a decision that Fillmore made once he entered the presidency.[3]

---

[1] *The Congressional Globe: Official Proceedings of Congress, 31st Congress 1st Session* (Washington, D.C.: John C. Rives, 1850), 451-455.

[2] Guelzo, *The Crisis of the American Republic*, 48-49.

[3] Ibid., 48-49.

The bill dealing with the new fugitive slave law had been a hot topic of debate amongst the slavery supporters and the abolitionists. The abolitionists argued that if a slave made it to a free state, he was no longer the property of a slave-holder in a slave state. On the other hand, the pro-slavery forces contended that such a slave had not gained his or her freedom according to the laws; therefore, the slave was still the property of his or her owner, even if he or she was now living in a free state, and must be returned promptly. This idea was put forth in *Prigg v. Pennsylvania*, where the Supreme Court essentially stated that, based on the Constitution, it was the duty of the federal government to enforce the fugitive slave law already outlined in the founding document. Though it was mentioned in the Constitution, the federal government never put any force behind it. In fact, the Underground Railroad, which was a series of safe-houses used to hide runaway slaves as they made their way to free states, had been operating for years without much interference from federal authorities. The new bill, as a part of the Compromise of 1850, actually created a unit to track down runaway slaves and bring them back to their owners. These bounty hunters received five dollars if they let captured runaways go free, but were paid ten dollars by the owner if they returned them. Fillmore, making the greatest mistake of his political career, signed it into law; his action now had a strong rippling effect on his own political party. Northern abolitionists were now disillusioned with the Whig Party and soon built a new organization with which to promote their ideals.[1]

The Whigs were slowly dissipating, just as the Federalist Party had done some thirty years earlier. The Southern Whigs were suspicious of the Northern wing for their support of the antislavery cause. The Northern Whigs distrusted the Party not only because the Southern wing tended to be slave owners, but also because many in the Party establishment refused to back their platform. By 1852, most of the Southern Whigs had migrated to the Democratic Party, and their Northern counterparts had found other parties from which to further their goals. An example was the xenophobic American Party, which gained a foothold in the Northeast due to the massive increase of immigrants from Germany and Ireland in those years. Supporters of the American Party tended to not only be anti-immigrant but also anti-Catholic. They claimed that they were going to elect "representatives fresh from the people," and, when asked about their views on national issues, they responded by saying, "I know nothing." This expression led to the party's nickname, The Know-Nothings. Members of the party, as well,

---

[1] Malcolm Moos, *The Republicans: A History of Their Party* (New York: Random House, 1956), 28.

supported the cause of Prohibition because many of the foreign-born citizens they opposed were considered heavy consumers of alcohol. The Know-Nothings had a great deal of support among Northern groups, and even one of the leaders of the Congressional Republicans during the Civil War, Thaddeus Stevens of Pennsylvania, joined their ranks for a brief time after he left the Whigs.[1]

The Free Soil Party, which had run Van Buren in the 1848 election, was a minor party at this time. The party was a vehicle by which disenchanted Northern Whigs could vote for an antislavery candidate. Their one main issue was antislavery, as was stated in their platform: "We inscribe on our banner, 'Free Soil, Free Speech, Free Labor and Free Men,' and under it we will fight on and fight ever, until a triumphant victory shall reward our exertions."[2] Without question, the rise of the American Party and the Free Soil Party during the 1850s signified the downfall of the Whigs. The party received its final blow when its two most prominent members, Henry Clay and Daniel Webster, died in 1852, leaving an opening for a new party to form to unite the old Whigs behind an agreeable platform for all of its factions.[3]

The formation of the Republican Party did not begin with the fall of the Whigs but with the controversial Kansas–Nebraska Act of 1854. Two years earlier, Democrat Franklin Pierce, a slavery sympathizer, had been elected president, and many Southerners knew that he would defend (or at least not hinder) their push to expand slavery beyond the South. Due to this fact, Southern representatives understood that they could accomplish their goals and that they held the ultimate power in the United States. The Kansas–Nebraska Act was a strong example. Illinois' Democratic Senator, Stephen Douglas, wanted a railroad through his state that would reach the expanding West. In order to have such a railroad built, some of its tracks would have to run through the state of Missouri; consequently, Douglas had to persuade his fellow Democratic colleague from the state, David Hutchison, of the benefits this would bring. Hutchison agreed on Douglas' proposal on the condition that the Illinois senator would denounce the Missouri Compromise, which established the boundary between slave and free states at thirty-six degrees latitude and thirty degrees longitude. If he were to do so, the states of Kansas and Nebraska, which were both located above the compromised line, had the authority to determine their future through popular sovereignty.

---

[1] George H. Moyer, *The Republican Party 1854-1964* (New York: Oxford University Press, 1964), 27-28.

[2] *1852 Free Soil Party Platform.*

[3] Guelzo, *The Crisis of the American Republic*, 48-49.

Based on the original compromise created in 1820, Kansas and Nebraska were to be free. Douglas accepted the conditions and passed a bill that permitted the two states to choose whether to be slave or free states by popular sovereignty.[1]

The result of the Kansas–Nebraska Act was both disastrous and deadly. Proslavery forces and abolitionists flooded into the area to vote for their side of the debate. People fought each other, and, in some instances, killed one another to further their beliefs. The most notable instance was the Pottawatomie Massacre. Radical Ohio abolitionist John Brown, the son of a minister, believed that he was a messenger of God sent to destroy the institution of slavery. He and a few of his supporters captured a slave owner and his family and beheaded the males with a sword. Brown escaped capture and migrated to the East to continue his work. He would later be captured and put to death in 1859 by the United States for his rebellious attempt of a slave revolt at Harper's Ferry. Before his death, he famously said that he was "quite certain that the crimes of this guilty land will never be purged away, but with Blood. I had as I now think, vainly flattered myself that without very much bloodshed, it might be done."[2]

Brown's actions, in addition to other fighting, led to the area being dubbed "Bleeding Kansas." Some Northern congressional representatives, upset and troubled by the actions of their proslavery associates, decided to take action against the rising tide of the peculiar institution throughout the nation.[3]

Among Northern congressmen, two Democrats, Salmon Chase and Joshua Giddings, attempted to sway fellow members towards their anti-Kansas–Nebraska Act position. Chase and Giddings authored *Appeal of the Independent Democrats in Congress to the People of the United States*, in which they expressed their scorn for the tragedy occurring in the formation of two new states. In the document, Chase and Giddings said that they wanted to rescue the West from becoming "a dreary region of despotism, inhabited by masters and slaves." They also denounced the Kansas–Nebraska Act, claiming that it was "a gross violation of a sacred pledge; a criminal betrayal of precious rights." Continuing to promote the idea of freedom for all men, they contended that "the fundamental maxim of Democracy" was "EQUAL RIGHTS AND EXACT JUSTICE FOR ALL MEN." The document concluded by pronouncing,

---

[1] Moos, *The Republicans*, 27-28.

[2] Stephen B. Oates, *To Purge This Land With Blood: A Biography of John Brown* (New York: HarperCollins, 1970), 379.

[3] Moos, *The Republicans*, 27-28.

For ourselves, we shall resist it by speech and vote, and with all the abilities which God has given us. Even if overcome in the impending struggle, we shall not submit. We shall go home to our constituents, erect anew the standard of freedom, and call on the people to come to the rescue of the country from the domination of slavery. We will not despair; for the cause of human freedom is the cause of God.[1]

Indeed, Chase and Giddings paved the way for the formation of the new party as their diatribe sparked a movement among some congressional representatives devoted to either stopping the spread of slavery, or to ending its entire existence.[2]

After reading the document, Alvin E. Bovay led a meeting held in Ripon, Wisconsin, in February 1854. Deciding to form a new political party, Bovay chose the name "Republican" from Thomas Jefferson's former party, the Democrat-Republican. He wrote to famed newspaper publisher Horace Greely explaining why he chose the name "Republican,"

Advocate calling together in every church and schoolhouse in the free states, all opponents of the Kansas–Nebraska Bill, no matter what their party affiliations. Urge them to forget previous political names and organizations, and to band together under the name I suggested to you at Lovejoy's Hotel in 1852. I mean the name "Republican." It is the only one that will serve all purposes, present and future — the only one that will live and last.[3]

The Grand Old Party was born, and members soon were elected to congressional seats; Republican parties sprang up in most states as a counter to the Democrats and to the institution of slavery. "That in the view of necessity of battling for the first principles of republican government," read the Michigan Republican Party platform, "and against the schemes of aristocracy the most revolting and oppressive with which the earth was ever cursed, we will co-operate and be known as Republicans until the contest is terminated."[4]

In 1856, the Republicans nominated John C. Fremont, the great explorer of the Oregon Trail from Savannah, Georgia, as the party's first presidential nominee. He ran under the slogan, "Free Soil, Free Labor, Free Speech, Free Men, Fremont!" Although coming in third and losing to Democrat James Buchanan, Fremont's

---

[1] Joshua Giddings and Salmon P. Chase, *Appeal of the Independent Democrats in Congress to the People of the United States*, 19 January 1854.

[2] Moos, *The Republicans*, 28.

[3] Myers, *The Republican Party*, 43-44.

[4] Lewis L. Gould, *Grand Old Party: A History of the Republicans* (New York: Random House, 2003), 14.

campaign showed that the G.O.P. had a strong following and could represent a great challenge to the Democrats in 1860.[1]

One major event in Republican history occurred in May of 1856 on the floor of the United States Senate. Feeling threatened, Southern supporters of slavery lashed out at the antislavery forces forming in the North. One of the main champions of slavery was a man from John C. Calhoun's home state of South Carolina, Andrew Butler. Butler continuously attacked antislavery individuals while defending the institution. Republican Senator Charles Sumner of Massachusetts, however, was not willing to remain quiet on the issue and took to the Senate floor to give one of the most famous speeches in United States history — "The Crime Against Kansas." In it, Sumner derided the Kansas–Nebraska Act, calling it a mistake that had cost lives and prevented freedom. Being a strong opponent of the legislation, the Massachusetts Senator verbally assaulted those who backed it, along with slavery; most notably, he attacked Butler. Sumner poked fun at Butler's speech problems related to a stroke he had previously suffered, and metaphorically stated that he "has chosen a mistress to whom he has made his vows, and who, though ugly to others, is always lovely to him; though polluted in the sight of the world, is chaste in his sight... the harlot Slavery." In essence, Sumner compared the ugliness of slavery to a prostitute that Butler seemed to be willing to defend no matter the circumstance.[2]

South Carolina Representative Preston Brooks, a relative of Butler, was enraged by these comments. Feeling that Sumner had insulted his family's honor, Brooks entered the Senate chamber to confront Sumner directly. After exchanging a few words, Brooks pulled out a cane and proceeded to beat Sumner many times over the head; by the time members were able to stop him, Brooks had broken his cane and Sumner was severely wounded. He would not be able to return to the Senate to perform his elected duties for three years.[3]

In the North, sympathy formed not only for Sumner but also for the antislavery cause. They viewed the beating as a barbaric act by a person representative of the Southern region, and, the thinking went, if they treat political rivals in this uncivilized manner, then how were they treating black slaves? In the South the story met with a complete opposite reception. Brooks was given a hero's welcome, and many admirers sent him canes to replace the one he broke over Sum-

---

[1] Myers, *The Republican Party*, 43-44.
[2] David Herbert Donald, *Charles Sumner, Part I: Charles Sumner and the Coming of the Civil War* (New York: Da Capo Press, 1996), 285.
[3] Ibid., 285-286.

ner's head. The House of Representatives, however, had to take action against Brooks and voted whether or not to expel him. Despite having almost killed a fellow Congressional member, the House voted against expulsion. Brooks, nonetheless, had a different plan as he told the members of the House,

> They have written me down upon the history of the country as worthy
> of expulsion, and in no unkindness I must tell them that for all future time
> my self-respect requires that I shall pass them as strangers. And now, Mr.
> Speaker, I announce to you and to this House, that I am no longer a mem-
> ber of the Thirty-fourth Congress.

After making this statement, Brooks left Congress and returned home to South Carolina, where he died less than a year later.[1] Sumner would return to the Senate and remain a key figure for the Republican Party during the Civil War and Reconstruction period of American history. His beating had a strong effect on the formation of the Grand Old Party; more Northerners became sympathetic to the antislavery cause and were now voting for Republicans.

Dealing with the slavery issues, most Republicans fell into two camps: stopping the spread of slavery or all-out abolition. This issue, however, was not the only topic that consumed them. Economic development was an important aspect of the Republican Party's overall platform, and members tended to accept the old economic policies of Clay and his "American System." For instance, the 1860 Republican Party platform called for an increase in tariffs and enhancement of the national infrastructure, such as a railroad to the Pacific Ocean and harbor improvements. Their strong support of these economic ideals was one of the main reasons why most Republicans spoke out against the bondage of African Americans. In their view of the capitalistic system, slavery was an opponent, as it hindered a group of people from improving themselves economically and enjoying the fruits of their labor. In order to fulfill the principles of the "American System," slavery had to be removed, and, in its place, a class system by which individuals could choose or earn their economic standings and not be forced into an economic system they deemed oppressive.[2]

Without a doubt, Republicans upheld the principles of capitalism created by Hamilton and smoothed out by Clay. As author Allen C. Guelzo noted, "The new Republicans saw themselves as the party of an enterprising white middle-class."[3]

---

[1] Preston Brooks, "In Defense of His Attack on Sumner," 22 August 2009, http://www.bartleby.com/268/9/15.html.

[2] *1860 Republican Party Platform.*

[3] Guelzo, *The Crisis of the American Republic,* 59.

Similarly, in the essay, "Thaddeus Stevens: An American Radical," T. Harry Williams pointed out that Republicans promoted "the economic aspirations of Northern capitalism." In essence the Republicans, at least economically, were the former Whigs, and many of them opposed any internal taxation, including an income tax.[1]

The Republican Party achieved a milestone with the Election of 1860. The G.O.P. nominated former Whig Congressmen Abraham Lincoln. A corporate lawyer for the railroad industry and opponent of slavery, Lincoln seemed to be the perfect candidate for abolitionists because of his history of attacking the institution in debates and policy; Lincoln felt, like other Whigs, that slavery was an enormous obstacle to the sustainment of the capitalistic system most prevalent in northern industrial cities. In fact, he continually condemned the practice during his senatorial campaign against Stephen Douglas two years earlier. He warned in his speech accepting the Republican nomination for the Senate seat in Congress that the slavery issue had to be dealt with or it would continue to fester. He famously professed,

> A house divided against itself cannot stand." I believe this government cannot endure, permanently, half slave and half free. I do not expect the Union to be dissolved — I do not expect the house to fall — but I do expect it will cease to be divided. It will become all one thing or all the other. Either the opponents of slavery will arrest the further spread of it, and place it where the public mind shall rest in the belief that it is in the course of ultimate extinction; or its advocates will push it forward, till it shall become alike lawful in all the States, old as well as new — North as well as South.[2]

Lincoln, though, continually explained that he did not wish to eliminate slavery entirely, but to prevent its expansion into new territories. "I have no purpose, directly or indirectly, to interfere with the institution of slavery in the States where it exists. I believe I have no lawful right to do so, and I have no inclination to do so," he stated in his First Inaugural Address, seeking to calm the fears of people living in slave states.[3]

---

[1] T. Harry Williams, "Thaddeus Stevens: An American Radical," *Commentary: A Jewish Review* 21 (1956): 580.

[2] *Roy P. Basler, ed.,* Collected Works of Abraham Lincoln, *vol. 2 (New Brunswick: Rutgers University Press, 1953), 461-68.*

[3] Abraham Lincoln, *1st Inaugural Address*, 4 March 1861.

The Democrats were not as unified behind one candidate as the Grand Old Party was that year. Instead, there was infighting between the Northern and Southern wings over the issue of slavery. The national convention was held in Charleston, South Carolina, and Southerners demanded that the party not back Stephen Douglas for president; they were suspicious of Douglas because of what happened during his debate with Lincoln in Freeport, Illinois, in 1858. He was noncommittal in his support for slavery and said so in the debate. In what became known as the Freeport Doctrine, Douglas put forth the idea of popular sovereignty and suggested that states could outlaw slavery, even though in the *Dred Scott* Decision the Supreme Court said that slavery could not be prevented in any territory. In effect, Douglas tried to appease the proslavery and antislavery factions in Illinois, but many Southern Democrats viewed him as weak on the slavery issue and demanded that the party nominate somebody who would certainly represent their interests. When the party bucked their request, Southerners, led by William Yancey, walked out the convention and nominated John C. Breckenridge for president. The split among the Democrats allowed Lincoln to receive the majority of electoral votes even though he only won roughly forty percent of the popular vote.[1]

With Lincoln's election to the presidency, many Southerners believed that slavery was heading towards its final chapter in United States history. Lincoln tried to appeal to them in his First Inaugural Address. He said,

> We are not enemies, but friends. We must not be enemies. Though passion may have strained it must not break our bonds of affection. The mystic chords of memory, stretching from every battlefield and patriot grave to every living heart and hearthstone all over this broad land, will yet swell the chorus of the Union, when again touched, as surely they will be, by the better angels of our nature.[2]

Southerners, however, understood Lincoln's previous positions on the issue and preferred not to remain in the Union and witness the fulfillment of their ultimate fear — the end of slavery (though slavery was not the only issue that led to the hostilities between the two regions). In December of 1860, South Carolina became the first state to secede, with several Southern states following its lead before Lincoln's inauguration day. South Carolina's Ordinance of Secession, which was ratified on December 20, 1860, stated in part,

---

[1] Charles P. Roland, *An American Iliad: The Story of the Civil War* 2nd ed. (Lexington: University Press of Kentucky, 2002), 27-33.

[2] Lincoln, *1st Inaugural Address*.

> We, the people of the State of South Carolina, in convention assem-
> bled do declare and ordain, and it is hereby declared and ordained, That
> the ordinance adopted by us in convention on the twenty-third day of
> May, in the year of our Lord one thousand seven hundred and eighty-eight,
> whereby the Constitution of the United States of America was ratified,
> and also all acts and parts of acts of the General Assembly of this State
> ratifying amendments of the said Constitution, are hereby repealed; and
> that the union now subsisting between South Carolina and other States,
> under the name of the "United States of America," is hereby dissolved.[1]

The Southern states founded a new nation which based most of its laws from
the United States Constitution but guaranteed the right to own slaves. They
formed the Confederate States of America and elected former Mississippi Senator Jefferson Davis as president and Alexander Stephens, the Georgia senator, as
vice president.

Davis explained the reasoning of the Southern states for breaking away from
the Union. He stated that the United States Constitution, to the "judgment of
the sovereign States now composing this Confederacy," had been "perverted from
the purposes for which it was ordained, and had ceased to answer the ends for
which it was established, a peaceful appeal to the ballot-box declared that so far
as they were concerned, the government created by that compact should cease
to exist." Like most Southerners, Davis felt the Constitution had been violated
by Northerners given the facts that the document counted slaves as sixty percent
of a person, it did not outlaw slavery, and the Supreme Court had ruled in favor
of slavery with the *Dred Scott* Decision. They believed they had a Constitutional
right to own slaves, and they thought Lincoln was seeking to deprive them of
that.[2]

Southerners began to remove most United States federal government workers from their offices in the South, but one place remained untouched — Fort
Sumter. When food and supplies began to diminish, the commander of the fort,
William Anderson, requested more supplies from Washington. The Confederates not only did not want the fort to be re-supplied, they wanted the U.S. forces
to relinquish the fort. Instead Lincoln sent the ship *Star of the West* to re-supply
Anderson and Fort Sumter. A Southern commander, Pierre G.T. Beauregard, commenced an assault on the ship and on Fort Sumter. Unable to defend themselves,

---

[1] *South Carolina Ordinance of Secession*, 20 December 1860.
[2] Jefferson Davis, *1st Inaugural Address*, 18 February 1861.

the Union had no other option but to surrender the fort to the Confederacy. This battle was the first in a civil war that lasted four years and threatened the United States with annihilation. It also presented a new challenge for both sides: how to finance such a massive endeavor.[1]

Throughout the Civil War, the Grand Old Party mainly focused on winning the conflict and dealing with the institution of slavery. The income tax seemed like a small, nearly insignificant item compared with other issues of the day, yet a hatred for the tax was stirred up such that many Republicans ever since then have fought to bring it to an end. To the Republicans, it may have been a necessary evil during the war; after the victory over the Confederacy, it became a horrid nuisance and an obstacle to their definition of free market capitalism.

---

[1] Roland, *An American Iliad*, 33-39.

CHAPTER 3. THE FIRST FEDERAL INCOME: 1861

"I am inclined very much to favor the idea of a tax upon incomes." — Senator
William Fessenden (Republican — Maine)
"I am in favor of an income tax as against any other kind of tax that can be
assessed." — Senator James Grimes (Republican — Iowa)

After the siege on Fort Sumter, the Union and Confederate armies hastily
pulled together their forces. Lincoln appointed General Irvin McDowell to command the Army of the Potomac, while the Confederates' first hero, Beauregard,
marched his troops northward in search of a quick all-out victory. With twenty
thousand volunteers heading out from Richmond, Beauregard met with McDowell at the small village of Manassas Junction, otherwise known as Bull Run. On
July 21, 1861, the battle commenced, and neither side appeared to be able to gain
the upper hand. Joseph E. Johnston and his command of twelve thousand Confederate soldiers, however, reinforced Beauregard. With five thousand soldiers
dead, twenty-six hundred wounded and no extra forces to help him, McDowell
reluctantly retreated back to Washington, D.C., and the Confederate forces cel-
ebrated an important second victory, increasing their momentum. The defeat led
Lincoln to replace McDowell with General George B. McClellan as leader of the
Union Army.[1]

---

[1] Allen C. Guezlo, *The Crisis of the American Republic: A History of the Civil War and Reconstruction Era* (New York: St. Martin's Press, 1995), 114-115.

The First Bull Run battle left a sinking feeling with many Northerner people. Some had predicted that the war would be over in a few months because the North had more people and was far more industrially advanced than the agricultural states that comprised the Confederate States of America. Indeed, Lincoln and the Republican-controlled Congress came to the realization that the Civil War might last longer than expected and that it would have to be financed adequately — somehow. They understood that heavy taxation was a necessity, but they wondered what forms of taxation would be most palatable to the electorate. Taking positions similar to those of Hamilton and Clay, most Republicans looked towards tariffs as a simple solution to the stark dilemma; direct taxation was not an idea they could implement with enthusiasm.[1]

Lincoln turned to his Secretary of the Treasury, Salmon P. Chase, to employ a new program of taxes to fund the war. Chase considered all options, but finally settled on new internal taxes to levy on the public. From the beginning, he grasped the enormity of problems that could arise as a result of enacting direct taxes; he said, "he has read history to little purpose who does not know that heavy taxes will excite discontent."[2] Even so, his plan, which called for twenty million dollars to be raised by internal taxes, did not originally call for the creation of a personal income tax on every citizen. Historian Steven R. Weisman remarked that the income tax's "first incarnation came as Abraham Lincoln and his Treasury Secretary, Salmon Chase, sought to raise money to save the Union."[3] This statement by Weisman was misleading because Chase did not even propose a tax on incomes to finance the federal government during the national crisis. Instead, on July 4, 1861, he asked for revenue "by direct taxes or from internal duties or excises or both," mainly from bonds, loans and tariffs.[4] To Chase, direct taxation in the United States Constitution was to be collected on real estate and dispersed among the states based upon population. The Constitution's Section Two

---

[1] Heather Cox Richardson, *The Greatest Nation of the Earth: Republican Economic Policies During the Civil War* (Cambridge: Harvard University Press, 1997), 112; Alexander Harris, *A Review of Political Conflict in America, From the Commencement of the Anti-Slavery Agitation to the Close of Southern Reconstruction: Comprising also a Resume of the Career of Thaddeus Stevens, Being a Survey of the Struggle of Parties, Which Destroyed the Republic and Virtually Monarchized Its Government* (New York: T. H. Pollock Publishers, 1876), 296.

[2] Frederick J. Blue, *Salmon P. Chase: A Life in Politics* (Kent: Kent State University Press, 1987), 144.

[3] Steven R. Weisman, *The Great Tax Wars Lincoln to Wilson: The Fierce Battles Over Money and Power that Transformed the Nation* (New York: Simon & Schuster, 2002), 4.

[4] Joseph A. Hill, "The Civil War Income Tax," *Quarterly Journal of Economics* 8 no. 4 (July 1894): 417.

---

of Article I stated, "Direct taxes shall be apportioned among the several states which may be included within this Union, according to their respective numbers." Chase took this section seriously and did not want to create any tax that could possibly be unconstitutional; he wanted collection of only "those forms of taxation which this term, as used in the Constitution, would include — namely, capitation taxes, taxes on real estate."[1] Therefore, he preferred to tax by the old system instigated by Hamilton.[2]

Not long after Chase made his bold proposal to finance the Union forces, the Chairman of the House Ways and Means Committee, Thaddeus Stevens of Pennsylvania, submitted H.R. 71. In the committee debate, members altered the final amount to be collected by direct taxation to thirty million dollars, which would be gathered among the states loyal to the Union according to their respective populations. Since a direct tax of this kind, according to the Constitution, had to be assessed on land, many Republicans grew increasingly upset over it. Most of them viewed it as an iniquitous attempt to harm the poor farmers of the Midwestern states, as the wealthy industrialists not only escaped most of the tax but also prospered as the high tariffs on foreign goods drove more business to their domestic sources. Republicans from states that relied heavily on farming (mainly, the Midwest) cried out against it. "I do not think it right to tax the holder of land," remarked Owen Lovejoy, an Illinois representative and brother of slain abolitionist, Elijah Lovejoy, "and allow the owner of the note or mortgage to escape... I think it is objectionable to tax agricultural lands and not tax merchandise, bank notes, bonds, and mortgages."[3]

Ohio Congressman Sidney Edgerton, who served briefly in the Civil War once leaving office, held a similar view on the situation. He commented on the House floor,

> I tell you a more odious bill cannot be devised, and one which the
> people will more promptly discard. Will you tell them that their lands are
> mortgaged, and at the same time tell them that the wealth of the country,
> the personal property of the country, the money and the merchandise of
> the country go free?... I ask if the farmers of the country are to have their
> lands pledged as security for the payment of this debt, while the great

[1] Ibid., 417.

[2] John Niven, ed. *The Salmon P. Chase Papers, Volume 3: Correspondence, 1858-March 1863* (Kent: Kent State University Press, 1996), xxii.

[3] *The Congressional Globe: Official Proceedings of Congress, 37th Congress, 1st Session* (Washington, D.C.: John C. Rives, 1861), 248.

stockholders, the money lenders, and all the great capitalists, are to go free, and bear none of these burdens.[1]

Edgerton, like many Republicans from Midwestern states, criticized the notion that the income tax was to be assessed on land, which would hurt the farming communities in their states, and not on personal property, such as salaries or stocks. To them, it was simply unfair.

Making a similar argument, Schuyler Colfax of Indiana, who would later serve as Vice President of the United States under Ulysses Grant and would be tarnished by the Crédit Mobilier Scandal in the 1870s, declared, "I cannot go home and tell my constituents that I voted for a bill that would allow a man, a millionaire, who has put his entire property in stock, to be exempt from taxation, while a farmer who lives by his side must pay the tax." Colfax also claimed that "If you want the people to come up fairly and squarely to support this war, to give their money freely,...give them a tax bill which they can recognize as fair and equitable, under which the wealthy man and the poor man will pay their share."[2] Ohio Representative James Ashley pointed out that the "only proper mode for any Government to raise money is to tax property of all kinds according to what it is worth," as he enthusiastically challenged taxes on land.[3]

Utilizing the average farmer as their rallying point, a good number of Republicans felt that the direct land tax wrongly burdened the middle- to lower-income agriculturalists who struggled by their intense labor to feed their families and make themselves a decent living. The industrialists, most from the Northeast, had very little land and chiefly invested in stocks and bonds that were, under Chase's program, exempt from any taxation. Because of this loophole, the poor farmers of the Midwest would finance the entire Civil War. Republicans in Congress saw this as unacceptable and wished to apply another tax in its place — an income tax.

During the initial debate, several Republicans demanded the taxes to be proportioned equally across the nation, judging that it was the only reasonable and just thing to do. "A taxation on real estate," noted William Kellogg of Illinois, "as well as personal property, would be more just, more equitable, more reasonable, and would fall alike on the resident and non-resident property holders." He wished "to equalize and make more just the taxation which is necessary to carry

---

[1] Ibid., 282.
[2] Ibid., 306-307.
[3] Ibid., 248.

on the war and to raise money for the support of the government."[1] Thomas Edwards of New Hampshire asked the question, "Why should we not impose the burdens which are to fall upon the people of this country equally, in proportion to their ability to bear them?"[2] In a related fashion, William Cutler suggested that if real estate and property taxes became too high, the government needed to tax incomes to equalize the tax burden. "If the proportion is too heavy...on real estate, let that be reduced," the Ohioan said, "and a corresponding increase made in the tax upon personal property — such as moneys and credit bonds, stocks, and, if necessary, resort to an income tax."[3] Undeniably, although they supported implementing taxes for government revenue, some in the G.O.P. were not anxious quite yet to get behind progressive taxation, preferring to levy duties in equal proportion upon the citizens.

A few days later, Republican members of the House of Representatives added to the bill a three percent tax on incomes that exceeded six hundred dollars a year. They hoped that this tax would help equalize the burden and alleviate the harsh tax that was to be placed on land. "Let us make those persons who control that property help carry on this war," declared Frederick Pike of Maine. "If five per cent is not sufficient to give the requisite amount, make it ten; and if ten is insufficient, make it fifteen." In his opinion, this was the only "fair way" to collect adequate revenue to conduct the Civil War. "A tax upon incomes," Pike added, "arising from real estates, and from personal property, is assessed as directly upon the property of the country as any tax can possibly be. You have, then, this advantage from an income tax."[4]

Samuel Shellabarger, the grandfather of the famed fiction writer with the same name, concurred with Pike, stating,

> No financial measure will be sustained ultimately and permanently as a war measure, by the country, which does not have as its basis an equitable apportionment of the burdens of taxation upon all the interests of the country according to their relative and respective ability to pay the enormous taxes which must be imposed... an income tax assessed on the revenues of each individual or corporation in the country is the nearest

---

[1] Ibid., 249.
[2] Ibid., 283.
[3] Ibid., 283.
[4] Ibid., 252.

approximate that can possibly be made, at least at this session, to a just
and fair apportionment of taxes among the people.[1]

Shellabarger knew that the tax, as presented in the bill, would be viewed by
the majority of people in the United States as biased due to the fact that it placed
such a large encumbrance on landholders and not on the wealthy who lived in
the cities and, most likely, did not own land. If the tax were not made equal, it
would later be difficult to collect the same tax again.

Illinois Representative Isaac Arnold, as well, displayed a hesitancy to vote
for the bill as it was currently written. Expressing his willingness "to contribute
the last man and the last dollar to crush out this wicked rebellion," he noted
however that "this tax shall be apportioned fairly justly and equitably.... Such tax
should commend itself to the justice of fairness of the people, in order that it may
be willingly and cheerfully paid." Akin to his fellow Midwestern representatives,
Arnold protested, "The wealth of the country is in the East — in New England
in the great Empire State of New York, and in the great Keystone State of Pennsylvania; and yet by this bill, there, where the wealth is, the burden of taxation
is made to fall lightest."[2] With their words, Arnold and the other Midwestern
Republicans successfully petitioned for modifications in the bill to benefit their
constituents.

The income tax allowed for an equalization of the revenue burden, but some
G.O.P. House officials showed a slight hesitation in putting an income tax into
the law books because it was a radical new step in the history of the nation. Indiana Representative William Dunn, who had served as an aide to George Mc-
Clellan in 1861, did not want any direct taxation to commence during this session
of Congress. He said, "It is with a view of avoiding this very difficulty of direct
taxation that I favor the policy of issuing notes bearing a good rate of interest.
I am not afraid but that we can get along in some way until the next session
of Congress without a resort to direct taxation."[3] Believing that Congress might
be moving too hastily to solve the problem without looking into other options,
Dunn preferred to utilize the same forms of revenue collecting that had been in
place since the time of George Washington rather than support an untried and
unknown income tax.

---

[1] Ibid., 271.
[2] Ibid., 326.
[3] Ibid., 271.

A constant opponent of the income tax was Roscoe Conkling, a representative from New York who later attacked the income tax as a powerful member of the Senate. He explained to his associates that he was ready at any moment to vote for bills to aid in the repression of the rebellion of the Southern states, including bills dealing with revenue. He described his eagerness by saying, "I am ready to vote all the money needed to throttle rebellion... for any tax, today or any day, requisite to the earliest and most complete attainment of the nation's purpose." In spite of this, Conkling was not keen on these types of taxes because the people, he believed, would see the collectors as agents of an overbearing and oppressive government.[1]

Others illustrated the possible unreliability of a tax on incomes in a capitalistic system. Alexander Diven, another veteran (he served for a few months in 1862) sitting in Congress from New York, observed, "So as to the merchant who one year is successful and makes $10,000, and the next year is unsuccessful and loses $10,000 — one year up and another down — how are we to fix his income?... Let the first thing this Congress does be to place the credit of the country upon a secure foundation."[2] Similarly, John Covode, a Pennsylvanian and former chairman of the committee that had attempted to impeach President James Buchanan in 1860, noted that income from year to year was erratic, and that the Civil War had the undesirable potential of causing financial ruin for many people throughout the nation. "The country is patriotic; but it is too much to impose such a heavy burden on the people, who are producing nothing. I would ask what you are to get from the income tax, where there is no income tax accruing?" he asked. "There are no incomes to tax."[3] To these Republicans, the government did not need the tax at the present time nor could they depend on the tax to bring in a constant flow of money to the treasury. In essence, a tax upon incomes was pointless and unwise.

Before its final passage, most Republicans conveyed their support for the bill's final passage. "The indirect or income tax which is to be raised by this bill will be, in my judgment, at least twice as much as what we shall raise by direct taxation," Vermont Representative Justin Morrill said.[4] Valentine Horton of Ohio supposed that "there can be no valid objection to the bill, for, if I am not grossly mistaken,

---

[1] Ibid., 272.
[2] Ibid., 282.
[3] Ibid., 330.
[4] Ibid., 330.

it bears equally and fairly upon every interest of the country."[1] William Sheffield of Rhode Island also fervently backed the bill. "The people of Rhode Island," he declared, "are willing to assume the responsibility which may be properly and justly imposed upon them by the Federal Government for the purpose of speedily and effectually putting down that rebellion."[2]

One original supporter of the income tax, Stevens, understood the problems that quite possibly could arise from creating such a radical new way to collect revenue for the United States government. He expressed his disdain for the tax. "We are all conscious that this bill is a most unpleasant one," the former member of the Know-Nothing Party remarked to his colleagues. "The Committee of Ways and Means are conscious that it is a most unpleasant duty for them to propose such a measure; and that it must be a most unpleasant duty for the House to adopt it."[3] Though he displayed some skepticism towards the income tax, Stevens knew that it had to be done for the survival of the Union. Acknowledging that "this bill will come to them with a very distasteful sound and aspect," Stevens believed that the tax was necessary, even if "the army of collectors are odious everywhere."[4] He came to the conclusion that the country had a choice between levying new forms of taxation upon the people or allowing the Union to lose the war.

Without a doubt, Stevens was ready to do what was necessary to ensure a Union victory over the Confederate forces; he, along with other backers of the bill, viewed it as the fairest way to tax the people without making conditions worse for poor people or exciting discontent among the different economic classes. The final vote on the bill in the House of Representatives was sixty-seven Republicans voting yes (80%), while seventeen voted against it (20%).[5] The bill placed the three percent on incomes over six hundred dollars, and all direct taxes were expected to raise twenty million dollars to finance the war. Many of those Republicans who voted against it were from Midwestern states and did not particularly like the tax on farmland and who wanted the income tax to collect

---

[1] Ibid., 323.
[2] Ibid., 270.
[3] Beverly Wilson Palmer and Holly Byers Ochoa, *The Selected Papers of Thaddeus Stevens, Volume 1: January 1814-March 1865* (Pittsburgh: University of Pittsburgh Press, 1997), 215.
[4] *Congressional Globe*, 37th Congress, 1st Session, 307.
[5] Ibid., 330.

much more revenue from the wealthy capitalist centers — namely, the cities of the Northeast.[1]

On July 25, 1861, James Simmons, a Republican from Rhode Island and Chairman of the Senate Finance Committee, introduced the House bill. He, like many Republicans in the other chamber of Congress, sensed it was the best policy to tax incomes instead of land. "Let us," he explained, "tax property, in the last resort, when we have to reach the poor as well as the rich, people of small means as well as those who have large; but I do not believe this country has come to pass to be driven to a resource of such extreme measures." In his view, land taxes were detrimental to individuals who sought to make a new home and life for themselves in the booming Western states. Their wealth, however, had not come to fruition quite yet, so it would be ill-advised to heavily tax them and run them into bankruptcy. Simmons concluded, "I think, with what we can collect by a moderate duty on importations and a moderate tax on incomes exceeding $1,000 we can meet all the exigencies of the public service." Agreeing with his Republican colleagues in the House, Simmons suggested that the United States needed a tax upon incomes in order to shift the burden to the wealthier individuals in society, for they were better able to handle such a payment than the struggling farmers.[2]

Future Secretary of the Treasury William Fessenden, of Maine, echoed the same sentiments as Simmons. "I am inclined," he added, "very much to favor the idea of a tax upon incomes, for the reason that, taking both measures together, I believe the burden will be more equalized on all classes of the community, more especially on those who are able to bear them." He was "perfectly aware that, if we should resort to a tax upon incomes instead of those which are proposed in this bill... the burden, if burden it is, will fall most heavily on the Atlantic and Middle States. I am willing that it should be so." Arguing that the rich had much more resources in which to finance the government, he also alleged that the "tax will be more lightly felt by the people generally." Indeed, he deduced that if the Congress were to impose the tax on the upper class, which made up such a small portion of the overall population, the masses of people throughout the country would be taxed almost nothing. It was a more logical step to take than to leave

---

[1] Edwin Robert Anderson Seligman, *The Income Tax Part 2* (New York: The Macmillan Company, 1911), 433.
[2] *The Congressional Globe, 37th Congress, 1st Session*, 254.

a rich person's wealth untouched while taxing those who have little means in which to pay it.[1]

Four days later, Simmons put forward an income tax higher than the House's recommendation: five percent on incomes above one thousand dollars with absolutely no tax on land. After introducing the amendment, Simmons announced,

> When we tax land, we tax poverty; that is, we tax the poor the same
> as we do the rich; but when we tax income, we tax nobody but those who
> can pay it... I know of no way that that amount of money can be raised
> with so little of public distress, that has ever been devised by man.[2]

Restating the same argument, Simmons wanted only to tax the rich and remove any load that could quite possibly fall on the poorer classes. No Grand Old Party senator challenged his statements; in fact, most of the debate on the bill occurred over sections not pertaining to the income tax. For instance, Massachusetts Senator Charles Sumner lashed out against the increase in tariff duties. As Chairman of the Senate Foreign Relations Committee, he feared that higher tariffs would anger European allies whom the United States would need to secure victory over the Confederacy. It was just one of several minor issues against the bill.[3]

Democratic Senator Trusten Polk of Missouri offered to strike out the section of the bill dealing with the imprisonment of those individuals who refused to pay taxes. Republicans were split on this issue. "Everybody that owns stock," protested John Hale, the New Hampshire Republican and one-time Free Soil Party candidate for president, "everybody that has money, everybody that has property of any kind, that is not real estate and visible, will be disposed to conceal it from taxation. They always have done so, and they always will." Though he knew that it would be difficult to force people to pay the tax and fruitless to imprison them, Hale wanted the section to remain in the bill. He said, "If you strike this out, you let the richest men in the country, who have stocks and large incomes, stare you in the face when you ask them for their taxes, and you will get them off poor men who cannot help themselves."[4]

In addition, New Jersey Senator John Ten Eyck concurred with Hale's statements. "I would never vote," he told fellow senators, "in this age of the world, to imprison a man for debt." To him, the poor should never go to jail because they

---

[1] Ibid., 255.
[2] Ibid., 314.
[3] Ibid., 314.
[4] Ibid., 320.

simply could not afford to pay taxes. It was unfair, in his mind, to do so, but Ten Eyck had no problem arresting a rich man for not paying his share to help with the survival of the Union. He proclaimed, "If a man, rolling in wealth and bloated with stocks, at this period of time, refuses to pay taxation for support of this Government, and to save the nation from the consequences of this rebellion, he ought to go to prison; and he will be better in prison than out of it."[1]

Fessenden reiterated the same points, observing "that many men who are rich...resort to every possible evasion to get rid of the payment of taxes." He deemed the amendment allowing the government to arrest those who do not pay taxes to be both fair and just. "This bill," Fessenden concluded, "in the first place, gives to such persons an opportunity to come forward and state under oath what their income is," and that if "they do not chose choose to do that, then the asses-sor has the right to say how much their income is."[2] Senators such as Fessenden, Hale and Ten Eyck saw no problem with imprisoning men who were, by declin-ing to pay their taxes, not aiding in the effort to win the Civil War. If the federal government could not raise the necessary funds to supply Union forces, it would certainly mean death and defeat. To them, it was the patriotic duty of the wealthy class to pay some portion of their revenue, and, if they refused, they deserved time behind bars.

Some Republicans, on the other hand, viewed it as an unnecessary and un-precedented measure for the federal government. John Sherman of Ohio frankly stated, "I will not vote to imprison a man, deprive him of his liberty, for refusing to pay taxes." If any person chose to defy the legislation, there were ways to get the necessary funds from him or her. Arresting people was too strict because if "a man has real property it can be seized; if he has stocks they can be sold."[3] Without question, other options remained for the government to recourse the injustice of a wealthy man not paying his taxes than simply throwing him in jail. Sherman offered an alternative by having the government take property and stocks and selling them for funds. Sherman, nonetheless, was part of a small minority within the party as most Republicans supported imprisonment for those who cheated by not paying their taxes.

After the initial debate, Simmons decided on August 2 to drop the tax from five to three percent. He, as well, placed a moderate tax on property so that all

---

[1] Ibid., 320.
[2] Ibid., 320.
[3] Ibid., 320.

classes in the Union would be taxed justly. "We lowered the rate upon incomes," he said, "because we imposed direct taxes on property, and thought it was right to migrate, in some degree, the burdens of the people."[1]

Almost all G.O.P. senators backed the idea of an income tax. James Grimes of Iowa, who would be one of only a handful of Republican senators to vote for President Andrew Johnson's acquittal in 1868, professed, "I am in favor of an income tax as against any other kind of tax that can be assessed."[2] Likewise, Sherman added, "I think, on a whole it is a fair compromise of the various elements to be consulted in a tax bill."[3] Minnesota Senator Morton Wilkinson explicitly explained his reasons for supporting the tax bill. "I shall vote for this bill," he remarked, "notwithstanding, I believe it will operate very hard on the people of the new States, where it is known they have no money." Although he regretted this undeniable fact, he was "relieved somewhat from the embarrassments which seemed to press upon me as a representative of one of the newest States of the Union, by the provision of this bill in relation to an income tax." Had the bill not contained a tax upon incomes, Wilkinson would have voted against it.[4]

Some patriotic Republicans were not eager for an income tax, but were willing to vote for the bill as the apparent best means to vigorously support the Union cause. Ten Eyck proclaimed, "We have got this stern and stubborn reality before us, and we have to 'face the music' or give it up ... I am willing to stand or fall, so far as I am concerned, by it."[5] Preston King of New York, who, sadly, committed suicide in 1865, said, "I am myself disposed to vote for all the measures which are, in the judgment of the majority, deemed necessary, whether my own individual opinion accords with them or not, for I believe we should be united in our action."[6]

The Republicans in the Senate remained a cohesive group as one hundred percent of them voted in favor of the tax bill. With the bills differing upon how much should be exempt from income taxation, a conference committee met on August 5 and decided to keep the tax at three percent and exempt incomes under eight hundred dollars. It was a monumental step taken by the Congress as a new form of government revenue was put into action by this bill. A problem arose with the

---

[1] Ibid., 397.
[2] Ibid., 321.
[3] Ibid., 398.
[4] Ibid., 400.
[5] Ibid., 399.
[6] Ibid., 399.

bill that forced the Congress to take another look one year later: the income tax was never collected.[1]

Most newspapers in the Union showed fondness for the income tax. *The New York Herald* wrote,

> The necessity of a great war have forced upon us a measure which we had hoped to avoid. The interest of the immense loans that have been authorized by Congress has to be provided for, and as our revenue from imports can no longer be relied upon, and the public land will, in all probability, be all absorbed by the grants made to officers and soldiers or our army, no option is left us but to resort to it.[2]

The paper admired the fact that "Millionaires like Mr. W.B. Astor, Commodore Vanderbilt ... and others, will henceforth contribute a fair proportion of their wealth to support of the national government."[3] The newspaper understood the income tax was going to be unpopular with the people, "but its simplicity and certainty are strong recommendations in its favor as a measure of expediency at the present time." It ultimately expressed faith, though, that the income tax would not be a permanent fixture in American finance law.[4]

The New York Times also promoted positive aspects of the income tax, quashing all of the arguments presented against it. "The next most important point," a columnist observed, "as it is generally argued, is the unpopularity of this mode of raising revenue. Why is it so? Who are those that most cry out against it? Certainly it is not the poor man, for he would, by the $500 minimum, be exempt." Calling into question individuals who protested the tax, the paper explained that other taxes at the local levels were collected in the same fashion. It asked, "Why should the millionaire object to it; is he not compelled to pay the State, City, and County on the same basis of the value of property; why then should he not pay the General Government in the same way?"[5]

The *The New York Times* noted that an income tax was a necessity for war and needed to be properly levied so as to be felt minimally by people paying it. "The correctness of the principles on which an income tax is advocated," declared the

[1] Seligman, *The Income Tax Part 2*, 434.

[2] *New York Herald*, 5 August 1861.

[3] Elmer Ellis, "Public Opinion and the Income Tax, 1860-1900," *The Mississippi Valley Historical Review* 27 no. 2 (September 1940): 226.

[4] *New York Herald*, 6 August 1861.

[5] "Some Suggestions in Regard to Direct Taxation—An Income Tax," *New York Times*, 26 July 1861.

paper, "we think can not be converted, and their adaptation into a law so as to equalize the public burdens, promote harmony and good feeling, establish justice and strengthen our republican institutions, would seem neither difficult nor doubtful."[1] Even the economically conservative Horace Greeley and his *New York Tribune* espoused support for the new income tax law. The paper stated, "We do not strenuously object to direct taxes, though we prefer to raise money by Excise rather than by indiscriminate Income and Property Tax." Despite the fact that the paper loathed the income tax in principle, it was still prepared to accept and promote the idea if it assisted the Union in destroying the Confederate threat.[2]

As the income tax became part of the overall revenue landscape to finance the Civil War, it would eventually morph into a partisan issue between certain sections of the country; it also would split the Republican Party along economic and regional lines. Historian John F. Witte observed in *The Politics and Development of the Federal Income Tax* that the 1861 income tax led to a division which pitted the wealthy industrial North and Northeast against the poorer agricultural regions in the rest of the country...a simple response to different economic circumstances: the Northeast favored first tariffs... and excise, license, and land taxes if needed; the South and West resisted all these taxes, whose impact fell disproportionately on them, and favored taxes on income and wealth, of which they had little.[3]

These differing opinions later fueled hostility between the Northeast/West and Midwest/South, but, for the time being, each side gave in a little, hoping to make certain that the Union would be victorious over the Southern rebels. A moderate income tax, along with a moderate land tax, they felt, should enable the government to collect enough money to sustain the Union forces until the next Congress met and made changes to strengthen the revenue flow.

Although the income tax was never really implemented in 1861, passage of the bill did allow the federal government to step, temporarily, out of its normal function in times of dire emergencies. Republicans expressed some hesitation with starting such a radical move, but most just desired to show loyalty and patriotism to the Union cause. They remained united for this one bill, but soon the sectional partisanship would be on display in Congress as each fervently rep-

---

[1] "Thoughts on Taxation," *Barre Gazette*, 24 January 1862.

[2] Ellis, "Public Opinion and the Income Tax," 226.

[3] John F. Witte, *The Politics and Development of the Federal Income Tax* (Madison: The University of Wisconsin Press, 1985), 68.

resented its best economic interests. Future bills dealing with the income tax would divide the Grand Old Party on not only how to levy it, but also whether to levy it any more.

CHAPTER 4. THE REVISION OF 1862

> "The weight must be distributed equally — not upon each man an equal amount, but a tax proportionate to his ability to pay." — Representative Justin Morrill (Republican — Vermont)
>
> "I think that a Federal tax is always odious to the people; that a tax of any kind is always odious to the people." — Representative John Stratton (Republican — New Jersey)

A year into the Civil War, the Union forces suffered massive defeats in some of the conflict's most critical battles. After having to surrender Fort Sumter to Beauregard and retreating at the First Bull Run encounter, a sense of fear and dread swept across not only the federal government but also the general public. It seemed that they might very well lose to the Confederacy. The Union appeared to have righted its ship when Lincoln replaced McDowell with the dashing General George McClellan. A military genius, McClellan was the man the President hoped would put a swift end to the awful rebellion by the Southern states, but some in the government were unsure they could place their trust in McClellan because of his political ties to the Democratic Party and sympathy towards the slavery cause. Despite these concerns, Lincoln assured his fellow Republicans that McClellan was the correct choice to head the Army of the Potomac.[1]

The Confederate Army as well had a new commander, but not because of any incompetence in leadership. Joseph Johnston, the general who saved Beauregard

---

[1] Allen C. Guelzo, *The Crisis of the American Republic: A History of the Civil War and Reconstruction Era* (New York: St. Martin's Press, 1995), 115.

at the First Bull Run and leader of the Army of Northern Virginia, received serious wounds at the Battle of Seven Pines, forcing him to leave his position. Confederate President Jefferson Davis replaced him with Robert E. Lee, a Virginia slaveholder and graduate of West Point. Lincoln had personally recruited Lee to take charge of the Union forces at the start of the war, but Lee declined, citing his love for his home state over his loyalty to the United States.[1]

Devising a campaign based in Maryland, Lee planned to march his troops into the North to win one clash after another and completely demoralize an already stunned nation. However, Lee had placed a set of battle plans in a cigar box, which eventually a Union soldier discovered; he delivered them to McClellan. This enabled McClellan to know Lee's strategy before the battle commenced, as he met him at the town of Sharpsburg, Maryland, near Antietam Creek. However, McClellan failed to fully capitalize on the South's enormous blunder and took a conservative stand; he did not force Lee to retreat from his position. Although he knew Lee's strategy, McClellan allowed the Confederate army to continue fighting, and, as a result, he had to pull his forces back over the bridge. This was one of the bloodiest battles of the entire conflict, and the Union endured thirteen thousand deaths. Embarrassed and angry over McClellan's failure to boldly attack and crush Lee's forces, Lincoln remarked, "If General McClellan does not want to use the army, I would like to borrow it for a time."[2] He had let the Confederates slip away without a significant victory for the United States, and McClellan's ineptness did not help the President's standing in Congress.[3]

The Battle at Antietam Creek, however, was not a complete defeat for the Union as it gave Lincoln the perfect opportunity to accomplish an objective that had been prominent throughout most of his public life — ending slavery. Many historians have debated his ultimate reasoning for abolition, but, in the end, it would be an important aspect of the war and its aftermath. On January 1, 1863, Lincoln issued his Emancipation Proclamation. Although it was an extremely significant document for the liberty of the African Americans, it only freed slaves currently residing in Confederate states; it did not emancipate the slaves in states that had remained loyal to the United States, such as Missouri and Kentucky. Nonetheless, the Emancipation Proclamation helped to end the "necessary evil" once and for all. As it stated,

[1] Charles P. Roland, *An American Iliad: The Story of the Civil War* 2nd ed. (Lexington: The University Press of Kentucky, 2002), 70.
[2] "George McClellan," 22 August 2009, http://en.wikipedia.org/wiki/George_B._McClellan.
[3] Roland, *An American Iliad*, 80-83.

And by virtue of the power, and for the purpose aforesaid, I do order and declare that all persons held as slaves within said designated States, and parts of States, are, and henceforward shall be free; and that the Executive government of the United States, including the military and naval authorities thereof, will recognize and maintain the freedom of said persons.[1]

In the South, another deadly battle made Lincoln and his administration nervous. Albert Sidney Johnston, heading a force of Confederate soldiers in the state of Tennessee, attacked a Union squad near a small church known as Shiloh (which ironically means "place of peace" in Hebrew). The commander in-charge was Ulysses S. Grant, another West Point alumnus, who was celebrating the capture of two Southern forts along the Tennessee River. During the initial assault, Grant was further up the river and unable to assist the vulnerable Union forces. Albert Sidney Johnston, the commander of the Army of the Mississippi, pushed the Union forces back from the area, but lost his life in the process; Beauregard replaced him.[2]

Grant arrived a few hours later and one of his subordinates, William T. Sherman, suggested for the Union forces to retreat. Throughout the war, Grant had always been impressed by the way Sherman handled himself. He later wrote about the Battle of Shiloh,

I feel it a duty, however, to a gallant and able officer, Brig. Gen. W. T. Sherman, to make a special mention. He not only was with his command during the entire two days' action, but displayed great judgment and skill in the management of his men. Although severely wounded in the hand the first day his place was never vacant. He was again wounded, and had three horses killed under him.[3]

Still, Grant refused Sherman's suggestion and ordered the soldiers to continue assaulting the Confederates. By the next day, Beauregard drew back, and the Union forces stood victorious. This battle boosted the reputation of Grant, even though his preliminary response nearly led to defeat and the loss of thirteen thousand Union soldiers.

Grant understood that the Confederate force was not going to be easy to defeat. "Up to the battle of Shiloh," Grant later wrote, "I, as well as thousands of other citizens, believed that the rebellion against the Government would

---

[1] Abraham Lincoln, *Emancipation Proclamation*, 1 January 1863.
[2] Guelzo, *The Crisis of the American Republic*, 156.
[3] Ulysses S Grant, *Report of Major General U.S. Grant on the Battle of Shiloh*, 9 April 1862.

collapse suddenly and soon if a decisive victory could be gained over any of its armies... I gave up all idea of saving the Union except by complete conquest."[1] Indeed, the Union had won the Battle of Shiloh yet suffered the loss of more than ten thousand soldiers. Lincoln was so thoroughly impressed by Grant's actions that he said, "I can't spare this man; he fights." The fact that the Union lost so many soldiers at Shiloh, coupled with the defeat of McClellan at Antietam, raised the awareness of Congress that much more revenue would be needed to stop the South from winning independence.[2]

Thus in the midst of the war, the Lincoln Administration moved to increase the money flow to the federal treasury. With heavy losses and innumerable deaths even in victory, the Union was depleted of resources. Late in 1861, Secretary Chase, one of the founders of the Republican Party and future Chief Justice of the Supreme Court, sent a request for fifty million dollars to be raised by internal taxation, but failed again to offer the creation of a tax on incomes. In his annual report to Congress, Chase professed,

> Considering, however, how large a proportion of incomes after the deductions sanctioned by law will fall within the exemption limit of $800 a year, and considering also what numerous questions will certainly perplex its assessment and collection, he respectfully submits whether the probable revenue affords a sufficient reason for putting in operation, at great cost, the machinery of the act, with a view, should the states assume the direct tax, to the collection of the income tax alone.[3]

He judged that it was neither feasible nor worth the money, time and effort, to establish the offices and officers to collect a tax which most Americans would not have to pay because their annual income fell below the exemption. To him, it would be a waste of governmental assets at a time of national crisis. Chase was, in fact, open to all practical suggestions when it came to the country's finances, especially as the Union armies were fighting for the nation's preservation. He sincerely felt that the government "must not shrink from a plain statement of the actual necessity of the situation." Chase showed a willingness to take the required steps to make certain that the government had a strong financial footing, including instigating an income tax.[4]

---

[1] C.C. Buel and R.U. Johnson, eds., *Battles and Leaders of the Civil War vol. 2* (New York: T. Yoseloff, 1956), 485-486.

[2] Guelzo, *The Crisis of the American Republic*, 156.

[3] *Report of the Secretary of Treasury for the Year 1861* (Washington, D.C.: 1861), 15.

[4] Joseph A. Hill, "The Civil War Income Tax," *The Quarterly Journal of Economics* 8 no. 4 (July 1894): 421.

A year earlier, the Congress had passed a bill creating an income tax of three percent on eight hundred dollars, yet the federal government had failed to put it into action. This time, Congressional Republicans sought to make it a substantial part of the revenue flow. On March 3, 1862, Stevens reported a bill, H.R. 312, which taxed incomes exceeding six hundred dollars at three percent. The bill was not brought up for discussion until March 12, when Morrill, a leading figure on the Ways and Means Committee, detailed all of its features. He even articulated why he supported the income tax. "The weight must be distributed equally — not upon each man an equal amount, but a tax proportionate to his ability to pay," he succinctly stated. "The income duty is one, perhaps, of the least defensible that, on the whole, the Committee of Ways and Means concluded to retain or report." Morrill knew the tax would only fall on a small percentage of the overall population, yet he was of the opinion that it was fair as well as crucial; it also forced every citizen to bear some responsibility of the cost of the war. He added,

> The income tax is an inquisitorial one at best; but, upon looking at the considerable class of State officers, and the many thousands who are employed on a fixed salary, most of whom would not contribute a penny unless called upon through this tax, it has been thought best not to wholly abandon it.

Morrill, in essence, came to the conclusion that the tax was worth implementing even if the people might object to its collection. He argued, "Ought not men, too, with large incomes to pay more in proportion to what they have than those with limited means, who live by the work of their own hands or that of their families?" Morrill noticed that to meet the needs of the government, Congress had no option but to put into practice an income tax that burdened the wealthier classes more for support of the war.[1]

Other Republicans admitted, too, that the people would perceive an income tax negatively, and felt it was extremely important to make certain that its creation and execution were flawless, or they risked a backlash from the country. William Wordsworth of Kentucky objected to the bill, stating,

> The bill now under consideration calls upon the people of the United States for vast sums of money, and imposes unusual burdens. We ought to be very careful, indeed, in the details of the bill when we approach the people to demand from them a portion of the necessaries of life, as this bill does; but, above all, we ought to be still more careful to inspire the people

---

[1] *The Congressional Globe: Official Proceedings of Congress, 37th Congress, 2nd Session* (Washington, D.C.: John C. Rives, 1862), 1194-1196.

of this country a confidence that their hard-earned wealth is to be devoted alone to the preservation of the liberties which are their alienable rights.[1]

Another Republican pointed to the fact that it did not matter what type of tax the Congress requested the people of the United States to pay because all taxes for the support of the government were determined by them to be dreadful. "Perhaps there is no duty and no debt which the people are called upon to pay which they pay more reluctantly than a tax for the support of the government," John Stratton, a Princeton alumnus and Representative from New Jersey, commented. "I think that a Federal tax is always odious to the people; that a tax of any kind is always odious to the people."[2] Similarly, Ohio Congressman John Hutchins observed, "Taxation is odious, and that individuals, corporations, counties, and States will shirk as much as possible the payment of all taxes. All men are anxious that all men but themselves shall be taxed."[3] Morrill, Stratton, Hutchins and some Grand Old Party members alleged that creating an income tax could lead to potential conflict, yet they must consider it as a valuable way to increase the revenue to sponsor the war effort.

During the debate, Republicans were not excited about eliminating the income tax provision from the bill. In fact, none of them even recommended its removal, mostly arguing over minor points within the bill. For instance, on April 3, Robert McKnight offered an amendment to strike out the section that allowed for a tax upon real estate. "A person whose whole income may be derived from real estate is first taxed upon real estate, and then he is taxed upon the income which he derives from it," declared the Representative from Pennsylvania. "It will make the owners of real estate pay more than their fair share of the burdens of the Government."[4] In a sense, there was a double taxation on real estate, and he called for that portion of the bill to be removed.

Most Republicans, though, did not feel it appropriate to meet McKnight's request. Stevens, for instance, opposed the measure because, "it will exempt all incomes from real estate."[5] He believed it unreasonable to not tax property while taxing incomes. Morrill repeated Stevens' sentiments. "If all classes of the community are not included, it would be hardly worth while to have an income tax at

---

[1] Ibid., 1198.
[2] Ibid., 1222.
[3] Ibid., 1224-1225.
[4] Ibid., 1531.
[5] Ibid., 1531.

all."[1] Stevens and Morrill insisted that if the federal government was to initiate an income tax, it must also be even handed, and tax real estate so that every class in the United States would, in one way or another, pay for the war.

Republicans were not as content with some ideas presented by their Democratic counterparts. When the income tax was nominally debated, Democrat George Pendleton of Ohio introduced an amendment on April 4 to tax all incomes below the six hundred dollars exemption. The proposal angered G.O.P. representatives who argued that a real estate tax would cover those individuals whose income fell below the limit for the income tax. From their viewpoint, this scheme represented double taxation, for the poorer classes of society would not only have to pay a tax on their property, but also a portion of their income to the federal government. Stevens summed up the Republican stance on this issue. "I am willing," the Chairman of the Ways and Means Committee lividly remarked, "to tax the people as much as they will bear if necessary to carry out this war; but I am not willing to tax them twice over in the same bill... If the pending amendment is adopted, we ought to strike out the income tax altogether, and insert this in its place."[2] Indeed, it appeared as though Republicans wanted to tax the people minimally for financial support of the conflict; Stevens clearly articulated the reluctance of many in the party to "tax the people to death" in order to achieve maximum revenue for the government. The tax on real estate was enough for the lower classes to pay; requiring them to pay an income tax in addition to it would be, in his view, unjust.

Cornelius Leary, a Democrat from Maryland, presented his own amendment to exclude government bonds from being taxed as income. Stevens rebuffed this idea, saying, "I cannot see the difference between putting the burdens of this taxation upon a man who buys $100,000 of United States bonds, and he who buys $100,000 worth of my bonds." Leary's amendment was vehemently rejected by the House of Representatives.[3]

That same day, Alexander Diven inserted an amendment to the bill that defined income as investments that produced profits and not on money earned by labor. "What I desire is to have the income tax confined to the production of investments. That is what is meant by income tax the world over." His amendment, unlike Leary's, was adopted into the bill.[4]

---

[1] Ibid., 1533.
[2] Ibid., 1545.
[3] Ibid., 1531.
[4] Ibid., 1533.

On April 8, the tax bill moved towards final passage, and almost all of the Republicans in the House of Representatives supported the measure. Albert White of Indiana proclaimed, "It is of the highest importance that this tax should be made effective."[1] Stevens gave his final thoughts on the measure and urged his comrades to vote yes on the legislation. "If it should become a law, it will undoubtedly be a subject of comment among well-meaning people, and be used as an engine of mischief by unprincipled men, who prefer the possession of power to the prosperity of the country," he said. Stevens accepted there were several problems with the formation of an income tax, maintaining that it "has been found very difficult to adjust so as to escape double taxation." Besides this factor, Stevens, a man who suffered with a clubbed foot his entire life, illustrated the importance of putting the tax into action. "But the committee thought," he continued, "it would be manifestly unjust to allow the large money operators and wealthy merchants, whose incomes might reach the hundreds of thousands of dollars, to escape from their due portion of the burden." He ultimately conveyed what a majority of Republicans thought of the application of an income tax: it was necessary so as to make the burdens of the Civil War proportionate among all classes in the nation. The Pennsylvania Representative concluded his remarks by saying,

> I have no fear that the loyal people of the free States will complain of any burdens which may be necessary to vindicate the authority of the Union, and establish on a firm basis the principle of self-government and the inalienable rights of man. While the rich and the thrifty will be obliged to contribute largely from the abundance of their means... no burdens have been imposed on the industrious laborer and mechanic; that the food of the poor is untaxed; and that no one will be affected by the provisions of this bill whose living depends solely on his manual labor.[2]

With that statement, little else was added to or denounced in the bill, and a final vote was taken on its passage. Republicans eagerly voted for it, with the exception of financial conservative James Buffinton of Massachusetts who was the only Grand Old Party representative to vote no (he was also the only member of the party to vote against the income tax in every tax bill during this period).[3] The final House bill levied a three percent tax on incomes above six hundred dollars while also putting into place a direct property and inheritance tax. The bill

---

[1] Ibid., 1577.
[2] Ibid., 1576-1577.
[3] Ibid., 1577.

moved next to the Senate, where Republicans found even less to debate when it came to the income tax.[1]

The new Chairman of the Senate Finance Committee, William Fessenden, reported the bill on May 6, but the deliberation was held off until May 21. Senate Republicans, in the same approach as their associates in the House of Representatives, mostly agreed that the income tax was a correct way to collect revenue from the people. Their proposal, however, differed from the House's as it created progressive rates of taxation as an individual's wealth increased. They presented a tax of three percent on incomes above six hundred dollars, five percent on incomes over ten thousand dollars and seven and one-half percent on incomes exceeding fifty thousand dollars. No rejection of these tax brackets came from the G.O.P., and no amendments altering the rates were ever offered by them.[2]

The strongest objection to the bill came from Wisconsin Senator Timothy Howe, who disputed the one and one-half percent tax on government bonds because it discriminated against private sector bonds as well as incomes that were to be taxed at three percent. Various Republicans gave reasons in support of that provision. "That income tax has existed until the present time. The object of that provision was to induce persons to invest in the public securities.... We desire that the people should take the public securities in preference to other investments," said Fessenden.[3] He insisted that if the government bonds were taxed less than private bonds, it would make capitalists, wealthy individuals and foreigner investors more inclined to invest in the government, which, inevitably, would help the war effort. Moreover, it allowed the federal government to keep the income tax, tariffs and property taxes at lower rates, relieving the bulk of the population from having to pay enormous sums of money.

James Simmons, a former Whig, added, "If the Senator from Wisconsin will look into the income tax of other countries, he will find it is invariably the case that the tax on investment in the national securities is always made lower. It is sound public policy to do so."[4] Zachariah Chandler of Michigan went even further than Simmons and Fessenden on the issue, aiming to have absolutely no income tax on government bonds. "Here is the best security in the world, and we offer them to the world, and we proclaim to the world if you take these bonds

---

[1] Steven R. Weisman, *The Great Tax Wars Lincoln to Wilson: The Fierce Battles Over Money and Power that Transformed the Nation* (New York: Simon and Schuster, 2002), 40.

[2] *The Congressional Globe, 37th Congress, 2nd Session,* 2255.

[3] Ibid., 2449.

[4] Ibid., 2449.

they shall never be taxed," stated the future Secretary of the Interior under President Grant. "I declare that I believe it to be for the interest of the Government to proclaim in advance that there shall never be a tax of any sort, kind or description, upon these bonds which we are now offering to the world in such immense quantities."[1] Republicans wanted people to purchase these bonds, and they tried to create strong incentives for them to do so.

Howe, nevertheless, claimed that the tax created an unnecessary tax shelter for those individuals who were looking for income tax loopholes; they could simply take their money and place it in government bonds, alleviating themselves of paying the tax. On June 2, he told senators that he wished for the tax either to be equal or to be struck out of the bill altogether. Howe said,

> Is it good policy? Why, sir, if by discriminating in this taxation you can induce any capitalists to buy your bonds at a price enhanced beyond the discrimination, then do it. I do not think you will succeed in that enterprise. The truth about it is, you put your bonds into market, and you sell them at what capitalists can afford to pay for them, what they are willing to pay for them, or what they can get them at. Their property, their money has got to pay, or ought to pay, taxes in some shape, just as much if invested in your bonds as if invested in your lands, or in your manufacturing stocks or your banking stocks.

In effect, Howe, who was later nominated for the Supreme Court by Grant, worried that due to the reduced tax on government bonds wealthy individuals would place all of their income in those bonds, thus avoiding the three percent tax on incomes. He felt that it was every person's duty to pay taxes to the federal government since it was the government who provided security and freedom to them. Howe thought that the "liability to pay taxes to meet the wants of the Government is an obligation due from every citizen to the Government.... Every individual has an equal interest and owes and equal debt." In his view, if the government did not tax securities, the loss of revenue to the government would eventually be shifted to the farmers and poorer classes. It was unfair to allow that to happen, so the tax on government bonds had to be the same as the income tax. Despite Howe's pleas, Republicans kept the tax the same as first presented in the bill, as their objective was to gain as much revenue as possible and this tax provision, in their view, achieved that goal. Instead of collecting a tax on incomes, Republicans felt that collecting it through the purchase of government bonds

---

[1] Ibid., 2550.

would be sufficient for the needs of war. To them, they were just collecting the same money in a different manner.[1]

Three days after his first objection, Howe recommended an amendment to collect fifty million dollars from the income tax alone and increasing the percentage on each income bracket. He preferred this to taxing property or capital which would immediately affect those in the lower classes. "I want to submit that it is true of the nation as it is of any individual in the nation, that its expenses must be met either by its income or by its capital," he explained, "and if you exhaust any portion of the capital of this nation, you head it towards bankruptcy." As Howe pointed out, the overwhelming majority of the loyal states had citizens who did not have incomes to tax, having invested what wealth they had in the land they owned and worked. He yearned to shift that encumbrance from them and place it solely on rich people who had incomes that exceeded the minimum exemption of six hundred dollars. By increasing the tax rates and the amount to be collected overall, Howe assured them that the federal government would have enough revenue without destroying the farmers of America. The Senate, however, later rejected his scheme.[2]

Before voting on the measure, Fessenden and Simmons gave their final thoughts on H.R. 312. "I believe after all that has been said, and strengthened by what I have seen," joyfully proclaimed Fessenden, "there is the best disposition everywhere to meet this matter boldly, strongly, with stout hearts and calm minds, and a willingness to take... this additional burden upon them, and more, even, if the necessities of the country require it."[3] Simmons too believed that the people did not mind bearing the burdens for the war, even if many items of necessity were being taxed. "I think, however we could bear it better in the shape of an income tax," he noted, but threw his support behind its final passage as Senate Republicans voted one hundred percent in favor of the bill.[4] The Senate's version placed a three percent tax on incomes over six hundred dollars, five percent on ten thousand dollars, seven and one-half percent on fifty thousand dollars and an inheritance tax on one thousand dollars.[5]

In the conference committee, the only change made to the tax bill was to strike out the seven and one-half percent bracket and leave it at five percent. As

[1] Ibid., 2449.
[2] Ibid., 2574-2575.
[3] Ibid., 2610.
[4] Ibid., 2611.
[5] Weisman, *The Great Tax Wars*, 41.

Stevens pointed out, "We did not agree to that provision imposing seven and a half per cent on incomes over fifty thousand dollars."[1] The final legislation kept the three and five percent sections the same; created a three percent tax on corporations, railroad dividends, banks, trust companies and insurance companies; a five percent tax on incomes of Americans living abroad; a one and one-half percent tax on government bonds; suspended direct taxes for two years;[2] and created the Internal Revenue Bureau to collect all of the tax imposed by the federal government.[3]

Unlike the first bill that introduced the tax on incomes, this measure would be enforced by Congressional Republicans and the Lincoln Administration because of the heavy losses experienced by Union forces. With the momentum on the Confederates' side, the United States government desperately needed the funds.

Northern newspapers were split on the effectiveness of the new income tax bill. For example, two of the largest papers in New York, the *Herald* and *Times*, resembled the division within the media at the time on the particulars of the legislation. "The Tax bill," stated the *New York Herald*, "has been found defective in very many particulars, and will require much amendment in the Senate, if it should not be suspended there by the substitution of an entirely new bill."[4] Conversely, *The New York Times* took a less negative view on the creation of an income tax, adding,

> The income taxes so framed as to place the heaviest burthen upon that
> portion of the people who have the largest material stake in the country
> and the nearest interest in the integrity, public faith and lasting stability
> of the Government; the men of money and of productive stocks and other
> income paying securities.[5]

The *Herald* felt that the government made a law that was not equal in its implementation of the income tax, while the *Times* contended that the income tax should be unequal and placed upon the shoulders of the upper class.

Other newspapers were also divided on not only the implementation of the income tax, but also the language utilized by Congress in the bill. "Never did a

---

[1] *Congressional Globe, 37th Congress, 2nd Session*, 2891.

[2] Edwin Robert Anderson Seligman, *The Income Tax Part 2* (New York: The Macmillan Company, 1911), 437-438.

[3] Heather Cox Richardson, *The Greatest Nation of the Earth: Republican Economic Policies During the Civil War* (Cambridge: Harvard University Press, 1997), 116.

[4] *New York Herald*, 13 April 1862.

[5] "The Internal Tax Bill," *New York Times*, 4 March 1862.

people," explained the *San Francisco Bulletin*, "almost ignorant of what taxes were, face a gigantic system of taxation with such good heart before. If the system is judiciously shaped the burden will rest so equally upon all that after the first year it will scarcely be recognized as a burden."[1] *The Weekly Patriot and Union* instructed its readers to patriotically pay the income tax even if they believed it to be unjust or a harsh financial affliction. It demanded of its readers, "Make fair returns — pay your assessment without grumbling. The necessity growing out of this glorious war in which we are engaged require it — the necessities of the poor enslaved negro require it — and these necessities must be met."[2] *The Crisis* newspaper supported the income tax, but opposed the definition of income in the legislation because it stated that income was everything a person made without subtracting his or her expenses. The newspaper wrote,

> It would be wrong to tax a mechanic, farmer, or other person the gross
> amount that might come to him, without considering and deducting his
> outgoes, and call that "gains, profits and incomes" subject to taxation.
> Such a construction would repress industry and prevent improvement.[3]

To most media, it was easy to see that the country would benefit from an income tax as part of national revenue collection; but this was certainly a radical step that had not been asked for but pushed upon society by the secessionist states.

Historians had one defined view as to why Republicans chose to support such a drastic new measure as a tax upon the vast incomes in the United States: they believed that the Grand Old Party did so to keep the extreme viewpoints away from the political process by bending somewhat to their pressure. As Robert Stanley noted in his text, *Dimensions of Law in the Service of Order: Origins of the Federal Income Tax, 1861-1913*, "The early income tax was designed to preserve imbalances in the structure of wealth and opportunity, rather than ameliorate or abolish them, by strengthening the status quo against the more radical attacks on that structure by the political left and right."[4] Similarly, in *Refinancing America: The Republican Antitax Agenda*, Sheldon Pollack observed that Republicans would rather vote for a small income tax than have a far-reaching progressive tax that

---

[1] "The Coming Era of Taxation," *San Francisco Bulletin*, 31 May 1862.

[2] "The Income Tax," *The Weekly Patriot and Union*, 14 May 1863.

[3] "Income Tax," *The Crisis*, 10 September 1862.

[4] Robert Stanley, *Dimensions of Law in the Service of Order: Origins of the Federal Income Tax, 1861-1913* (New York: Oxford University Press, 1993) viii.

treated each economic class differently.[1] Republicans feared that if they did not champion an income tax measure, radicals would push their agenda and change, in some way, the capitalist system of the United States. They might have taken the opportunity to demand a redistribution of wealth. The G.O.P. chose, there-fore, to swallow their objections and allow an income tax to pass and defuse such arguments.

The 1862 bill was America's first glimpse as to the positive and negative as-pects of an income tax. Never before in the United States had the national govern-ment directly reached into the pockets of average citizens for funding. Certainly, they had indirectly taxed the public through tariffs and excise taxes, but most of the population had not openly witnessed the government collecting revenue from them. Republicans were fully supportive of the tax, but, within two years, some congressional representatives put forth the concept of progressive rates of taxation. This notion did not sit well with some Republicans who viewed it as a violation of basic equality in the United States, and many of these opponents to progressive rates would be the first to call for the ultimate repeal of the income tax after the Civil War.

[1] Sheldon D. Pollack, *Refinancing America: The Republican Antitax Agenda* (New York: State University of New York Press, 2003), 24.

Chapter 5. The Fracture Begins: 1864 Revenue Law

"It seems to me that it is a strange way to punish men because they are rich." — Representative Thaddeus Stevens (Republican — Pennsylvania)

"I do not like and cannot approve the discrimination, the distinction in the rates of assessment or taxation upon incomes." — Senator Solomon Foot (Republican — Vermont)

By 1864, the tide was turning in favor of the Union as the Confederates experienced deep defeats and setbacks from which they never fully recovered. The deaths of several popular and skillful leaders were a major factor in the sinking spirits in the Rebel South. After a successful campaign at Chancellorsville in 1863, Thomas "Stonewall" Jackson received fatal wounds when a small group of Confederate soldiers accidentally shot him as he patrolled at night. Doctors amputated his arm to prevent infection, but Jackson succumbed to pneumonia. Not long after Jackson's demise, J.E.B. Stuart, the handsome soldier who helped Lee capture John Brown at Harper's Ferry in 1859, lost his life at the Battle of Yellow Tavern. Without a doubt, the loss of these important commanders demoralized the South and denied the Confederate military of prominent and intellectual leadership; they placed all of their hopes with Lee, but even he, by this time, was feeling the winds of defeat at the hands of the Union forces.[1]

---

[1] Allen C. Guelzo, *The Crisis of the American Republic: A History of the Civil War and Reconstruction Era* (New York: St. Martin's Press, 1995), 266.

In mid-1863, Lee devised a daring strategy in order for the Confederacy to achieve its desired independence. Conquering the Northern states was neither a desirable nor a feasible goal; rather, Lee calculated that if he won a few battles in the region, the people of the Union might grow weary of the Lincoln Administration and vote him out of office the next year. This would allow for the Peace Democrats, also known as "Copperheads," to occupy the White House and seek a treaty with the Confederate States of America, recognizing it as a sovereign nation.

Accordingly, Lee chose to march his troops into Pennsylvania, and, while searching for better shoes, they met with an unexpected assault. Union forces, under the command of General George Meade, attacked on July 1 at the town of Gettysburg. Deadlocked, neither side could gain the upper hand. Then an ill-fated decision doomed Lee and his soldiers. For reasons unknown, and still debated to this day, George Pickett and his company charged the Union army, suffering a loss of 1,100 soldiers and failing to achieve anything positive for the Confederates. Lee conceded the battle and retreated his forces back to Virginia. As the Union stood victorious at Gettysburg and the momentum of the conflict shifted in their direction, Lee, on the other hand, came to the stark realization that he would probably never be able to win any battles in the North. The Confederates had won some battles in early fighting, but almost all on their home turf, and Lee understood that was not enough to secure a definitive victory. Twenty thousand Southern soldiers had lost their lives at Gettysburg, and they were not the only spirits dead by the end of the battle.[1]

The devastating battle at Gettysburg gave Lincoln an opportunity to speak about the war in terms that strongly assumed that the tide was turning in favor of the Union. Four months after the battle, he addressed the people with words that have become famous in United States history:

> But, in a larger sense, we can not dedicate...we can not consecrate...we can not hallow this ground. The brave men, living and dead, who struggled here, have consecrated it, far above our poor power to add or detract. The world will little note, nor long remember what we say here, but it can never forget what they did here. It is for us the living, rather, to be dedicated here to the unfinished work, which they who fought here have thus far so nobly advanced. It is rather for us to be here dedicated to the great task remaining before us that from these honored dead we take increased

---

[1] Ibid., 267-268.

devotion to that cause for which they gave the last full measure of devotion that we here highly resolve that these dead shall not have died in vain
that this nation, under God, shall have a new birth of freedom and that
government: of the people, by the people, for the people, shall not perish
from the earth.[1]

With the Gettysburg Address, Lincoln helped to rally the public to continue
the fight to block the secession of the Southern states.

The Southern cause appeared all but lost, especially with the surrender of
Vicksburg by General John Pemberton to General Grant around the same time.
The South simply did not have the strength and numbers to defeat the North on
its own land, and now it also had to face the fact that the Union controlled the
Mississippi River. It would not be too much longer before the Confederate States
of America surrendered its forces, its government and, eventually, its way of life.[2]

As the United States marched towards the finish of the Civil War, the federal
government still needed more revenue to keep the military strong and vibrant.
By this time, the income tax had been in operation for two years, and not only
members of Congress but also the individuals who collected the tax praised its
success, even though most understood that it was, in a sense, an unequal burden.
The Commissioner of Internal Revenue, Joseph J. Lewis, acknowledged this fact
in his annual report,

> This tax though as fair in theory as any that can be laid, has been found
> by the experience of other countries to be incumbered with practical dif-
> ficulties in the assessment which have deprived it of all claims to public
> favor... People of this country have accepted it with cheerfulness, to meet a
> temporary exigency, and it has excited no serious complaint in its admin-
> istration. In order that it may not be felt to be inquisitorial in its character,
> the instructions issued by this office of required that the returns of in-
> come shall not be open to the inspection of others than officers of revenue.
> Some doubt having been entertained whether a proper construction of
> the law sustains the instructions, I recommend that the doubt be removed
> by express enactment.

Throughout the entire report, Lewis showed how effective his government
entity was in collecting the tax upon incomes. To prevent any sort of problems
and complaints against the tax, he and his agency tried to remedy many of its
faults. He protected against personal financial statements becoming public, and

---

[1] Abraham Lincoln, *Gettysburg Address*, 19 November 1863.
[2] Guelzo, *The Crisis of the American Republic*, 268-269.

he underscored the United States citizens' acceptance of the burden as a direct contribution to the Union cause. The income tax, in his judgment, was working to perfection, yet more money was desperately needed to maintain the war effort.[1]

On April 26, 1864, the House Committee of Ways and Means introduced H.R. 405, which they hoped to raise two hundred and fifty million dollars through the internal taxes already in practice. Augustus Frank, a Republican and former banker from New York, proposed to keep the three and five percent tax rates, but also offered an amendment for a ten percent tax on incomes exceeding twenty-five thousand dollars a year.[2] "I offer the amendment," Frank said, "because I think it is just, right, and proper that those having a larger amount of income shall pay a larger amount of tax. I believe, with the Secretary of the Treasury, that the larger tax we pay at this time the safer we are and the better will be the securities of the Government."[3]

Iowa Representative and Minister Josiah Grinnell, who Horace Greeley famously urged to "go West" in 1865, reiterated Frank's arguments when he said,

> I am opposed to any discrimination unless there is something that looks like meting out justice to all parties who must pay this tax ...[I] could not in justice to myself and to our country advocate anything else in this time of high living for the masses.... I am in favor of increasing the tax on large incomes. I am speaking for justice in this regard. I say, that a man who has an income of over ten thousand dollars should be required to live out of that income in time of war, and not be able to lay aside more than ninety per cent of his income and to pay only ten per cent of it to the Government, is only reasonable.

Attacking the upper class for not contributing a fair portion of its wealth to finance the government, Grinnell, a friend of abolitionist John Brown, complained, "They do not contribute to the Government a proportion anything like that paid by those who are worth a less sum of money who have gone into our Army." He concluded, "It is time that extravagance in gewgaws, snobbishness in display, and that large class whose great care is to safely compound their hundreds of

---

[1] Edwin Robert Anderson Seligman, *The Income Tax Part 2* (New York: The Macmillan Company, 1911), 439.

[2] Joseph A. Hill, "The Civil War Income Tax," *The Quarterly Journal of Economics* 8 no. 4 (July 1894): 423.

[3] *The Congressional Globe: Official Proceeding of Congress, 38th Congress, 1st Session* (Washington, D.C.: John C. Rives, 1864), 1876.

thousands, should feel that there is war and a demand which they have not yet felt on their purses and on their patriotism."[1]

Rufus Spalding of Ohio, a Yale graduate, simply stated, "I can see no injustice in thus graduating the tax." Those Republicans who resided in Midwestern and Western states, which did not have much income and wanted the wealthier areas, such as the industrial Northeastern states, to bear more of the revenue burden, mainly supported Frank's idea. Both Spalding and Grinnell represented states in the Midwestern region and thus proclaimed proudly their support for graduated income tax rates in favor of taxes on land or property.[2]

Republicans in the Northeast, however, were not keen on the concept presented in Frank's bill. In fact, they were openly hostile towards it, citing the unequal treatment of those in different economic classes as the key reason why it was incorrect policy. Justin Morrill saw this injustice and stated on the House floor,

> No one doubts our constitutional power to levy this tax, and the question is one merely of policy in relation to revenue. Experience under the provisions of the old act on this subject shows that people who are taxed unequally on their incomes regard themselves as being unjustly treated, and seek all manner of ways and means to evade it. This inequality is in fact no less than a confiscation of property, because one man happens to have a little more money than another.[3]

John Hubbard also recognized the underlying problem with graduated rates of taxation. "I very much dislike the discrimination provided for in the amendment offered by the gentleman from New York," the Connecticut Representative added. "In my judgment it is wrong. By the bill as it stands the poor man is required to pay nothing and the man of modest means little or nothing, while the wealth of the country is taxed for the purpose of revenue."[4] In essence, Hubbard was increasingly upset with those who did not desire to tax the poor equally with the affluent; instead, he believed the wealthy class had been forced to finance the government through their income while the working class escaped its portion of the tax bill.

Besides these men, Thaddeus Stevens was the most ardent opponent to the implementation of the amendment. In a harsh diatribe, the Dartmouth alumnus

---

[1] Ibid., 1876-1877.
[2] Ibid., 1876-1877.
[3] Ibid., 1876.
[4] Ibid., 1877.

charged that the tax was not only unequal but also hindered the economic progress of industrious individuals. "It seems to me that it is a strange way to punish men because they are rich. I do not know but that there ought to be an indictment against every man who ventures to go above $600 in income," he pointed out to his fellow congressional representatives. "If any man dare go above a certain amount, more than I am worth or any other member, then we should take it all." Stevens felt that the wealthy already paid their amount to the federal government, noting, "The rich man pays according to his wealth. If he is made to increase the tax according to his wealth, it is a punishment." Congress and the government must treat each economic class as equals, in his view, and make "no distinction between one man and another because one is richer than another. That is right and just." Without any doubt, in Stevens' mind, the tax rates of three and five percent were sufficient and equal, but a graduated income tax system "amounts, at last, to nothing more than a punishment of the rich man because he is rich." Expressing the sentiments of the Republicans on the Ways and Means Committee, Stevens, a strong ally of the railroad corporations, finished his remarks by saying that they "were of the opinion that the principle was a vicious one. I think the principle of taxing a man worth $20,000 more in proportion to his wealth is an unjust one.... If he is worth over a million dollars we might as well provide that the Government shall take the surplus."[1]

Republicans who opposed the idea of graduated, or sometimes referred to as progressive, rates had a united opinion as to why it was ultimately wrong: it was unequal, which would inevitably lead to problems in the overall economy. The inequality inherent in Frank's proposal, from their stand point, would cause wealthier people to think the government was treating them wrongly; it would encourage them to either withhold money to be taxed or prevent them from moving upward in the capitalistic system. They therefore argued for a flat tax.

Immediately, Henry Dawes of Massachusetts, a backer of Frank's amendment, complained to Stevens about his argument. Dawes saw it as fair and moral to tax different levels of wealth with different rates. "Does the gentleman from Pennsylvania," quipped Dawes, "call it punishing the rich men to make them pay their share of the burdens of taxation, or does he think that the poor should pay the taxes for the rich?" He, like many other Republicans, rejected the notion that progressive tax rates discriminated against economic classes and bred jealousy.

---

[1] Ibid., 1876.

The debate ended for that day, but picked up soon afterwards with greater tensions forming between to the two sides.[1]

Two days later, on April 28, Samuel Hooper of Massachusetts, the father-in-law to Senator Charles Sumner, proposed an addition to Frank's amendment, which had passed a House vote. In it, the government would have the graduated rates for one year, and then the tax would become uniform at eight percent. With this amendment, Hooper exhibited his disdain for Frank's idea. "I object," he said, "to the introduction of the principle of the gentleman from New York, selecting certain men of wealth to be taxed as a class at a different rate." Undeniably, Hooper opposed the idea in principle because it sought to "crush down rich men"; he was unable, though, to persuade his colleagues to vote for his motion and it went down to defeat, and the graduated tax rates remained the same in the original amendment.[2]

On the day of the vote in the House of Representatives, Morrill knew that he did not have enough votes to stop the introduction of progressive tax rates into the system of internal revenue. In his speech, he made one final point on his belief that Frank's measure was unjust.

> On all other subjects we tax every man alike. This provision goes upon the principle of taxing a man more because he is richer than another. The very theory of our institutions is entire equality; that we make no distinctions between the rich man and the poor man. The man of moderate means is just as good as the man with more means, but our theory of government does not admit he is better.

Deeming that it "is seizing property of men for the crime of having too much," Morrill described what would inevitably occur if the Congress adopted progressive taxation upon the affluent class: the people of that class would think that the federal government was discriminating against them and therefore would feel justified in making every attempt to hide their fortunes to avoid paying the tax. In the end, Morrill feared that the effect of the policy would be the denial of much-needed funds for the war effort.[3] The House, nonetheless, ignored his plea and not one Grand Old Party representative voted against the tax bill. It was supported by even those who denounced the graduated income tax rates as inequitable, because Republicans, such as Stevens, Morrill and Hooper, did not want to appear to be against the war by voting no on any revenue-seeking legislation.

---

[1] Ibid., 1876.
[2] Ibid., 1938.
[3] Ibid., 1940.

Therefore, they chose to back the bill even if they opposed one feature of the bill, due to the fact that they were content with almost everything else in it.

The final House bill created three different rates of taxation: five percent on six hundred dollars, seven and one-half percent on ten thousand dollars and ten percent on twenty-five thousand dollars. Not only had they established a graduated system, but also boosted the percentage in the first tax bracket from three to five percent. Indeed, the income tax, with the help of Republicans, was taking shape throughout the nation as this new concept was increasingly becoming more expansive in its reach each year it remained a part of government revenue collection. The bill next moved to the Senate, where there was much more antagonism towards the idea of progressive taxation among the Republicans in the chamber.[1]

Fessenden reported the bill to the full Senate, but the Finance Committee struck out the ten percent provision and left it at the two rates of five and seven and one-half percent. Immediately, G.O.P. senators came to the floor to criticize the idea of graduated income tax rates. Fessenden confessed, "my own opinion is not exceedingly well fixed on this yet," but understood that any income tax "at best is a discrimination." He rationalized the concept of progressive rates, stating, "I have been in favor of making some discrimination as against large incomes." Despite his own opinion, Fessenden believed, "there is and ought to be a sort of conservative sentiment to protect property." If the government, in his view, taxed the wealthy class exceedingly, the overall wealth of the nation would surely dissipate, causing society and people to be more impoverished. He explained further,

> While in times of emergency especially we call upon it to pay largely, it is believed by many that it ought not be unreasonably harshly burdened... It is for the interest of the community that men should be incited in every possible way to accumulate, because as much as they accumulate by their industry they add to the national wealth.

Fessenden took a similar position as Stevens, thinking that punishment of success would only lead to less individuals seeking to achieve higher standards of living due to fear of it being seized through taxation. "For this reason," Fessenden added, "while we adopt the principle that those having very large incomes can afford, and perhaps better afford than those who have smaller ones, to pay a tax, a large tax, and the discriminating tax, if you please, there are limits even to that."

---

[1] Robert Stanley, *Dimensions of Law in the Service of Order: Origins of the Federal Income Tax, 1861-1913* (New York: Oxford University Press, 1993), 33.

Deducing that the idea of progressive rates infringed on citizens' property rights, Fessenden held that excessive rates of taxation had to be curtailed to maintain a productive and vibrant economy.[1]

Vermont Senator Solomon Foot joined Fessenden in condemning progressive tax rates. He firmly rejected the principle, exclaiming,

> I do not like and cannot approve the discrimination, the distinction in the rates of assessment or taxation upon incomes as proposed in the House bill. I cannot but regard it as a wrong and indefensible in principle, and I think it will prove to be odious in practice. It is calculated to excite jealousy and disaffection, and I apprehend that it will prove, upon experience, if it shall be suffered to stand, productive of harm, much more than of benefit, in its operation.

Foot asserted that if these graduated rates were placed in the law books, the upper, middle and lower classes would clash with one another because of the differential treatment of each class by the government in the rate of taxation. The wealthy would despise the lower class for not paying any tax and the middle class for paying less in percent of taxation. To avoid these inevitable societal problems, Foot believed that the income tax must be a flat rate so as to be uniform. The economic classes "expect, however, as they have a right to expect, that these taxes shall be levied upon all classes alike, according to their several ability and means to pay, without prejudice upon the one hand or favoritism upon the other." Holding to the concept that progressive tax rates bred jealousy and hatred among the economic classes, Foot feared that only conflict would be the result, splitting a nation that had to be unified during the battle against Southern rebels. People in those classes who were forced to pay more in proportion to their wealth would cry out and feel as though they were not getting an equal break from the national government; hostility was the last thing the government needed at that time. He asked the supporters of this idea, "upon what principle of ethics or of equity would you impose a higher rate of taxation upon one of the parties than upon the other?" Foot admitted that he was more than willing to vote in favor of increasing the income tax, but the rates had to be "uniform; otherwise, it is discriminating against one class, and that a small class, I am aware." Foot had no quarrels about taxing people more to pay for war debts, but it had to be a flat tax rate and not progressive as was put forth in the bill.[2]

---

[1] *The Congressional Globe, 38th Congress, 1st Session,* 2513.
[2] Ibid., 2514.

One of the most shocking objections to the graduated income tax rates was a senator who vehemently pushed for the creation and continuance of the tax — John Sherman, the relative of Civil War hero William T. Sherman. Even though he supported taxing incomes as part of the nation's financial structure, he deemed that progressive were wrong in theory and in practice. The Ohio Senator noted,

> I think discriminations in the rates of duty are objectionable.... All discriminations between rates of taxation on incomes tend to promote perjury and lead to abuse. I do not think that because a man is wealthy he ought to pay a higher rate of taxation. The effect of such a proposition is generally to induce a man to resort to subterfuges to decrease the apparent amount of his income, so as to avoid the payment of the tax.

Like many of his fellow Republican senators, Sherman was aware of the vast inequality present in forcing citizens of different economic classes to pay taxes on a different scale. He also knew that, when faced with this reality, the wealthy class typically avoided paying the tax altogether, thus decreasing the whole revenue flow to the treasury. "All taxes," he added, "are paid more readily when people believe that they are paid more equally by all classes of citizens. Because a man is wealthy, I do not think a different rule of taxation should be applied to him any more because he is poor."[1]

Likewise, the ardent abolitionist Charles Sumner criticized the bill and predicted that it was going to do more harm on the American people. He said, "The tax that is proposed by the House of Representatives and which our committee proposes to strike out would not be very productive, and I have reason to believe that it would be odious. I do not think that we shall accomplish enough by it to pay for what it will cost." Sumner not only pointed out that the cost of executing this structure would outweigh the benefits gained from it, but also that it was inherently unequal to distinguish between people based upon their wealth. At the time, they waged a war so that African Americans were to be seen not as slaves, but as citizens of the nation; in the same manner, many Republicans, as well, did not want to make a distinction of individuals based upon their economic classes with the federal tax code.[2]

During the debate on the bill, Massachusetts Senator Henry Wilson, a Civil War veteran and future Vice President under Grant, authored an amendment that prevented the head of household from spreading his wealth to other family

---

[1] Ibid., 2513-2514.
[2] Ibid., 2515.

members in order to get under the six hundred dollars exemption. His proposal allowed him the opportunity to speak out against the tax code, especially the exemption clause. "I am against this $600 exemption. I regard the whole thing as a cover under which the great mass of the income of the country protects its self from taxation," he griped. "Men who own property worth thousands of dollars get exempted under it wholly and entirely." He without question showed discontent over the tax system, claiming that the exemption of six hundred dollars was too much, and that all classes in society needed to pay their share of the taxes. He continued, "I believe great frauds are perpetuated under this exemption as it now stands; that wealthy persons divide their property among their wives and children, and thus getting exempt from tax under this $600 clause." Wilson felt that it generated a tax shelter allowing rich people to avoid paying the income tax during a period of great turmoil in United States history. To him, they disgraced the country, hiding their money by giving it to their families and not honestly stating their true wealth. With this amendment, Wilson, too, wanted to tax incomes fewer than six hundred dollars at three percent, but the Senate voted down his entire amendment.[1]

On June 6, Wilson presented another amendment to alter the rates in the tax bill: a six hundred dollar exemption, a five percent tax on incomes between six hundred dollars and two thousand dollars, and a seven-and-one-half percent tax on incomes exceeding two thousand dollars. Although he realized that the tax discriminated against economic classes, Wilson theorized that most wealthy individuals probably would not mind paying it since "it will reach so large a class in the community, so many men who are able to pay, that I think there will be no objection to this form."[2] Several Republicans agreed with his estimation. "I am perfectly content to vote for the amendment of the Senator from Massachusetts, if we should carry out a system of graduation and let the big fellows who get from $25,000 up to $100,000 a year pay a proportionate rate," said James Grimes.[3]

Other Republicans, such as Fessenden, did not sense that Wilson's amendment was a good idea. He thought that it was "too much of a tax on such small incomes." Despite objection, Wilson's proposal was accepted as part of the revenue bill.[4]

---

[1] Ibid., 2515-2516.
[2] Ibid., 2759.
[3] Ibid., 2759.
[4] Ibid., 2759.

That same day, Grimes offered an amendment to reestablish the ten percent rate taken out originally and impose it on incomes that exceeded ten thousand dollars. He justified his motion,

> I propose to carry that principle out to a little greater extent, and cause these men who have large fortunes and derive them from large incomes to pay a little amount, only 2 ½ percent, in addition to the rate paid by the small men who exhaust nearly all this income in the support of their families... If there is any class of men that the distinctions ought to be made in favor of and not against it is the very class of men we have discriminated against, and now we reach a class of men who have a surplus over and above the money that is necessary to meet their family expenses, and it is that class I propose to reach and tax.

From Grimes' standpoint, wealthy people could easily afford a ten percent tax rate because their finances were exuberant enough to pay the government, yet not feel much of the burden.[1]

His plan, though, met with some stiff opposition from his fellow G.O.P. senators. "It seems to me," asserted John Henderson of Missouri, "that perfect justice requires that the same tax shall be levied on the same amount of property anywhere." Emphasizing the same themes used by many Republicans in the Senate on the first day of debate, Henderson, the coauthor of the Thirteenth Amendment that abolished slavery, essentially thought that the federal government had the obligation and duty to tax every person exactly the same. He added, "I do not see exactly the justice of imposing a tax so heavy upon incomes... we exempt $600, that is for the poor man; and beyond that it seems to me that incomes ought to bear the same rate." This argument presented by Henderson, however, failed to win sufficient support as Grimes' proposal passed by a slim margin.[2]

The bill passed the Senate the same day of Grimes' amendment. It placed a five percent tax on six hundred dollars, seven and one-half percent on five thousand dollars, and ten percent on fifteen thousand dollars. After the conference committee discussed the bill, they agreed on each graduated rate, but altered the top rate to be taxed at ten percent at ten thousand dollars, instead of fifteen thousand dollars, and limited its collection to the year of 1870.[3] The bill additionally

---

[1] Ibid., 2760.

[2] Ibid., 2760.

[3] Sidney Ratner, *American Taxation: Its History as a Social Force in Democracy* (New York: W.W. Norton and Company, 1942), 85.

put a five percent tax on banks, trust companies, insurance companies, railroad companies, canals and turnpikes.[1]

Besides Congressional Republicans, other members of the Grand Old Party showed support for the income tax but in limited ways. On June 20, 1864, Chase wrote to new Secretary of the Treasury William Fessenden, "Better, it seems to me, a tax of ten or even twenty per cent on all incomes than the rapid accumulation of National debt attended, as it must be, by the rapid deterioration of National credit."[2] Lincoln, as well, identified the importance of creating an equal tax system for the national government to collect substantial revenue to continue towards a victorious end of the Civil War. "It is fair," he told the 164th Ohio regiment, "that each man shall pay taxes in exact proportion to the value of his property; but if we should wait before collecting a tax to adjust the taxes upon each man in exact proportion with every other man, we should never collect any tax at all." He appeared to be a backer of the idea of graduated income tax rates, but admitted, because they did not treat all economic classes equally, there would be "some irregularities in the practical application of our system."[3] The Republican-leaning *Chicago Tribune* put it simply this way, "the rich should be taxed more than the poor."[4] The national Republicans were supportive of any measure that helped to end the bloody conflict raging between the North and South and that included discriminating against certain groups of society who made more money and had more assets than another group.

Some historians are somewhat misguided by the facts of the debate over the graduated income tax rates by Republicans in Congress. For example, Sheldon Pollack contended that the idea "provoked intense objections among a number of Republicans of the injustice the graduate tax rate would inflict on the wealthy." It was true that Republicans such as Stevens insisted that the tax wrongly punished rich individuals, but they pointed out the inequality of the tax and were not necessarily the advocates of the upper class. In each remark to describe it, they utilized the words "inequality" and "discrimination," and they did not clamor

---

[1] Seligman, *The Income Tax*, 444.

[2] John Niven, ed., The *Salmon P. Chase Papers, Volume 4: Correspondence 1863-1864* (Kent: Kent State University Press, 1997), 400.

[3] Roy P. Basler, ed., *The Collected Works of Abraham Lincoln: Volume 7* (New Brunswick, Rutgers University Press, 1953), 505.

[4] Lewis L. Gould, *Grand Old Party: A History of the Republicans* (New York: Random House, 2003), 32.

about how the wealthy should not be taxed at all as suggested in Pollack's assessment.[1] Another example was Robert Stanley, who noted,

> During the income tax debates two rhetorical profiles emerged, sharply disparate in their style of argument, because the law struck simultaneously at so many economic fault lines, including regional hostility, rural/urban tensions, and, most clearly, class anxieties. Proponents of the tax focused on the hard empirical facts of economic disparity and the complicity of the law in its creation, while opponents sought to divert attention from these themes by focusing on the alleged intrusive effects of the tax, and claiming that as the sole creators of their fortunes, taxpayers owed no compensation.[2]

As was seen by the arguments given against the graduated income tax features by Congressional Republicans, they opposed the tax because it was unequal in its application not because of its intrusiveness or basic implementation. Certainly, later debates focused on whether or not the tax should be kept in practice, but the opponents were not as concerned about its invasive features as its injustice towards all economic classes in America.

The bill of 1864, which introduced the concept of graduated income tax rates, commenced a decline in support of the tax by many in the Republican Party. Without question, members of the G.O.P. still backed the measure and argued for its continuance so that the Union could crush the rebels with sufficient resources. Progressive tax rates, however, made some Republicans uneasy, especially those who represented wealthier areas in the Northeastern United States. The foundation of support was slowly slipping away, and this bill exposed the distinct contrast in thinking between different factions of the Republican Party. Never again in its history would the Grand Old Party stand unified in favor of a federal income tax.

---

[1] Sheldon D. Pollack, *Refinancing America: The Republican Antitax Agenda* (New York: State University of New York Press, 2003), 23.

[2] Stanley, *Dimensions of Law*, 46.

CHAPTER 6. THE ATTEMPT OF A FLAT TAX RATE: 1865–1868

"In this country we neither create nor tolerate any distinction of rank, race, or
color, and should not tolerate anything else than entire equality in our taxation."
— Representative Justin Morrill (Republican — Vermont)
"So far as the Constitution speaks of taxation at all it says that it shall be equal." —
Representative James Garfield (Republican — Ohio)

By 1865, victory was all but certain for the Union Army. With victory in the
air, Lincoln had won reelection in November of 1864 over the Democratic nominee and his famous foe, George McClellan, for a second term.[1] On March 4, 1865,
he gave his most important speech — his Second Inaugural Address, where he
declared that the United States government would show

> malice toward none; with charity for all; with firmness in the right, as
> God gives us to see the right, let us strive on to finish the work we are in;
> to bind up the nation's wounds; to care for him who shall have borne the
> battle, and for his widow, and his orphan—to do all which may achieve
> and cherish a just and lasting peace, among ourselves, and with all nations.[2]

Lincoln resumed his policies to crush the Confederate secession movement
with his lieutenant general, Grant, concocting a scheme of total war on the South.
He gave William T. Sherman the freedom to destroy almost every city and town
in Georgia and South Carolina with his "March to the Sea." (Sherman once fa-

---

[1] Charles P. Roland, *An American Iliad: The Story of the Civil War* 2nd ed. (Lexington:
University Press of Kentucky, 2002), 241-244.
[2] Abraham Lincoln, *2nd Inaugural Address*, 4 March 1865.

mously declared in front of an Ohioan crowd, "There is many a boy here today who looks on war as all glory, but, boys, it is all hell.") Grant understood that the strategy would horribly demoralize not only the Confederate troops, but also the people and the government. And the more the citizens of the Confederacy turned against the war effort, the more easily victory would come for the Union.[1]

In the Northern theater, Lee was engaged in his last campaigns as Union forces were closing in on him. After the United States Army captured the Confederate capital of Richmond, Lee knew that his fighting days were numbered. In April, Lee finally surrendered to Grant at Appomattox Courthouse, ending four years of conflict, injury and the loss of life (six hundred thousand in all).[2] General Lee gave an impassioned speech to his defeated subordinates on April 10, 1865,

> After four years of arduous service marked by unsurpassed courage and fortitude, the Army of Northern Virginia has been compelled to yield to overwhelming numbers and resources. I need not tell the survivors of so many hard fought battles, who have remained steadfast to the last, that I have consented to the result from no distrust of them. But feeling that valour and devotion could accomplish nothing that could compensate for the loss that must have attended the continuance of the contest, I have determined to avoid the useless sacrifice of those whose past services have endeared them to their countrymen. By the terms of the agreement, officers and men can return to their homes and remain until exchanged. You will take with you the satisfaction that proceeds from the consciousness of duty faithfully performed, and I earnestly pray that a merciful God will extend to you his blessing and protection. With an unceasing admiration of your constancy and devotion to your Country, and a grateful remembrance of your kind and generous consideration for myself, I bid you an affectionate farewell.[3]

The Union cheered. Lincoln rejoiced at the fall of the Confederate States of America but did not live to see the Union put back together. A few days after Lee's surrender, Lincoln attended the play "Our American Cousin" at Ford's Theater in Washington, D.C. While the Lincolns were sitting in the presidential box, John Wilkes Booth, a Southern actor, opened the door behind Lincoln and shot him in the back of his head. Booth jumped from the box, breaking his leg as he fell onto the stage. Standing on his injured leg, Booth shouted to the stunned

---

[1] Roland, *An American Iliad*, 241-244.
[2] Ibid., 241-244.
[3] Robert E. Lee, *Farewell Address*, 10 April 1865.

crowd, "Sic Semper Tyrannus!," which, in Latin, means "Thus always to tyrants." The quote was not only the motto of Virginia, the headquarters of the Confederacy, but also supposedly was said by Brutus upon the murder of Julius Caesar. He added as he limped off the stage, "I have done it, the South is avenged!" and proceeded to escape the theater through a back exit. Booth then mounted his horse and rode out of Washington.[1]

Lincoln was transported out the theater and rushed to the Petersen House across the street. There, he lay dying as members of his Cabinet and fellow Republicans visited him over the next few days. Booth's plot also included the killing of Secretary of State William Seward and Vice President Andrew Johnson, a Southern Democrat. Seward survived his assault with the help of a metal neck brace that he wore due to a previous injury in a carriage accident. The man appointed to assassinate Johnson refused to go through with the plot, staying in a local bar in Washington and getting drunk. Lincoln, however, was the main target, and Booth succeeded in his plan to rid the nation of him and avenge or boost the pride of the Southern people.[2] When Lincoln died, Secretary of War Edwin Stanton proclaimed, "Now he belongs to the ages."[3]

Booth, however, remained the most wanted man in the nation; he was the first person ever to assassinate a United States president. He spent the next week in the swamps of Virginia and Maryland, having had his leg splinted by Dr. Samuel Mudd on the night of Lincoln's murder. During his time on the lam, Booth wrote of his experiences and attempted to explain his rationale for killing Lincoln. "I know how foolish I shall be deemed for undertaking such a step as this, where, on one side, I have many friends and everything to make me happy ... to give up all ... seems insane; but God is my judge. I love justice more than I do a country that disowns it, more than fame or wealth," he wrote in a letter to his sister. He also believed that "African slavery is one of the greatest blessings that God has ever bestowed upon a favored nation," and that Lincoln was purposely trying to destroy the Southern way of life. Federal authorities eventually found Booth in a barn where he was shot and killed.[4]

---

[1] George H. Mayer, *The Republican Party 1854-1964* (New York: Oxford University Press, 1964), 124.

[2] Ibid., 124.

[3] David Herbert Donald, *Lincoln* (New York: Touchstone, 1996), 599.

[4] "John Wilkes Booth," 6 September 2009, http://en.wikipedia.org/wiki/John_Wilkes_Booth.

Lincoln's passing, just as his idol Henry Clay's death did, left a void within his own party, along with fear, as a Democrat who once owned slaves in Tennessee was now the overseer of the Reconstruction process. During this same time, a small fight was brewing among Grand Old Party members dealing with the income tax and whether or not it should be graduated, flat, or completely removed from the law books. It was a fight that would not conclude until 1872.

With fears of the war slowly dwindling, some individuals, mostly industrial and capitalist supporters, became weary of having to pay the income tax. It was acceptable to foot the bill of the conflict, but the fighting had come to an end, and there was no more need for such monumental government expenditures. Wealthy and commercial forces, mainly in Northeastern metropolitan areas, formed anti-income tax associations in protest. They believed that there was inherent injustice of any type of tax upon incomes. Members signed petitions, held rallies, and even sent representatives to lobby Congressional leaders and testify against its continuation.[1] "The income tax has, since the time that it was first levied and imposed, produced great discontent," said the New York Anti-Income Tax Association's address. "It is a burden felt to be oppressive and unjust."[2]

The Northeast, as was evident by where most of the anti-income tax associations commenced, made the loudest clamor for its repeal, and the newspapers of the region also expressed much contempt for it to remain as a permanent vehicle for government revenue. *The Nation* said,

> No fact speaks so well, for the loyalty of the American people, and in support of their determination to pay their debts as readiness with which they submit to the payment of war taxes in times of peace... It is a tax that can be defended only by the necessity of the case, seeing that it bears hard upon men of moderate means, and that it is by its nature essentially inquisitorial.[3]

It pointed out, as well, "every one's business and mode of life is at the mercy of the tax gatherers, who in all ages have been regarded as the most odious of mankind."[4] Similarly, the *New York Tribune* noted, "The Income Tax is the most

---

[1] Elmer Ellis, "Public Opinion and the Income Tax, 1860-1900," *The Mississippi Valley Historical Review* 27 no. 2 (September 1940): 229.

[2] "Down with the Taxes; Formation of an Anti-income Tax Association, Organization and Address to the Public," *New York Times*, 30 March 1871.

[3] Charles Adams, *Those Dirty Rotten Taxes: The Tax Revolts that Built America* (New York: The Free Press, 1998), 141.

[4] Ibid., 185.

odious, vexatious, inquisitorial, and unequal of all our taxes."[1] The *Philadelphia Evening Bulletin* denounced the income tax as "the most onerous and odious of all taxes," and that it "should be removed."[2]

The Weekly Patriot and Union, as well, sought to generate outrage against the tax from its readers. "We all know how grinding this excessive taxation has been, and how much more grinding it will be if it must be submitted to another year," the paper stated. It believed that the income tax "is one of the most, if not the most, oppressive of all taxes, and should have been greatly reduced if not altogether abolished weeks ago."[3] *The New York Herald* made a compelling argument for the "unconstitutionality of the income tax,"[4] while the *New York World* called it a "gross usurpation," and that it was "lawless from the beginning, besides being a swindle, and it was denounced by the democracy as such."[5] *The New York Sun* contended, "every man who pays the income tax pays an unconstitutional tax, levied contrary to law, and which could not be legally collected of him."[6] Indeed, these Northern areas, which were witnessing the growth of commerce and wealth, chose to oppose the tax because, to them, it was unequal and hindered economic activity, thus deflating the prosperity that could be generated by capitalists. These industrialists and "captains of industry" tended to vote for Republican candidates due to their unwavering support for high protective tariffs. The support for tariffs migrated to the party by former Whigs, as stated earlier, who viewed it as a way to keep prices of American products low against cheaper foreign competition. As they voted Republican, and with the completion of the Civil War, capitalists influenced the G.O.P. agenda, and this sway would be seen during the debate over the income tax.

In addition, some newspapers not from the Northeastern section of the United States wanted the income tax to go. For instance, the *Salt Lake Daily Telegraph* stated that the income tax was "unconstitutional and cannot rightfully be collected of any man."[7] Besides them, the *Daily Iowa State Register* simple said, "The revenue law or execution needs overhauling."[8]

[1] Steven R. Weisman, *The Great Tax Wars Lincoln to Wilson: The Fierce Battles Over Money and Power that Transformed the Nation* (New York: Simon and Schuster, 2002), 97.

[2] "Abolish the Income Tax," *Pittsfield Sun*, 31 January 1867.

[3] "Unnecessary Taxes," *Weekly Patriot and Union*, 17 May 1866.

[4] "Unconstitutional Legislation of Congress – Mr. Bartlett's Argument on the Income Tax," *New York Herald*, 9 April 1868.

[5] "The Income Tax," *The Sun*, 13 April 1868.

[6] "The Income Tax and Its Illegality," *Flake's Bulletin*, 15 May 1868.

[7] "Invalidity of the Income Tax Law," *Salt Lake Daily Telegraph*, 28 May 1868.

[8] "Inequality of the Income Tax," *Daily Iowa State Register*, 7 January 1868.

A few newspapers, at this point, saw the need to maintain the income tax even if some opposed its retention. Despite the fact that the war was drawing to a close, they judged that the tax helped alleviate the debt that had mounted as a result of the war. *The Sun* in Baltimore said that a "tax system fully enforced now would release the people from heavy taxes when the reaction of peace should lessen the profits of industry." To them, if the debt was not taken care of at this point, taxes inevitably had to be raised in the future to meet the demands of the government. *The Sun* completed the article by saying that "every sentiment of patriotism demanded that the largest taxation now be fearlessly assessed and impartially collected."[1] The *San Francisco Bulletin* backed keeping the income tax, but also aimed at having a flat tax of five percent. "The raising of the limit to $1,000 will be a great relief to thousands of our industrious citizens, and will tend to equalize the burden imposed by the revenue law," the paper opined. "The rich will pay nearly as much, while the poor will not pay an amount disproportionate to their means."[2] *The New York Times* shared that same sentiment, explaining that they were "in favor of keeping the income tax in existence for the presence — though at a reduced rate."[3] Likewise, the *Philadelphia Inquirer*, who later staunchly contested maintaining the income tax, also expressed a need to preserve the tax for the present time. It realized that some people "grumble at the rates of taxes due to the United States under the internal revenue act," but that they should be satisfied that the tax was very mild and not overbearing.[4] The statements by these newspapers, nonetheless, eventually turned negative towards the tax as government expenditures decreased after the war ended.

Following the passage of the 1864 tax bill, Secretary of the Treasury William Fessenden issued his report to Congress in December on his observations and feelings towards the graduated income tax rates. He wrote, "the income tax should not be collected upon all, without exemption, as the law, as it is, opens the door to innumerable frauds; and in a young and growing country, the vast majority of incomes are small, while all participate alike in the blessings of good government." Though he thought that there should always be some exemption for poorer Americans, he believed there to be no problem with graduated income tax rates. "The adoption," he added, "of a scale augmenting the rate of taxation upon incomes as they rise in amount, though unequal in one sense, cannot be consid-

---

[1] "The Financial Question," *The Sun*, 1 March 1865.
[2] "Reduction of Income Tax," *San Francisco Bulletin*, 27 February 1867.
[3] "Congress and the Income Tax," *New York Times*, 27 January 1870.
[4] "Taxation in Rebeldom," *Philadelphia Inquirer*, 17 March 1865.

ered oppressive or unjust, inasmuch as the ability to pay increases in much more than arithmetical proportions as the amount of increase of income exceeds, the limit of reasonable necessity."[1] Fessenden, who later fell out of favor with Congressional Republicans for his vote against impeaching Johnson, argued, more or less, that taxes on income be made as to increase in percentage as a person's income swelled; he recognized, however, that graduated rates were essentially unequal as the burden of payment rested more on the wealthy class of society.

Joseph J. Lewis, the Commissioner of Internal Revenue, also demonstrated his support for both an income tax and a tariff because, when they were utilized in unison, every person in the United States paid some form of taxation. He justified his sentiments in his report to Congress,

> Many persons will escape assessment who could not escape payment through banks, railroad corporations and paymasters. But the duties on income will in general be assessed more exactly and collected more closely than heretofore... I am unable to see why a man who consumes his income should not be taxed for it as well as one who saves it.[2]

In his judgment, the middle and lower classes escaped the income tax due to the exemption clause, but tariffs allowed the federal government to receive a portion of the tax revenue from those classes. The tariff and income tax benefited the national government, and he considered it essential for Congressional leaders to maintain both after the end of the Civil War. Some Republicans, though, were not willing to heed Lewis' advice.

Less than a year after the passage of the 1864 tax bill, the House Ways and Means Committee reconsidered the graduated income tax rates with members fashioning House Bill 744, which put forward a flat rate of ten percent on incomes exceeding three thousand dollars. The architect of the flat rate, Justin Morrill, presented the legislation on February 9, 1865 and explained in his opening remarks,

> The income tax, intrinsically the most just of all taxes, is yet one extremely difficult of adjustment and collection. The fault found with our present law is that too many large incomes partially escape which ought to contribute more fully. Every man would be content, provided his neighbor paid his just proportion. This we have attempted to remedy by providing that in all cases returns shall be made under oath, and that even then this shall not be final unless the assessor shall be satisfied of their correct-

---

[1] "Report of the Secretary of Treasury," *New York Times*, 7 December 1864.
[2] *Report of the Commissioner of Internal Revenue for 1864* (Washington, D.C.: 1865), 13.

ness. We also propose that all incomes over $3,000 shall be assessed at ten per cent.

Morrill wanted this flat rate from the beginning, but the overwhelming majority of Republicans voting to employ the graduated rates silenced his arguments for it. With the war over, he now felt it possible to achieve a flat rate, which he felt was not only fair for all economic classes, but also gave wealthier Americans more incentive not to avoid payment.[1]

A few of his Grand Old Party associates were not too keen on the flat rate, preferring to keep the rates as currently assessed by the government. For example, Massachusetts Representative John Alley deemed the proposal of Morrill as nothing less than an attempt by the entire Ways and Means Committee to show its disinclination to tax the people. To him, the nation had to tax incomes more to ensure the credit of the United States remained solid and secure. The debt of the country grew steadily during the Civil War and, to remove any form of revenue collection now would be to invite instability and possible economic disaster. Alley stated,

> I have been surprised at their reluctance to bring in a bill which should tax the people of the country as I believe, and as I think I know, they want to be taxed... I believe that if there is anything the people desire more than another, it is that our taxes should be increased to such a degree that the credit of the country should be preserved and protected.[2]

One member of the Ways and Means Committee, Thaddeus Stevens, who previously communicated a distrust of graduated tax rates, challenged Alley's statement. "What burdens does the gentleman from Massachusetts expect it to put on the people?" he asked. "When we come to the income tax, I propose to increase the present rate on all incomes above $2,000 to fifty per cent. Will that gratify the gentleman from Massachusetts? Will the country demand more than that? If it does, I, for one, cannot stand it." Through his hyperbole, Stevens presented what he saw as an absurd argument put forth by his fellow Republican. In his view, the people had bore enough of a tax burden and deserved to be relieved of it, and the flat rate was fair and allowed for the continuation, in some form, of the income tax without resorting to its complete removal. Stevens could not fathom how the American people would want to be taxed more than they had

---

[1] *The Congressional Globe: Official Proceedings of Congress 38th Congress, 2nd Session* (Washington, D.C.: John C. Rives, 1865), 696.
[2] Ibid., 761.

been during the war. Indeed, he thought it was only right to suppress the burden by lowering the rates and creating a flat rate of ten percent.[1]

Some Republicans, conversely, argued in favor of completely removing the income tax because it was no longer necessary to finance the government. Civil War veteran and Ohio Representative James Garfield offered to strike out the entire section dealing with the tax; he despised the fact that it bore heavily on laboring classes. "I believe that this income tax, as now administered, is the very essence of injustice," complained the future President. "This mode of taxation is the very soul of injustice, and if the Committee of Ways and Means cannot devise some mode of adapting the tax to a better scale of justice than this we had better repeal it. There is no equality in this mode of taxation." Garfield found it to be unequal in two ways: it hurt the struggling worker who lived day-by-day on his hard labor, and it treated wealthier individuals wrongly by asking them to bear almost the tax's entire burden. From his standpoint, it had to be fixed to be more just, but, if it could not be adjusted to correct these wrongs, then it must be eliminated entirely.[2]

Morrill, moreover, rebutted the contentions of Garfield. He asked, "Is the gentleman from Ohio prepared to give up thirty-five or fifty millions of income tax and propose a tax directly upon the real estate of the country?" Morrill was not concerned over the small details of the income tax since the war still had not ended, and the Union required revenue in order to sustain itself and crush the rebellion. He was more willing to tax incomes and gain as much money at the present time than debate the wording of the bill.[3]

One section of Morrill's bill that received a great deal of attention was his definition of income. Democrat John Griswold of New York challenged the suggestion that considered profits as the definition of income; he believed property should be the true income determination. Joining him in this belief was Republican Representative George Boutwell of Massachusetts. According to Boutwell,

> The producers and consumers of the country pay the tax; and the only difference there is, and in the difference I find some advantage in the tax upon manufacturers and sales over the income tax, is that the consumers in this country are a larger class than the producers... the larger portion of the pecuniary burdens of this war should be upon property and not upon labor and laborers, for wherever you find a man poor you find a man able

[1] Ibid., 761.
[2] Ibid., 837.
[3] Ibid., 837.

to defend himself; but it is property, in and of itself, which is indefensible, and relies upon man for protection.[1]

Similarly, Massachusetts Representative Samuel Hooper indicated that if "it were possible, I would willingly exempt from taxation all who depend for their support upon their daily labor." These men thought it best to lay property or sales taxes upon the people rather than an income tax, which they described as taking away from the fruits of a man's labor.[2]

Morrill countered their arguments. "I believe that the more just mode of arriving at any income tax would be to levy it upon the amount of property held by every person," he admitted, "but not believing that it will be a part of the permanent policy of the country I think it better to go on collecting it as we are now, collecting it, upon profits." Indeed, Morrill illustrated an eagerness to accept the positions of Boutwell and Hooper, but recognized the fact that citizens unavoidably would hate a tax on property. In that light, Morrill persisted in defining income as profits and not property.[3]

On February 17, Illinois Republican John Farnsworth proposed an amendment to the bill that excused any military officer below the rank of brigadier general from paying the income tax. "All officers below the grade of brigadier general should be exempt from this income tax," he said. "Their pay is scarcely sufficient to maintain them." His amendment was agreed to in the House, as most Republicans had no quarrels about it. Morrill's promotion of the flat tax, as well as his overall bill, won favor with most G.O.P. members as it too passed the House of Representatives with little trouble.[4]

In the Senate, John Sherman introduced the bill on February 27, 1865, opening debate by informing the chamber,

> The changes in the income tax are necessary to prevent a repetition of the shameless and wholesale evasions of the special income tax. This is the only tax imposed on the accumulated property... It is the one that should have been paid most cheerfully, but its assessment and collection was a disreputable farce... It may be truly said of some of these taxes that they are mongrel. We can only reply that we need the money now, and must look more to the result of the tax in revenue... A tax system full enforced now will enable us to relieve our people from many taxes when the

---

[1] Ibid., 874.
[2] Ibid., 874.
[3] Ibid., 873.
[4] Ibid., 883.

reaction of peace shall lessen the profits of industry....We cannot increase our taxes after war — we must be prepared to reduce them...I therefore conclude that every dictate of policy, every sentiment of patriotism, demands of us the largest taxation now to be fearlessly assessed and impartially collected.[1]

With those words, discussion commenced on the bill, with most of senators objecting over small phrases and ideas.

Sherman pointed to the fact that if the income tax was completely collected at present, it would allow the government to reduce taxes after the completion of the war. Since the war had caused a large debt for the nation, Sherman thought it was imperative for the people to pay off the debt as quickly as possible rather than suffer the consequences of a country that was literally broke.

The only debate on the income tax in the Senate dealt with the subject of Farnsworth's amendment allowing military personnel not to pay the tax. Henry Wilson supported the measure, observing, "This tax has been put on since the mass of the Army was raised, and it goes pretty hard with them." He also observed that many soldiers "have not paid it yet and cannot pay it. I think with the small compensation our officers have we should not tax them."[2]

Unlike in the House of Representatives, many Republicans were not dedicated to this proposal. "I have had a good deal of intercourse with officers," explained James Grimes of Iowa, "and I have never heard any great complaints that they have made against the income tax."[3] The other senator from Iowa, James Harlan, contended that the amendment was perhaps "unconstitutional," reasoning that if "all taxes are to be 'uniform throughout the United States' I do not perceive how you can tax one class of officers on their salaries and exempt another class... I think that a tax ought to be uniform; if it is an income tax, it ought to be levied in a uniform mode on the incomes of all the people of the United States."[4] In a related fashion, John Henderson of Missouri believed there to be "a constitutional objection to it," and that it was "a very great impolicy to commence exempting anybody from a tax." The Senate voted down the amendment, and army officers were still required to pay the income tax.[5]

---

[1] Ibid., 11389-1139.
[2] Ibid., 1290.
[3] Ibid., 1290.
[4] Ibid., 1290.
[5] Ibid., 1290.

The bill eventually passed the Senate, with Republicans sponsoring the measure fervently. In its final form, the bill placed a five percent tax on incomes below five thousand dollars and a ten percent flat rate on incomes exceeding that amount. Although satisfied for the time being with this new system, Morrill sought to make the income tax entirely flat during the hard times of reconstructing the crumbled Southern states.[1]

On May 7, 1866, Morrill, now the Chairman of the House Ways and Means Committee, proposed H.R. 513 to subtract seventy-five million dollars from the national budget and ease the taxpayers of the financial encumbrances of the Civil War. The bill exempted all incomes under one thousand dollars from taxation while establishing a uniform rate of five percent on incomes over it. Having cried out against graduated rates, this afforded Morrill the opportunity to finally suspend what he perceived as the inequality in the income tax system. Speaking on behalf of the members of the Ways and Means Committee, Morrill showed how they had "proposed some modifications of the income law, but have not reached the conclusion that it can wholly dispensed with." From his perspective, as well as the committee as a whole, the time had not quite come yet to completely remove the tax from law. "If our income tax should be contemplated as a part of the permanent policy of this country it is not to be denied that it would need various and perhaps fundamental amendments," he said, "we have undertaken to lessen but not entirely remove the weight of the income tax." Utilizing the rhetoric of equality, Morrill detailed his opposition to progressive tax rates by proclaiming, "In a republican form of government, the true theory is to make no distinctions as to persons in the rates of taxation. Recognizing no class for special favors, we ought not create a class for special burdens." Undeniably, Morrill seized on the principle that no economic class in the United States should shoulder the financial burdens of the government disproportionally with other classes; therefore, a flat rate was essential because each person with this system paid the same percentage on his or her income.[2]

This idea by Morrill was definitely controversial among the Republican congressional representatives. In fact, a rift formed between Republicans in the Northeast and West who, for the most part, supported industrial interests and

---

[1] Joseph A. Hill, "The Civil War Income Tax," *The Quarterly Journal of Economics* 8 no. 4 (July 1894): 425.

[2] *The Congressional Globe: Official Proceedings of Congress, 39th Congress, 1st Session,* (Washington, D.C.: John C. Rives, 1866), 2437.

wealthy individuals, and Republicans in the Midwest and South who supported homestead farmers and the working class.

Not all Republicans from these regions, however, were monolithic in their beliefs. For instance, John Raymond rebuked Morrill, claiming that a tax upon incomes was "the fairest of all subjects for taxation." The New York Representative revealed his conviction that "income is the first thing, so far as industry and the products of industry are concerned, which should be taxed" due to the fact when incomes were taxed, the government needed no other taxes. He explained that, without a tax on incomes, the government resorted to taxing goods and necessary items for sustaining life, which actually forced people to pay more. From his standpoint,

> If you encourage your people in their labor... in producing wealth, then after they produced it and have the net proceeds in their pockets, it is quite just and fair and proper for the government to claim a proper share of these profits to meet its own necessities. The Government should not trench upon the necessities of the great mass of its people. The absolute necessities of people should be spared, should be held sacred from the hand of the tax collector. The people should be allowed to enjoy undiminished so much of their earnings as they need to supply those necessities... I know that this may fall heavily upon portions of the community, but fortunately they will be those portions of the community which can best afford to bear it, and those portions of the community, I will add, which have thus far borne all taxation with the utmost readiness, and which show no signs of complaint at the taxation to which they are subjected... I am confident that this nation, with its resistless enterprise, its boundless resources, its rapidly increasing population, will meet the emergency for which it is now required to provide with the same degree of honor and success that has attend its conduct of the war.

Raymond, a cofounder of *The New York Times*, threw his support behind graduated income tax rates, especially at ten percent; he came to the conclusion that since the rich could best afford to pay the income tax, the correct action to take by Congress was to tax them more to pay the debt. Not only did he feel that this was proper, but also that they, being patriotic citizens, were eager to pay their share of the burden.[1]

---

[1] Ibid., 2440.

Raymond was not alone in the Republican Party on this issue of maintaining graduated income tax rates. On May 23, 1866, Frederick Pike of Maine offered an amendment to Morrill's bill that created a five percent rate on those making between one thousand and five thousand dollars, and a ten percent tax on all incomes above five thousand dollars. Pike defended the measure by saying,

> Every laboring man in the country pays a tax upon what he eats, drinks, and wears. And until we come to the point of relieving the great body of people in the country from onerous taxes upon everyday's consumption it is a question whether or not men who are able to pay should not pay this increased proportion of their income to the General Government... I have not yet heard of any remonstrance from any gentleman whose tax is more than five per cent, according to existing law. No one of this class has ever sent a request of this Congress to be relieved from taxation.

Pike preferred to tax incomes rather than consumption because the tax liability had to fall more on the wealthy than on the middle or poorer classes. The majority of Republicans accepted the views of Pike to a limited degree; when Republicans from Midwestern states offered larger tax rates for the more affluent, a true fracture materialized between party members.[1]

Substantial tax rates for Morrill's bill were launched with Pike, but others presented additional taxes. For instance, Lewis Ross, a Democrat from Illinois, recommended an amendment to initiate a twenty-five percent tax on individuals making more than sixty thousand dollars a year. Morrill grew angry over this proposal. "In this country," he bitterly shrieked, "we neither create nor tolerate any distinction of rank, race, or color, and should not tolerate anything else than entire equality in our taxation." Morrill attempted to clarify his argument for a flat rate; since the United States had just finished a war predicated on the idea of equality and race neutrality, it was not only an injustice, but also hypocritical to now allow the government to treat its citizenry unequally based upon their economic situation. Asserting that the "proposition cannot be justified on any sound principle," he criticized the scheme of progressive taxes because it "is saying to the man of wealth, 'You have got the money and we will take it because we can make a better use of it than you will.'" Morrill continued his barrage by revealing a fear that wealthy individuals, if taxed disproportionately, always found ways to avoid paying their taxes. He alleged that heftier tax rates on rich people had a tendency "to create a great amount of fraud and false swearing." Morrill said

---

[1] Ibid., 2783.

it was only natural for people who were taxed differently than others to react negatively and not pay the tax at all, explaining that

> [A] man who is taxed only as high as his neighbor upon the amount he possesses is willing to pay his tax,....in a republican form of government we cannot justify this inequality of taxation....I do not see how gentlemen after they have accumulated a certain amount of property, will be willing to continue their adventures thereafter for fear of becoming subject to the tax. It will have the effect, too, of creating absenteeism. When men have acquired a large fortune they will be very apt to go elsewhere to expend it.

Morrill accepted the notion that if the government handled wealthy people differently than other classes, they would not cooperate with the government. He viewed this as a major problem because the United States needed these individuals, more than any other group, to help finance the debts from the war.[1]

To reach a compromise, or possibly take credit for the success of graduated income tax rates, Ohio Republican Rufus Spalding put forth a compromise amendment: thirteen percent tax on incomes over six thousand dollars. Spalding noted,

> [T]he tax is equal while the means of payment are unequal. The man who has the higher income has the greater means of payment and feels the tax less. The difference is in his favor. The poor man, to the extent of his modicum, pays his full tax. If he had a larger income he would of course be happy to pay the increased tax.[2]

Joining Spalding in support was only a small amount of his Republican Party members. Ithamar Sloan of Wisconsin, for instance, backed Spalding's idea; he acknowledged, however, that it was the goal of him and his other Republicans to seek equality in taxes wherever possible. He stated,

> I suppose if a perfectly just system of taxation could be devised and put in force, every man would be taxed just in proportion to his ability to pay the tax; not perhaps in proportion to the amount of property he may have, or what he may produce, but in proportion to his ability to pay his tax; in proportion to the excess which he has left after meeting all the legitimate demands upon him.

Sloan believed that more relief could come from taxes on items such as food and cotton than on incomes. "There are many items in this bill," he said, "where relief can be afforded more justly and more equitably and more in accordance with the interests of the whole country, than by the change proposed by this

---

[1] Ibid., 2783-2784.
[2] Ibid., 2784.

committee." Indeed, some Republicans sought other ways (namely, cutting consumption taxes) to provide tax breaks to the people rather than by cutting income tax rates or creating a flat tax.[1]

Scores of Republicans, in contrast, were not too ecstatic on the high progressive rates offered by Spalding or Ross. In truth, the G.O.P started to splinter somewhat over this issue, especially between the Northeastern and Midwestern politicians. Most Republicans, though, contested the high rates in Spalding's amendment. "I have been from the first opposed to the principle of the tax," stated Morrill. "Our urgent necessities during the war having ceased, I think we ought to relieve ourselves at the earliest moment from such a tax. The particular effect of it is to harass men of great enterprise in the country."[2]

Morrill was positively not alone in his views on the amendment. Iowa Representative Hiram Price lashed out at the Spalding's idea, "I do not think it at all equitable. I do not think the amendment would make the tax bear equally upon all men, without regard to race or color." He informed the congressmen that they better "treat all men alike in this matter of taxation," and that if "one man is more economical than another, and saves his money, and so at the end of some years is in possession of more income in consequence of such economy, I do not think he should be punished for that which should be considered a virtue."[3]

Similarly, Thomas Davis of New York voiced his opinion on the floor of the House of Representatives,

> I believe the action of this House would be very unwise if we discriminate on the subject of tax on incomes...The capital of this country should be protected. It should be invited to investments of enterprise and industry. If we discriminate against capital, we interpose obstacles to business, because if men are successful we tax them unfairly and unjustly... You discriminate in consequence of the amount of property, which a man holds. You take away from the accumulation of industry that which would go into capital except for the interference of the Government.

Davis concluded his passionate observations by denouncing discriminatory tax rates as a hindrance to the prosperity and growth of American business.[4] Another representative from New York, Robert Hale, endorsed Davis' position through complaining, "I do not believe it is equal or just. It does seem to me that

---

[1] Ibid., 2784.
[2] Ibid., 2784.
[3] Ibid., 2784.
[4] Ibid., 2785.

the principle upon which these taxes have always been assessed has been upon a principle of equality... the rich men being in the minority shall have injustice done to them."[1]

Halbert Paine, a general in the Civil War who had a leg amputated, also conveyed his concerns about the equality of high income tax rates on the wealthy class. "What will be said of that discrimination," stated the Wisconsin Representative, "which compels a man to pay a tax when his income is over $1,000 and relieves him from taxation entirely when below that amount?" Without question, these Republicans underscored the dangers, and inherent inequality, in the graduated income tax proposal of Representative Spalding. Instead, those that opposed the measure deemed that all incomes had to be taxed at the same rate to maintain a sense of equality and avoid class envy and warfare.[2]

Spalding's amendment went down to defeat. Morrill's bill, with Pike's amendment, eventually passed with one hundred percent of Republican support in the House of Representatives. It established two tax rates: five percent on incomes above one thousand dollars and ten percent on incomes above five thousand dollars.[3]

In the Senate, William Fessenden introduced the bill on June 16, 1866. He said, "the House of Representatives propose many changes, the committee came to the conclusion that it would be better for this session to let the income tax stand as it is." [4] With little disagreement and debate, the Senate passed the legislation, with the only stipulation that the tax remain until 1870.[5]

Less than six months after the passage of House Bill 513, Morrill again made an effort to institute a flat tax rate for all citizens with House Bill 1161, which was brought forth to Congress on February 13, 1867. According to the legislation, one tax rate, five percent, would be placed on any person making more than one thousand dollars a year; there was no tax on anyone below that income. He indicated that the Ways and Means Committee

> have sought to afford the greatest possible amount of relief to the country consistent with the prudent regard to the public credit, and were led in the outset to consider what would be the most feasible mode of accom-

---

[1] Ibid., 2785.
[2] Ibid., 2784-2785.
[3] Ibid., 2865.
[4] Ibid., 3321.
[5] Edwin Robert Anderson Seligman, *The Income Tax Part 2* (New York: The Macmillan Company, 1911), 453.

plishing this object and leave at the same time the fewest impediments in the way of general industry.

He also related to the chamber that the last few years had been difficult on taxpayers due to the heavy burdens of war debt. Not only had the war destroyed families and nearly the Union, but also had confiscated the hard-earned money of the people to ensure victory. The taxes for the past five years "have been excessive, and nothing but danger which menaced the life of the nation justified the heavy drain upon the pockets of our people." He gladly announced that the government had sufficient revenue and could afford to reduce the taxes for the country.[1]

Morrill, in addition, thought it was time to finally create a flat tax rate because it was, in his opinion, fair and equal. He argued,

If an income tax was to continue as a permanent tax it should be based upon the value of the whole property possessed by each person. I am disposed to think, however, that a tax of vexatious character which must adhere to an income tax should rightfully place it on a list of those to be abandoned first in order.

Although he desired to remove the income tax forever from the nation's memory, Morrill knew that it was still necessary to levy at that moment; the nation was in the middle of the reconstruction process, and revenue was needed to prolong the policies of the United States government. It was for this reason that he promoted the flat tax rate of five percent. He urged the Congress to halt

the manifest injustice of taxing incomes above $5,000 twice as much as below. To do more than this is to provoke controversy as to the constitutional right to do it, and to lodge in the mind of every man, who finds himself as he thinks unjustly oppressed, and excuse for understating his income to such an extent as will avoid the wrong with which he is threatened. To such persons it seems sheer confiscation, and if justifiable to the extent of five per cent, then justifiable to the extent of fifty per cent. They offset wrong for wrong... the role of perfect equality should be as immovable as the poles.

Utilizing the identical rhetoric, Morrill, once more, sought to eliminate progressive tax rates, which he deemed to be discriminatory, in favor of a small,

---

[1] *The Congressional Globe: Official Proceedings of Congress, 39th Congress, 2nd Session*, (Washington, D.C.: John C. Rives, 1867), 1216.

flat rate. Always the fighter, the Vermont Representative never gave up on this premise.[1]

Nine days afterward, Midwestern Republicans tried to compromise with Morrill and his Northeastern allies in the Grand Old Party. Illinois Republican Jehu Baker, who later in life became a Democrat, penned an amendment that put a five percent tax on people making between one thousand and six thousand dollars, and a ten percent tax on incomes above six thousand dollars. He deduced that "taxation should be imposed with some reference to ability to pay."[2] He was, however, in a minority as many Republicans roundly rejected progressive tax rates.

Their words became harsher by this time because a strong majority backed Morrill's idea. James Garfield reasoned,

> I believe in the first place, that it will be found to be not sound legislation... ultimately it will be declared unconstitutional to levy a tax at a different rate upon the incomes of different men... Because some men are poor and others are rich I do not believe that the poor man has the right to say to the other, 'You shall pay more tax per dollar upon all your income than I will pay.' I do not believe such a law will be considered constitutional.

Showing his interpretation of the United States Constitution, Garfield said that when it "speaks of taxation at all it says that it shall be equal."[3] Parallel to this argument, George Miller of Pennsylvania conveyed his observation on the topic. Noting, "all taxes should be uniform," Miller thought it wrong to penalize those who "by their industry have made large incomes" and not "those who are not industrious and who have made but a small income. Where is the justice in that? I cannot see it." Most Republicans agreed with these statements, and the House declined Baker's amendment.[4]

That same day, Indiana Representative Ralph Hill presented an amendment to Morrill's bill, which would have created a three percent tax on incomes above one thousand dollars, a five percent tax on incomes above five thousand dollars, and a ten percent tax on incomes over ten thousand dollars. "This is perfectly constitutional," he rationalized, "it is perfectly uniform in every aspect... There is no inequality in the tax at all. It applies equally to every man." Though several Re-

---

[1] Ibid., 1218.
[2] Ibid., 1482.
[3] Ibid., 1482.
[4] Ibid., 1483.

publicans supported his idea, Hill's amendment, just like Baker's, was defeated in the House of Representatives.[1]

Morrill's original legislation passed; when it came up in the Senate, Fessenden introduced it, and there was no debate on it. The chamber ratified the bill with a uniform rate of five percent on incomes above one thousand dollars.[2]

Historians have noted how the industrialists attacked the income tax through congressional collaborators, mostly within the Republican Party. "The attack of business classes," wrote Sidney Ratner in his book, *American Taxation: It History as a Social Force in Democracy*, "on the income tax... must therefore be seen as an effort to increase their profits by shifting the burden of taxes to the shoulders of the laboring and farming classes at a time when these classes were beginning to recoup some of the losses they had suffered during the Civil War."[3] In a similar manner, Steven R. Weisman stated in his work, *The Great Tax Wars Lincoln to Wilson: The Fierce Battles Over Money and Power that Transformed the Nation*, that the "industrialists and their allies in Congress went after the income tax."[4] The conclusions of most historians on this subject are substantially supported by the remarks made by Republicans on the subject of the income tax. As the shouts of disapproval over the income tax became louder in the Northern section of the United States, the party began to adopt the principle of lowering, and, in some cases, outright removing, the income tax to benefit their wealthier contributors; Republicans in the Midwest and South, though, still hoped to stop the swell of protests against the tax that was materializing within the halls of Congress.

The antagonism over the income tax steadily grew within the Republican ranks. During the Civil War, they perceived the tax as an uncomfortable but necessary duty to finance the debt that was accruing to defeat the Confederacy. Once the war was finished, nevertheless, numerous Republicans began to clamor for its removal. Originally, that hostility was aimed at the progressive rates, as some tried to make it a flat rate for all income levels. In time, several party members, despite the compromise of a flat rate, choose to support absolute removal of the tax. Through 1865 to 1868, a divide surfaced in the G.O.P. over the issue: Northeastern and Western members of Congress pushed to remove the income tax, while, at the same time, Republicans in the Midwest and South chose to

---

[1] Ibid., 1483.
[2] Ibid., 1941.
[3] Sidney Ratner, *American Taxation: Its History as a Social Force in Democracy* (New York: W.W. Norton and Company, 1942), 139.
[4] Weisman, *The Great Tax Wars*, 94.

support maintaining the tax as a revenue outlet for the federal government. This obvious division continued to manifest until the income tax was finally eliminated in 1872.

Chapter 7. A Deep Divide: 1870

> "The income tax ought not be continued in any form." — Representative Noah Davis (Republican — New York)
> "I favor the repeal of the income tax." — Representative William Kellogg (Republican — Pennsylvania)

After the death of Lincoln, skepticism emerged among Republicans about his successor, Andrew Johnson, and how he might lead the country in the Reconstruction era. For one, the Democrat Johnson once owned slaves. Although the only Southern senator not to join the Confederacy, Johnson struck fear in some Republicans that he may well offer too much leniency and side with the rebels on the important issues of how to heal the nation. Johnson promised to carry on the policies of his predecessor, but the worries of the Republicans soon materialized as Johnson turned into their worst nightmare.

The Republicans, and some in the Democratic Party who backed their effort, could claim success during this apprehensive period of American history. They passed the Thirteenth, Fourteenth and Fifteenth amendments to the United States Constitution. "Neither slavery nor involuntary servitude, except as a punishment for crime whereof the party shall have been duly convicted, shall exist within the United States, or any place subject to their jurisdiction," stated the Thirteenth Amendment, which outlawed the institution of slavery. The Fourteenth Amendment provided due process and equal protection under the law to all naturalized citizens, and the Fifteenth Amendment allowed African American men the right to vote in elections. It read, "The right of citizens of the United States to vote shall not be denied or abridged by the United States or by any State on account of race, color, or previous condition of servitude."

The Congress also established the Freedmen's Bureau, a government entity with its purpose to help educate newly freed slaves on jobs skills and literacy. Most Republicans in Congress thought African Americans needed some assistance in their new existence as independent men and women to prevent them from falling into a life of continual poverty and dependence that they had, unfortunately, been accustomed to for such a long period of time.[1]

Because of these important additions to the Constitution, the United States witnessed its first black congressional representatives. The first African American senators were from the state of Mississippi: Hiram Revels and Blanche K. Bruce. The House of Representatives, as well, had new black members, such as Robert Smalls and Joseph Rainey of South Carolina and Jefferson Long of Georgia. In all, seventeen blacks served in the Congress during Reconstruction: fifteen in the House and two in the Senate. The United States Congress would not have as many African American legislators serve in one era again until 1969.[2]

With all of these achievements, Reconstruction had, however, deep corruption, division and chaos. Many Southerners were not disposed to accept blacks as their equals, Radical Republicans tried to destroy any person, including the president, who prevented them from implementing their programs without compromise, and several carpet bagging governments in the former Confederacy swindled the citizens and seemed to not be interested in building up and maintaining order in a severely archaic Southern society.

President Johnson was none too keen on the Congressional Republicans' ideas for handling the reconstruction process. In fact, Johnson often showed outward hostility to their proposals. For instance, in 1866, the Republicans passed a Civil Rights Act that guaranteed equality for all citizens regardless of race. Johnson vetoed this bill; angered by his actions, the Congress overrode the veto, and the act, eventually, became the Fourteenth Amendment to the Constitution. This commenced a poor working relationship between the President and members of the opposing party.[3]

---

[1] Allen C. Guelzo, *The Crisis of the American Republic: A History of the Civil War and Reconstruction Era* (New York: St. Martin's Press, 1995), 366-399.
[2] Ibid., 366-399.
[3] Ibid., 366-399.

Johnson, as well, eagerly allowed former Confederate states and rebels to re-join the nation without much punishment or repercussions. Republicans viewed his terms as too relaxed for people whom they considered traitors to the United States. When former Confederate Vice President Alexander Stephens entered Congress as a senator, the Radical Republicans decided to take immediate action. They passed Reconstruction Acts to dismantle the Southern states and divide them into five military districts to make certain that their agenda was being properly implemented. Johnson made it known that he did not care for the actions of the Congress, and, after this point, the Republicans did everything in their power to damage and undermine his presidency.[1]

The Republicans authored bills to remove presidential authority from Johnson, passing legislation such as the Commander of the Army Act, which, when Johnson made a military move, forced him to take the decision to the head of the U.S. Army for approval. In addition, they approved the Tenure in Office Act, which prevented the president from firing any cabinet official without the endorsement of Congress. Using this act to protect Secretary of War Edwin Stanton, a Republican in Johnson's administration, they aimed at preventing opponents of Johnson from being dismissed from their jobs simply because he did not care for them. When Johnson fired Stanton anyway, the Republicans had had enough of him and commenced impeachment proceedings to oust him from office. Many Republicans used the rare opportunity to rail against the President and his actions toward their Reconstruction policies.[2] John Bingham attacked Johnson, proclaiming,

> May God forbid that the future historian shall record of this day's proceedings, that by reason of the failure of the legislative power of the people to triumph over the usurpations of an apostate President, the fabric of American empire fell and perished from the earth!...I ask you to consider that we stand this day pleading for the violated majesty of the law, by the graves of half a million of martyred hero-patriots who made death beautiful by the sacrifice of themselves for their country, the Constitution and the laws, and who, by their sublime example, have taught us all to obey the law; that none are above the law;... and that position, however high,

---

[1] Ibid., 366-399.
[2] Ibid., 366-399.

patronage, however powerful, cannot be permitted to shelter crime to the peril of the republic.[1]

The trial was an all-out assault on Johnson, his character, and his policies. The Republicans in both the House of Representatives and Senate, under the leadership of a Thaddeus Stevens and Charles Sumner, repeatedly scorned the President while attempting to persuade their Democratic Party colleagues to join in their cause. The Republicans, though, ultimately failed to convict him by one vote; Johnson left office in 1869, having not sought reelection.

Problems arose in the South due to the actions by the Republicans in government. As a result of their Reconstruction policies, ex-Confederates met in the state of Tennessee and formed the Ku Klux Klan in 1866. Originally construed as a social club, some chapters of the Klan grew increasingly violent against what they viewed as the harsh treatment of Southerners by the Congress. Riots and lynchings became all too common, forcing new President and Civil War hero Ulysses S. Grant to send more troops to squash these uprisings. Greater Union presence in states below the Mason-Dixon Line just fed the passions of many Southerners who still believed in their hearts that their revolution was right and that it was not over yet.[2]

Republicans, additionally, produced scandal after scandal throughout the whole process. In truth, the scandals damaged the Republican Party's image not only in the South, but also in most states of the Union. Some carpetbaggers enjoyed ripping people off, including a few who ran states as governors or legislators. This image hurt the G.O.P. in the former Confederate states, and Hiram Revels, a black Republican senator, chastised the corrupt carpetbaggers who came to deceive Southerners and take advantage of the black vote. "Since reconstruction, the masses of my people have been, as it were, enslaved in mind by unprincipled adventurers, who, caring nothing for country, were willing to stoop to anything no matter how infamous, to secure power to themselves, and perpetuate it," said Revels. He pointed out that Republicans told his fellow blacks "that they must vote for them; that the salvation of the party depended upon it; that the man who scratched a ticket was not a Republican. This is only one of the many means these unprincipled demagogues have devised to perpetuate the intellectual

---

[1] Douglas O. Linder, "The Impeachment Trial of Andrew Johnson," 7 September 2009, http://www.law.umkc.edu/faculty/projects/ftrials/impeach/imp_account2.html.

[2] Guelzo, *The Crisis of the American Republic*, 366-399.

bondage of my people."[1] In essence, Revels insisted that African Americans were hurt by these con artists, yet coerced, in many ways, to vote for these men by the Republican Party. To many Southerners, it was horrific enough that Republicans made them accept equality with African Americans, but the fact that some Republican governments were corrupt as well only deepened their hatred. This led, in the end, to greater activities by groups hostile to Reconstruction, such as the Ku Klux Klan.

The corruption within the Republican Party, additionally, extended outside of the Southern states. For example, the Grant administration and members of Congress embarrassed themselves by getting involved in fraudulent dealings and scandals, such as the Credit Mobilier, which destroyed the political careers of Representatives Oak Ames and Schuyler Colfax, and the Whiskey Ring, which members of Grant's cabinet were involved. These scandals tarnished the legacy of the Grand Old Party during a time when they could boast of many achievements that helped heal the nation.[2]

The era of United States history known as Reconstruction was a time of both triumph and tragedy. Many accomplishments could be found throughout the country; for instance, advancements in civil rights and the ending of slavery was needed and, in some cases, successful. The ills of this period, however, seemed to leave a more lasting legacy. It is debatable if Reconstruction can be deemed a success or if it was an utter failure of leadership by the United States government.

In the scope of problems facing the nation during Reconstruction, the income tax was a minute issue to say the least. Nonetheless, it created much debate within the halls of Congress. In Grant's own administration, a divide appeared between the collectors of the internal revenue and members of the cabinet. In an 1869 report, the Commissioner of Internal Revenue, Columbus Delano, wrote,

> My opinion is that, so long as a large internal revenue is required by the official necessities of the government, a portion of that revenue should be collected from incomes. The reasons for this seem apparent and forcible... I submit if it will be wise to abolish the income tax as long as the labor, industry and business of the country are directly or indirectly subjected to any considerable taxation.

---

[1] James Wilford Garner, *Reconstruction in Mississippi* (New York: The Macmillan Company, 1901), 399-400.

[2] Guelzo, *The Crisis of the American Republic*, 366-399.

He believed that the income tax had to be kept in some form if the government needed the revenue; its removal should only be considered when all other taxes had been cut or discontinued.[1]

Grant's administration, though, received many complaints from citizens in the more affluent classes of American society. Hamilton Fish, Grant's Secretary of State and a former governor of New York, obtained a letter from John C. Hamilton, a fellow New Yorker of considerable wealth, member of a Union League, and the son of the former Secretary of the Treasury, Alexander Hamilton. Hamilton was none to pleased to be paying a tax on his large income. "I wish the income tax could yet be repealed. Our Union League has denounced it unanimously. They contribute very largely to elections," he wrote to Fish.[2] Fish agreed with Hamilton's complaints and thought that the income tax must be halted. The head of the Internal Revenue Board, Alfred Pleasonton, also desired to see the tax gone, while President Grant spoke out in favor of retaining the tax, but only for three years and at a reduced rate.[3] "It may be advisable," the Eighteenth President remarked, "to modify taxation and tariff in instances where unjust or burdensome discriminations are made by present law... I also suggest the renewal of the tax on incomes, but at a reduced rate, say three per cent, and this tax to expire in three years." Grant later worked behind the scenes throughout the entire debate to repeal the income tax after the end of those three years.[4]

Even before Congress took up the measure, most major newspapers all through the country called for the removal of the income tax. Viewing it as only an obligation of war, they felt that the time was right to relieve the citizens of this tax. *The New York Herald* led the charge, explaining that a "personal income tax is odious in all countries... why should not the coming Congress abolish it at it at once?"[5] The *Herald*, as well, demanded that the government never again consider instituting an income tax on the people.[6] The *New York Tribune* believed that since only a small minority paid the tax, and most people did not, it was iniquitous to those who had to pay it. The newspaper indicated that "Congress will be wise not to extend it... it is not wise to oppress the few for the benefit of

---

[1] *Report of the Commissioner of Internal Revenue for the Year Ending June 30, 1869* (Washington, D.C.: 1869), xiii-xix.

[2] Allan Nevins, *Hamilton Fish* (New York: Dodd Mead, 1936), 606.

[3] Sidney Ratner, *American Taxation: Its History as a Social Force in Democracy* (New York: W.W. Norton and Company, 1942), 130-132.

[4] "The Income Tax," *Philadelphia Inquirer*, 13 December 1869.

[5] "The Income Tax – Why Not Abolish It?," *New York Herald*, 17 July 1869.

[6] "The Income Tax law Repealed," *New York Herald*, 9 March 1870.

the many."[1] *The Macon Weekly Telegraph* noted that an income tax was "universally acknowledged to be inquisitorial, oppressive and unconstitutional,"[2] while the *Pittsfield Sun* labeled it "unjust" and "unequal" for those who were forced to pay it.[3] The *Boston Post* described the tax as "unequal," an "unpopular burthen," and held that there was "quite enough discrimination against the labor and wages class now without superadding a statute like this."[4]

"Of all taxes a tax on income is the most obnoxious to our people, the most easily loaded by the dishonest, the most oppressive upon the honest," stated *Flake's Bulletin*. "We hope the tax will be discontinued."[5] Flake's Bulletin derided the tax and demanded that the Congress abolish it as soon as possible.[6] The *Philadelphia Age* referred to the tax as an "odious and inquisitorial system,"[7] and its sister paper, the *Philadelphia Inquirer*, was the most vocal opponent against retaining the income tax; it wrote more than 50 articles protesting the tax's retention. Calling it an "obnoxious burden,"[8] the *Inquirer* declared that the "time for its expiration has come and gone and it now exists without excuse or reason."[9] *The Sun* contended that the income tax had to be removed for the sake of equality among the economic classes.[10]

"We are opposed to the continuation of the income tax in any form whatever," said the *Idaho Statesman*.[11] "And we trust the case will meet with prompt action at the hands of Congress."[12] The *Morning Republican* referred to it as a "burdensome and onerous tax,"[13] the *Columbus Daily Enquirer* portrayed it as "an odious system of taxation,"[14] and the *Owyhee Avalanche* said that the income tax was unpopular across the nation.[15] The *Weekly Journal Miner*, in addition, labeled it "oppressive" and "odious."[16] It was an "odious income tax," according to the *Galveston News*, that

---

[1] "*The Sun*, the Income Tax," *Pittsfield Sun*, 2 September 1869.
[2] "The Income Tax," *Macon Weekly Telegraph*, 30 July 1869.
[3] "*The Sun*, the Income Tax," *Pittsfield Sun*, 2 September 1869.
[4] "The Income Tax," *Philadelphia Inquirer*, 13 December 1869.
[5] "The Income Tax," *Flake's Bulletin*, 1 December 1869.
[6] "The Income Tax," *Flake's Bulletin*, 4 May 1870.
[7] "*The Sun*, the Income Tax," *Pittsfield Sun*, 2 September 1869.
[8] "The Income Tax," *Philadelphia Inquirer*, 3 December 1869.
[9] "Wasting Time," *Philadelphia Inquirer*, 9 March 1870.
[10] "The Income Tax," *The Sun*, 16 December 1869.
[11] "The Income Tax," *Idaho Statesman*, 17 February 1870.
[12] "The Income Tax," *Idaho Statesman*, 30 April 1870.
[13] "The Income Tax," *Morning Republican*, 8 February 1870.
[14] "Republican, Radical," *Columbus Daily Enquirer*, 26 February 1870.
[15] "The Income Tax," *Owyhee Avalanche*, 27 January 1870.
[16] "Laus Deo!," *Weekly Journal Miner*, 16 July 1870.

needlessly delves into the affairs and finances of private citizens.[1] The *San Francisco Bulletin*, too, opposed the income tax because its "abolition, even for this, its last year, would meet with a heartier gratification than any other reduction that could be made."[2] Joining this chorus of newspapers against the tax was the *Houston Daily Union*, which was "glad to see all the leading papers of the country in accord with us on the propriety... of repealing the income tax."[3]

A few newspapers, though a minority, still supported the retention of the income tax. "It is really the fairest and most equitable form of taxation, for it exacts payment in proportion to income," wrote the *Trenton State Gazette*, "it is not yet time to repeal it entirely."[4] Moreover, the *Minnesota Herald* identified the tax as "the fairest and most equitable of all the internal federal taxes... the tax does produce revenue, and we can hardly afford to forgo revenue."[5] *The Weekly Patriot and Union* called it the "most just and proper" tax, and "a more equitable system than any other" enacted by the United States government.[6]

Despite the fact that some newspapers were supportive of the income tax measure, most print media universally despised it. Many of the newspapers that called for its extinction were published in the Northeast: *Herald, Tribune, Inquirer, Boston Post*, and *Pittsfield Sun*, just to name a few. This pattern also emerged in the debate by Republicans in Congress over the income tax; the bulk of Northeastern Republicans responded to the calls for repealing the income tax from their local newspapers and constituents.

By the year 1870, various Republicans did not just want the income tax reduced or made flat — they wanted it removed completely. A major split surfaced in the party due to the fact that Republicans from predominantly farming states, such as Iowa, Wisconsin and Nebraska, hoped to continue collecting the tax, though maybe in a limited form. They feared that elimination of the tax might lead to a government budget deficit, with the only remedy to increase consumption or property taxes that would bear harshly upon the cash-poor farmers. Republicans from the more industrialized states typically represented wealthier individuals and the business community, which mainly paid most of the income tax

---

[1] "Income Tax," *Galveston News*, 21 January 1870.
[2] "The Income Tax," *San Francisco Bulletin*, 25 March 1870.
[3] "The Income Tax," *Houston Daily Union*, 16 April 1870.
[4] "Tax and Revenue," *Trenton State Gazette*, 3 December 1869.
[5] "The Rich Restive Under the Income Tax," *Minnesota Herald*, 7 May 1870.
[6] "The Income Tax," *Weekly Patriot and Union*, 16 December 1869.

bill. This rift displayed itself clearly in the congressional debate over the future of the income tax.

In May of 1870, Ohio Representative Robert Schenck, a war veteran and participant in the First Bull Run battle, proposed House Bill 2045 to reduce internal taxes in the United States. The bill increased exemptions up to one thousand five hundred dollars of yearly income and charged a tax of five percent above that amount. "They know how cheerfully all through the war, and all through the period which has elapsed since the war, the people have paid that which was demanded of them in order to keep up the public credit and meet our Government liabilities," remarked Schenck, speaking about the American people. In his view, which corresponded with those on the House Ways and Means Committee, it was their duty "to make lighter the burdens which the people have to bear, whether cheerfully or not."[1]

Almost immediately, a chorus of Republican voices denounced the income tax as a whole and encouraged its total repeal. Some in the G.O.P claimed that the tax was simply a wartime measure. Dennis McCarthy was the first to condemn the tax, as he claimed that the people "demand strong, prompt and substantial relief — no half-way measures will satisfy." He generated the notion that the tax led, inevitability, to people eluding payment due to feeling discriminated by the government. He alleged that the income tax law was filled with "deception" and "fraud" by those who paid it, and removal was now the only remedy to the problem. "Now, sir, this income tax bears what no other tax bears upon its face, the evidence that it was only considered and passed as a war tax, being limited to five years in duration," explained the Republican representative from New York. "The five years are up; the war is over; our revenue will bear the reduction, and we can afford to let it die. I do not hesitate to say there is some dissatisfaction with this tax than any other." McCarthy also used an old argument that the tax was inherently unequal on its face because it treated one class of people differently than another. He said,

> Objections to its renewal are long, loud, and general throughout the county... This tax is unequal, perjury-provoking, and crime encouraging, because it is at war with the right of a person to keep private and regulate his business affairs and financial matters... Those who pay are the exception, those who do not pay are the millions; and the whole moral force of

---

[1] *The Congressional Globe: Official Proceedings of Congress, 41st Congress, 2nd Session* (Washington, D.C.: John C. Rives, 1870), 3496.

the law is dead letter... It creates curiosity, jealousy, and prejudice among the people... The people demand that it shall not be renewed, but left to die a natural death and pass away.[1]

Reiterating the same arguments were Noah Davis and Benjamin Butler. Davis, a fellow New Yorker and future presiding judge over the trial of the infamous Boss Tweed in 1873, absolutely deplored the income tax. He felt strongly that the Congress had to stop collecting the tax immediately due to the fact that it was originally "a war tax imposed for the purposes of war, and borne by patriotic people as one of the necessities of the war." From his standpoint, the promises of Congress to the people must be kept, or else a distrust of elected officials would manifest itself among the American people.[2]

Benjamin Butler, additionally, offered a similar argument to McCarthy. The Civil War veteran and author of the Civil Rights Act of 1871 believed

an income tax fairly and justly levied, in my judgment, is the most just and most equitable of all taxes; an income tax levied and collected as ours is is the most unfair, unjust, and inquisitorial of all taxes... a principle diffi-culty of our income tax is that it mistakes earnings for income. It treats as income the products of honest labor, whether mental or physical.

Butler also exhibited reservations against the tax assessors who collected the income tax from the people. "From this tax and the swarm of officers who assess under it the country ought to be and must be delivered," otherwise, in Butler's estimation, the members of Congress would be unemployed by the next election. To him, the implementation of an income tax was a major threat to his future political aspirations.[3]

The creator of Yellowstone National Park, William Kelley of Pennsylvania, expressed an utter hatred for the tax, but for a different reason: its tendency to probe in the private business affairs of citizens. Kelley abhorred the fact that the federal government utilized its authority to force individuals to turn over their financial statements to bureaucrats for inspection and payment. He stated that the people "ask that their private books and papers shall not be subject to the investigation of a rival house or an enemy upon the mere order of some irrespon-sible assistant assessor who challenges their correctness or calls upon them to produce their books at an assessor's office." Along with his supporters, Kelley insisted that his constituents "be relieved from the inquisitorial features of the

---

[1] Ibid., 3993.
[2] Ibid., 3996.
[3] Ibid., 3995.

income tax law, to be relieved from the necessity of exhibiting to the public view our entire income and its resources." Many Republicans, from the outset, conveyed their contempt for the income tax; it was not, however, unanimous.[1]

Other Republicans were not too thrilled with their colleagues who championed the destruction of the income tax, suggesting that the only reason why a faction within the Republican Party ranks so vehemently opposed the tax was that they represented the wealthier interests in United States society. Austin Blair of Michigan came to this conclusion when he objected to its elimination. "There has been a great deal of opposition to this tax developed in the country," he noted, "I attribute that mainly to the fact that those who pay it are a very influential class of people." He observed the denunciations of the income tax came from a "class of people, not that there is any very general opposition to the tax among the people as a whole. That could hardly be so, from the fact that the great body of the people are not reached in any way by this tax." Being fond of the tax because it was "a tax upon the accumulated wealth of the country," Blair discerned that if the tax burden were removed from the affluent, they had no other option but to place a larger tax load upon the backs of common laborers and farmers. He wished "to raise the exemption to $2,000," while also maintaining that the majority of the country requested the tax to be kept in some form because most people did not pay the tax anyway. He found no "good reason for abandoning the whole of this tax, for we cannot spare the revenue which can be derived from it... this is the most just and righteous tax of all the different taxes which are levied under our laws."[2]

Illinois Representative John Hawley, like Blair, wanted to raise the exemption rate so that less people paid the tax as a possible compromise to its total abolition. Hawley submitted an amendment to raise the exemption to two thousand five hundred dollars, which later went down to defeat in the House of Representatives. He expressed his opposition to the complete removal of the income tax, citing that "there is no other tax levied in this country which is so proper as is this tax, levied upon a proper basis and applied upon a proper principle." Hawley added, "I believe the tax should be so levied that it will fall upon the wealthy of the country, and not upon the poorer classes...The taxes levied in this country ought to be paid in proportion to the wealth and ability of the persons paying the tax." Distinctions would inevitably be made with taxing the incomes of citizens,

---

[1] Ibid., 3994-3995.
[2] Ibid., 3993-3994.

and Hawley would rather make those distinctions upon the wealthy few than the many poor.[1]

Jacob Ela of New Hampshire shared his sentiments, declaring,

> I believe the income tax as at present paid is one of the most just taxes laid, and affects no person who has not received a net income above the amount required for the reasonable support of a family, while most other national taxes, except those from succession of legacies, come from people who are struggling to get the means of support.

Ela knew that the complaints against the income tax came "mainly from the wealth of the country, and is expended to pay interest to that class, or to provide them with that protection which is the great expense of the Government." Ela did not care to see the tax removed, due to the fact that if it was, the federal government would have to unavoidably retain other taxes that he believed were far more arduous for the country. These Republicans — Ela, Hawley and Blair, did not advocate a tyrannical income tax — one that almost confiscated the private property of the people. To the contrary, they tried to make the tax as least oppressive as possible, and, for this reason, they offered to keep the tax with limited features, such as a low tax rate and a high exemption level. Their proposition to their Northeastern Republican associates, nevertheless, fell on deaf ears.[2]

On June 2, the vigorous debate continued in the House of Representatives where the lines were visibly drawn between the two camps in the Grand Old Party: total repeal or retention in a moderate form. The Republicans against the tax outright displayed their feelings as they persisted with their arguments that the income tax was not only unequal, but also oppressive. "I am for the absolute repeal of this income tax," stated Charles O'Neill of Pennsylvania. "I think the people are tired of it, more because of its inquisitorial character than on account of its amount." Deducing that the tax was an unnecessary nuisance for those unfortunate enough to pay it, O'Neill demand the government "to relieve them of this onerous burden."[3]

Stephen Kellogg, a veteran of the war and now congressional representative from Connecticut, trusted that "the House will strike out all these provisions for the continuance of the income tax, and end the obnoxious thing forever... The people demand at our hands a reduction of taxation, and they demand it now." He inquired of his colleagues, "Why not give relief to the people now, especially

---

[1] Ibid., 3996-3997.
[2] Ibid., 3997.
[3] Ibid., 4022-4023.

to those in moderate circumstances, whose chief means of support consist of their salaries or annual earnings?" According to Kellogg, the people in his home district demanded that the government dispense with the income tax as soon as possible to prevent any further protests against its continuance.[1]

Aaron Sargent, the first member of Congress to propose a women's suffrage amendment to the United States Constitution in 1878, also held strong reservations against the tax. The California Representative thought that the entire income tax system was a failure because it not only cost more to implement the collection, but the government also fell short of accumulating the amount due to evasion by taxpayers. He indicated that the people of his home state despised it, and their "spirit rebels against its inseparable features. They submitted to it as a war tax, as a patriotic duty. Now they demand its repeal. There is no division of opinion there. The unpopularity of this tax is universally amounting to loathing and hate." Contending it "demoralizes our people and makes them familiar with the idea of defrauding the revenue," Sargent identified the solution to the problem: "Strike out these sections entirely, and relieve the people of $19,000,000 taxes that they involve." He eagerly awaited the moment when he "shall vote to abolish this tax utterly, to wipe it off the statute-book."[2]

Republican opponents of the income tax persisted in their onslaught, with no one expressing more scorn for tax than Noah Davis. Having already spoken on the measure, Davis again took his shots at the tax in a rant on the House floor. He asserted, "the income tax is unequal, unjust, and oppressive," and believed it to be biased for some in the nation to pay the tax while others escaped from it. Affirming his opinion that unequal taxation was always discriminatory, Davis also judged that "taxation upon accumulated wealth is partially confiscation," and the income tax was "simply confiscation of one man's property for the benefit of another." From his standpoint, the Civil War was a great example of how the United States represented equality and justice, and, by showing prejudice based upon income levels, the country and the government was not living up to the ideals of the Constitution. He affirmed his opinion that the tax was not constitutional, and asked the question, "Is it not the duty of this House to let pass away forever by the period of limitation which its framers have attached to its life?"[3]

---

[1] Ibid., 4027.
[2] Ibid., 4030.
[3] Ibid., 4031-4032.

Thomas Fitch, one of the first senators from the state of Nevada, furthermore, articulated the need to rid the nation of the tax that some in the party deemed repulsive. Fitch called the tax "unequal," "oppressive," "unusual," "troublesome," and "unnecessary," and also felt it had to be removed as quickly as possible to relieve the people. "The country demands its abolition or reduction. The public press throughout the country clamors that it should cease." For these reasons, according to the Congressman, the government could justify repealing the income tax; there was no reason to keep it as a source of revenue, and the unequal quality of it could create hostility. "There is not a mechanic, a small tradesman, a clerk, a lawyer, a clergyman, or a physician in the land who does not feel that this tax is oppressive, and who does not know that it is unequal and unjust," he said.[1]

A former general during the Civil War, Nathaniel Banks of Massachusetts, thought that the tax was so egregious that people evaded it at all costs. During his turn on the House floor, Banks reasoned,

> I think this one proposition is universally dissatisfactory, and that, so far as I can judge of the temper and interests and opinions of the people I represent, it will do more to discredit the Government and its bonds than any other measure that could be proposed... I am opposed, sir, to the tax in any form whatever, and I shall vote for its abolition... It will excite discontent; it will be evaded, and it will produce a worse feeling in the public mind than almost any tax which we could impose... It is unequal; it is unjust; it forces men to pay it who ought not pay it, because they do not wish the condition of their business to be made public... The bulk of it is collected as a tax on wages, not on income of property, but on wages or salaries; and so far it is a measure to repress the productive energies of the country... Any measure that represses the productive energies of the country is far more injurious than beneficial... I do not want the tax revived in any form. I shall vote for its entire abolition.[2]

Some Republicans continued with the notion that the tax was only necessary to finance the war, such as New Jersey Representative John Hill, who held that, "The great necessity for the continuation of the tax has passed away, and the continued drain on the people by the taxation, as far as the income tax is concerned, is not now called for." Acknowledging that the people had paid vigorously during the war to patriotically support the Union and its troops, Hill sensed that the people were asking for, and deserved, to be relieved of having to further fund the

---

[1] Ibid., 4032.
[2] Ibid., 4032-4033.

federal government through the income tax. In his speech, he explained his motives for opposing the current income tax system,

When the income tax was first imposed it was in time of war, at a time and under circumstances that called for the immediate help to meet the expenses of the Government, and the citizens of our country responded cheerfully to the call made upon them by this tax... The very great inequality of the income tax law now in force demands the attention of the members of the House, and when it is called most fair, just, equal and popular tax all levied it must be that those who pronounce it such have not properly examined it in all its bearings or they would have discovered its inequalities and actual injustice... It is contended that the tax is a popular one because the revenue it produces comes from the rich and wealthy. The gentlemen who use such arguments forget that most of the rich and wealthy men who have incomes to return receive them from the profits of their business; and in the end a greater portion of it comes directly and indirectly from the workingmen... who in many instances are paid less wages in order that these taxes can be met and paid. Therefore, I hold that the income tax bears unjustly and hard on the most worthy and industrious class of citizens.

Hill loathed the tax, not because the wealthy were held more responsible in paying it, but how it injured the incomes of laboring people who worked for these wealthy individuals. Because the wealthy, in his view, gave more money to the government, they had less to pay in wages, which inevitably led to either laborers being given less money for their work or losing their employment altogether. He concluded by noting, "A large portion of the people are unwilling to endure this unequal and burdensome tax. We see no reason why the income tax should be continued."[1]

Scores of Republicans continued to assault the tax on the floor of the House of Representatives. Giles Hotchkiss, a New Yorker, claimed that

The unfair operation of the income tax is conceded on all hands... The people are universally clamoring against these taxes. Let us appease this clamor. It is my view of the duty of a Republican Representative to pay some heed to the voice of the people. We do not need this tax.[2]

Another Civil War veteran, Leonard Myers of Pennsylvania, stated that he was "opposed to its reenactment, and will do all I can to prevent it," because the

---

[1] Ibid., 4024-4026.
[2] Ibid., 4036.

war had come to an end, so the income tax was no longer necessary for the federal government to keep collecting. At the end of his speech, he declared, "Let us then lift the burdens from the people." To these Republicans, the tax was not required because the war was over, which was a compelling argument against it.[1]

One Republican believed that it was time for the United States to become an economic power within the world. William Kelley, a Pennsylvania representative, considered the tax to be an excessive burden on the American economy that was now trying to compete against other countries in Europe. He communicated his point of view by stating, "I favor the repeal of the income tax... relieve the capital and industry of the country of the weights which keep us behind other nations in the race for commercial supremacy." Similar to many of his like-minded Republican associates, Kelley could not see the tax as anything other than unequal in its application and burdensome in its administration. If it were to remain as a revenue source, Kelley deduced that it would remove money vital to the strength and growth of the United States economy, thus hindering the country from investing in future wealth that would help it develop into a world superpower.[2]

Just as passionate in the discussion were those Republicans that wanted to retain the income tax. One persuasive argument for its retention was that only a few wealthy people were stirring the calls for the tax to be killed, whereas the majority of the populace did not mind it. The uproar in favor of the abolition of the income tax, explained Pennsylvanian Representative Washington Townsend, was not coming from the rural and farming areas of the nation, and the people "do not demand the abolition of the tax." Believing it to be nothing more than a few influential individuals inciting discontent in a couple of states, Townsend pointed out, "It does not come from the masses of the people. It originated in the great cities, among men of gigantic capital, among the railroad monopolists, brokers and dealers in stocks, wholesale importers, mostly foreigners, and men of colossal fortunes and extraordinary incomes." Townsend supported the idea of increasing the exemption of the income tax to two thousand dollars. He argued,

> [W]e will relieve a large number of persons... on whom this tax is a
> burden, and who have to pay it out of their living, thereby depriving them
> of some of the necessaries of life, and we will tax only those who are in the

---

[1] Ibid., 4028.
[2] Ibid., 4034.

enjoyment of good incomes, and who pay the tax out of their surplus, and not out of their living.[1]

Charles Pomeroy of Iowa concurred with Townsend's assertion that only the moneyed people in the United States fought to remove the income tax through their elected representatives. Taking on directly those who pushed the agenda of the wealthy, Pomeroy said,

> The cry for repeal comes from the cities and from the metropolitan journals representing the wealth of the nation. The opposition to this tax comes from the men who are fattening on the capital of the country...The demand for its repeal comes only from the capitalists of the nation who control the public journals, and by means of those journals are able to get up an apparent public sentiment in favor of the repeal.

He believed the tax to be "more equitable than any other that can be imposed for the support of the Government," adding that just because a small minority of people demanded that the tax be abolished did not mean necessarily that the entire country supported the idea. To Pomeroy, there was no legitimate reason to quit gathering revenue from the income tax.[2]

Other pro-income tax members of the Grand Old Party insisted that the tax was the only avenue by which real wealth in the country was taxed. In their eyes, people paid taxes for their consumption but not their earnings; the income tax resolved that problem by allowing consumption taxes to be cut, and thus helping the working class. George McCrary, an Iowan and future Secretary of War under President Rutherford B. Hayes, thought "the income tax should be next to the last of the internal revenue taxes of this country to be taken off," because it was "the only mode by which a large part of the wealth of this country can be taxed at all." It was only correct to have the rich men of the nation pay the income tax "out of the surplus of their annual incomes." Rich people, according to McCrary, had the means by which to pay the tax and not be saddled with personal debt, and, as a result, the tax fortunately "operates less upon the mass of the people of the country."[3]

Hamilton Ward of New York, as well, believed in this ideal, as he was one of the few Northeastern Republicans defending the tax's preservation. "It is not apparent," proclaimed Ward, who later drafted the articles of impeachment against President Andrew Johnson in 1868, "what great evil there is to grow out

---

[1] Ibid., 4023-4024.
[2] Ibid., 4033.
[3] Ibid., 4022.

of the continuance of this income tax." Describing the income tax as "the only tax which reaches to any extent the large amount of personal property in this country," Ward supposed that if the tax no longer existed, the government lacked any way to properly tax property. He also objected to the fact that the tax protests came "mainly from the rich, from the men who live in palaces and have their thousands and millions of income." Ward considered it a better option "that the rich should pay it out of their abundance rather than the poor out of their poverty... I earnestly protest against that policy which protects the few at the expense of the many."[1]

German-born and Civil War soldier Gustavus Finkelnburg of Missouri went along with majority opinion of Midwestern Republicans when he said, "I entirely protest against its total abolition." Even though the tax may display some flaws, he understood it to be "the only tax which in some measure compels people to contribute very nearly in proportion to their pecuniary ability... It is a tax which does not enter the door of the needy."[2] In agreement was another Midwestern Republican, William Allison of Iowa. He made obvious his disappointment in the administration of the income tax since "the great majority of the people who pay this income tax manage in some way or another to transfer the payment to others." Alluding to the fact that wealthy people who owned businesses tended to raise prices or reduce wages in order to pay the tax, Allison thought it to be an abhorrent gesture by them. He continued with his argument in favor of retaining the tax by stating, "It is said that this is an unjust tax. In one sense it is an unjust tax and in another it is a proper tax, being a tax upon the accumulations of property." Allison yearned to have salaries spared as part of the definition of income, but realized that it was an impossible task. He reasoned, "while the income tax remains it ought to remain upon the accumulations of property, from whatever source that property may be derived." From his viewpoint, the income tax was still a necessary component of the revenue stream of the government and had to remain in place, not blotted from the law books.[3]

Wisconsin Congressman David Atwood added, "This income tax is a tax upon the real wealth of the country, and as such is the most just and least oppressive tax that is collected from the people... It does not reach the masses of the people, and those it does not reach certainly do not clamor for its repeal." At-

---

[1] Ibid., 4027-4028.
[2] Ibid., 4028.
[3] Ibid., 4029.

wood, as many of his like-minded Republicans, presumed that leading the charge against its extension were members of the affluent class; he also believed that if the Congress reduced or eliminated the income tax, no benefits would be given to the working class in response to those actions. "The fortunes of the rich," he explained, "are really earned by the labor of the poor... The rich would make no less money if the law were repealed; they would simply save more." Because of this fact, "the poorer classes would receive no better wages."[1]

Another line of reasoning used in favor of the income tax was the most simplistic — justice. A number of Republicans had faith that not only did the income tax garner enough revenue to sustain the government, but also that it was the most equitable. Civil War veteran Jacob Benton, now a leader from New Hampshire, said that he had

> no hesitation in declaring that in my judgment the income tax should be retained... it is a tax, in my judgment, more equitable and just than any other tax that is imposed in the whole catalogue of internal taxation... There is no other class in this country so well able to pay taxes imposed by the authority of Congress as those who pay the income tax... I am of the opinion that the people of the country believe the retention of the income tax is necessary, so as to diminish as far as possible the indebtness now resting upon the country.[2]

Many endorsed his opinion. "Every one will admit that the necessary taxes should be so levied as to bear with the most equal and exact justice to all, and such I certainly think is the income tax," remarked Logan Roots of Arkansas, another former soldier in the Civil War.[3] William Loughridge of Iowa, in no elaborate terms, held that,

> in the whole range of taxation there is no more equal or just system of taxation than this. It takes only from the surplus wealth. It does not press down with the leaden weight upon the head of poverty, or invade with ruthless hand the home of the poor to extort its pittance from the hard earnings of honest toil. It goes only to the house of opulence, and takes only where there is much left... I am in favor of lifting the burdens from the labor and the industry of the country.

[1] Ibid., 4034.
[2] Ibid., 4035.
[3] Ibid., 4038.

In concluding his speech, Loughridge espoused his expectation of retaining the income tax for future years.[1] This idea of fairness, more or less, was used by pro-income tax Republicans as a basis for keeping the income tax, but the term was not just relegated to their side. Both sides of the debate employed fairness in their arguments, yet with differing views on how to ultimately define it.

Still, some Republicans hoped to find a compromise between either conservatively keeping the tax as stood or radically rescinding it. Norman Judd, an Illinois representative, did not desire to see the income tax removed from the law books; instead, he recommended an amendment to House Bill 2045 defining income to mean invested capital rather than salaries or labor, thus staving off rejections that several Republicans had been making. He said about the income tax,

> Such a tax has been borne with the necessities of the country, and I may say its existence demanded it. But now that the time has arrived, as admitted on all hands, that more of the burdens of the people may be removed, these levies upon the industries of the country should be removed.

Judd refused to allow hard work or mental labor be defined as income and subjected to taxation. "To levy a tax upon the hands and brains of the man of industry," he explained, "the worker in this world's affairs, the producer of prosperity, and call it property can never be justified except in the case of absolute national necessity." His amendment, however, did not pass a House vote.[2]

Eugene Hale of Maine, believing that the eradication of the income tax was wrong in principle, recommended an increase in the amount of exemption while lowering the percentage rate of the tax. He pointed out that, by increasing the exemption, "the incomes above this amount are received by men who either have a certain and assured income, putting them above the necessity of a narrow rule of living, or by those who from trade or business derive large profits, enabling them to live luxuriously." He ultimately desired to see the income tax "cut off... at its lower stages, and retain it on the higher."[3] Ebon Ingersoll of Illinois made a modest effort to push this idea into the bill. "I do not think you can complain of this income tax if we raise the amount of exemption to $2,000, and we continue the tax upon all amounts above that sum," he commented. The House members, though, just as they had done to Judd, rebuffed Hale's proposal.[4]

---

[1] Ibid., 4040.
[2] Ibid., 4024.
[3] Ibid., 4027.
[4] Ibid., 4033.

When the bill came up to a final vote, pro-tax Republicans pleaded with their colleagues not to strike out the income tax. "I am in favor of continuing the tax," said John Farnsworth, an Illinois politician originally from Canada.[1] "I hope, sir, that the proposition to strike out will not prevail," stated Jesse Moore, a Civil War soldier from Illinois, who also supported increasing the exemption to two thousand dollars. The exemption gave relief to lower classes because those "whose incomes are annually above that amount are the opulent, the wealthy property holders; who are able to pay this tax."[2] William Stoughton of Michigan fought to "reduce the income tax so far as the income tax will allow." It was the duty of the wealthy to pay their share of the revenue needed to sustain the government, so Stoughton articulated his conviction that the income tax had to be "paid by those who have large incomes, are most able to pay, and are the most interested in the protection of property and the stability of public affairs."[3] Likewise, Illinois Representative Burton Cook noted, "But a tax upon property is the fairest of all taxes, and the fairest of all taxes upon property is that which bears the most just proportion to its productiveness." The income tax accomplished this, and it was for this reason that Cook opposed its total abolition.[4]

The amendment to completely remove the income tax was a fifty-fifty split among the Republicans: ninety-one for it, and ninety against it. Republicans from the Northeast and West thoroughly backed the idea, as fifty-four voted to eliminate the income tax (72%), and twenty-one voted to retain it (28%). The Midwestern and Southern G.O.P. members voted in a completely opposite manner: thirty-seven "yeas" (35%) to sixty-nine "nays" (65%). The amendment, though, failed to receive enough votes to be placed in the full bill. In the end, the pro-income tax Republicans gained the victory in the final vote count; the legislation passed to reduce the income tax, but not to completely remove it.

On June 22, John Sherman presented H.R. 2045 for Senate consideration. Once again, the battle lines were drawn between the two prevalent points of whether to eliminate the income tax or keep it, albeit in a narrower form. Those Republicans who opposed the tax in the Senate offered similar arguments with their House counterparts, with one of those arguments being that the tax had a repulsive and unjust nature. Roscoe Conkling, the head of the Republican Party machine in New York, absolutely despised the income tax and made no apologies

---

[1] Ibid., 4037.
[2] Ibid., 4036.
[3] Ibid., 4035.
[4] Ibid., 4407-4408.

for his analysis. The mentor of future President Chester Alan Arthur opened his remarks by stating,

> I am opposed to the revival of the income tax and am unwilling to vote for any provision which shall be an element of argument in favor of reviving a tax which is now dead, and which on every account I think is the most pernicious of all taxes that is proposed to continue or reestablish.

He also rebuked the tax for creating "more jealousy, more discontent, more invidious and odious discrimination, and more demoralization, I undertake to say, than any other tax enforced by law." Claiming that he spoke for the majority of his voters, Conkling told the Senate that he would support any other tax measure but the income tax.[1]

Henry Corbett of Oregon united with Conkling in pointing out what he viewed as the tax's abhorrent features. Viewing it as "a most pernicious and a most objectionable tax to the people," Corbett added that the government essentially was injuring the business community because they were the people responsible for paying the majority of the tax. He went on to say,

> I believe that if you went to make this tax so odious as that during another war you can never levy such a tax, you had better renew it, and then I assure you, you will never be able, even in that crisis, to establish or levy it again, in my opinion. The renewal of this tax will create such a feeling among the business community, and among the people who pay this tax, and those who have confidence in them, will have such and effect that you will never again levy such a tax in peace or war... Now, to continue this tax, when there are no real necessities of the Government, it seems to me is highly unwise; it is injudicious; it is wrong; it is treating this class of people who have borne this burden willingly up to the present time unjustly and unfairly.

Corbett blamed the tax for causing anger and jealousy among the people who had to pay for it and alleged that the "effect of this injustice toward them and this discrimination against them will be to cause that feeling of discontent to wish for a different form of government." Corbett also argued that if the Congress differentiated people based upon their economic class, they could do it for other aspects of society, which he believed to be a wrong ideal. Lastly, he described how the income tax turned honest men into dishonest ones because of their attempts to avoid paying their share of an unequal tax. In addition, he lashed out at

---

[1] Ibid., 4709-4711.

the fact of making business leaders and wealthy individuals open their financial books for government inspection; he perceived it to be an invasion into a person's private affairs. "This law is odious to the people by compelling them to show their books, when they may be in such a condition financially that it would rein for them to expose their condition," he said. "It has caused and will cause many a failure of success in business," and it has led "to more dishonesty than any other tax or any other system of taxation that has ever been adopted."[1]

One of the most shocking opponents of the tax was Senator Charles Sumner of Massachusetts, who had once promoted its formation during the Civil War. Now that the war was over, Sumner felt it was time for the tax to perish. The author of the Civil Rights Act of 1875 and creator of the Freedmen's Bureau demanded,

> the income tax must go. It must not be continued. It has already lived too long for the good of the country, and I think Congress should at once set itself in the way of reform. This whole bill should be modeled therefore on the prevailing idea, that the income tax is to go... Now, if the section before the Senate is in any respect dependent upon the income tax, or if it harmonizes with that, if it is supposed in any way to require the income tax or to anticipate the income tax, I hope it will not be adopted.

Sumner, a constant campaigner for equality and loather of oppression, was of the opinion that the income tax was not only unequal in its application, but also tyrannized those subjected to pay it; therefore, Sumner naturally resisted any prolongation of it as a revenue stream for the federal government.[2]

The Republicans from Midwestern and Southern states were just as eager to defend the income tax as a just and righteous entity for collecting revenue, and none was more passionate than Senator John Sherman of Ohio. In a zealous speech, he pointed out that every tax invaded the private income of the people, but that "the least inquisitorial of all is the income tax." Sherman noted that no tax had ever been devised to work equally or justly, so the income tax was no different from any other tax. It, to him, was "simply an assessment upon a man according to his ability to pay — according to his annual gains. What tax could be more just in theory?" Recognizing the fact that it certainly discriminated against some classes in society, he, nevertheless, claimed that "with proper exemption and proper guards there is no injustice in an income tax which does not apply

---

[1] Ibid., 4717-4718.
[2] Ibid., 4709.

to any other tax that can be levied in any form whatever." Sherman did not mind the biased features of the tax, so long as it would "discriminate in favor of the poor, in favor of the great mass of people." Sherman continually admitted that he preferred not to retain the income tax because it affected his finances, yet he also knew that "if you now repeal the tax on incomes you have to continue the taxes on the consumption of the poor." Sherman, who brought an end to monopoliza-tion with his antitrust act in 1890, saw a need to keep a tax on the wealthy so as to spare the poor from higher taxation. Warning his fellow Grand Old Party members that if they repealed the income tax it would force them to levy taxes against the impoverished, Sherman noted, "The property-holders of the country come here and demand the repeal of the only tax that bears on their property, when we have to tax everything for the food of the poor, the clothing of the poor, and all classes of our people." It was a monumental mistake, in his view, to take the side of the wealthy in this debate over the middle and lower classes in the United States; the poor would rise up against them, forcing members of Congress from their seats in the next election. He advised his colleagues,

> You must expect to meet popular clamor, not the clamor manufac-
> tured in the daily newspapers who receipts are large and productive, not
> the clamor that comes to us from cities or from the Union League, com-
> posed of gentlemen among the ablest and best in this country, whom I
> respect personally, but you will hear clamor coming from the mass of the
> people who will complain of the injustice and wrong, and their voice, al-
> though not often heard in the way of petitions, when it comes to you is
> more mighty than the waves of the sea.

Sherman gave Republicans a choice: tax a small percentage of people who can afford to give more, or remove the income tax and force the poorer class to shoulder the load of taxes. Of course, he thought the wisest course was to relieve the majority of Americans from internal taxes. He did not, however, rule out the possibility that the income tax could be removed if sufficient funds for the gov-ernment were obtained through other means.[1]

The debate recommenced the next day on the bill, with more Republican opponents of the income tax making their voices heard. Connecticut Senator William Buckingham declared his antagonism for the tax as unjust and unequal. One aspect of the income tax that disturbed Buckingham was the inspection of a person's or business' financial papers; assessing personal income "requires every

---

[1] Ibid., 4709-4716.

man at the end of the year to reveal the fact whether he has or has not made any money during the year." In his opinion, financial matters were not of the government's concern, especially a government predicated on the principles of liberty and freedom, and they need not pry into the personal business of an individual.[1]

Cornelius Cole of California, who still holds the record for oldest surviving former senator at one hundred and two years of age, branded the tax as prejudiced against the wealthy. Stating that his "judgment is based upon the unequal operation of the tax law," Cole proclaimed that he was going to vote for the entire repeal of the income tax, due to the fact that the government "can better dispense with this tax than we can with some other forms of taxation. It is, as we are all aware exceedingly unjust in its operations. It is inquisitorial in its character."[2]

Roscoe Conkling carried on with his barrage against the tax. "It is proposed to call back to life the one dead tax, the war tax, the unjust tax, the tax of doubtful constitutionality, the tax which the public faith stands plighted not to revive, the tax which is no longer needed," he lambasted.[3]

John Scott of Pennsylvania, like many other Northern Republicans, denounced the income tax as a mechanism by which politicians placed a wedge between the wealthy and lower classes; Scott disliked this type of demagoguery politics. "I always distrust that it is not solid ground upon which any legislator is standing when I hear him justify any measure by an appeal either to the rich or to the poor arraying them against it each other," he stated. He also contended that it was a dangerous precedent to set to allow certain people not to pay a tax while forcing others to do so. Deeming it to be bad policy, Scott feared it could lead to different types of discriminations, which the United States was supposed to condemn. He asserted,

> The safety of the poor man in this Government is the justice of the principle embodied in all measures of legislation. If you discriminate for him, you may discriminate against him; and perhaps it will not be too long, if we go on at this rate, basing our legislation upon the ground that we intend to impose the burdens of the Government upon the rich and exempt the poor from them, until some man may be found bold enough to claim that that doctrine shall be carried to its logical consequences, and that if the rich pay all the taxes taxation and representation shall go there.

---

[1] Ibid., 4757.
[2] Ibid., 4761-4762.
[3] Ibid., 4757.

Scott argued that since the rich paid the majority of the income tax, they may eventually plead to have greater representation since they would feel entitled to it. Scott did not want that form of favoritism to occur, so he could not vote to retain the income tax. Scott then recommended to those in the lower class to be careful about backing the tax because of his anxiety towards the possibility of discriminating in other aspects. "The poor man," he added, "who is appealed to for the purpose of imposing this tax upon others because they are rich, had better look to the ground upon which that principle of taxation shall be established." He repeatedly called the tax, like had so many other Republicans, "onerous," "burdensome," "demoralizing," and that it "can be dispensed with and must be abolished."[1]

Its promoters also fervently protested its repeal. Oliver Morton of Indiana called the tax both equal and impartial, noting that "it is the truest measure that has yet been found of the productive property of the country." The wealthy individual paid "out his abundance because he has got the abundance. If to pay this income tax is a misfortune, it is because he has the misfortune to have income upon which it is paid; and that is all." In his opinion, the tax "stands in comparably higher in justice and equity than any other tax that can be named." He latched on to the notion that most of the ruckus against the income tax did not come from the wide majority of states, but from the wealthy cities in the North, such as New York. In fact, Morton did not understand how those who had an abundance of resources complained about paying a fraction of it to support the federal government. He was more than willing

> to exchange with New York and agree that we would take her incomes and pay her taxes, if it would be agreeable. They pay the income tax because they have the capital there that accumulates from every part of the United States, because the wealth, the trade, and the commerce of the whole country are poured into her lap... Why, sir, they have to pay the income tax simply because the large incomes are there. If the large incomes were in Indiana the tax would have to be paid there.

Morton argued that it was best to tax a person's wealth because it had a known quantity and showed the overall productiveness of a person for the year. In contrast, a tax simply upon property did not guarantee productiveness due to the fact that a farmer, for example, may own the land but lost money on his crops or goods for that year. Morton believed it to be too detrimental, which was the

---

[1] Ibid., Appendix 518-520.

reason why he cautioned that its removal would be a huge mistake not only for the country, but also for the Grand Old Party.[1]

Indeed, the Midwestern Republicans butted heads with their Northeastern counterparts on this subject, and further discussion was pursued the next day, June 24, 1870; it was obvious neither side would back down. "The Republican party is a party of justice and equality," remarked Corbett. "It desires to do justice to all portions of the community." The income tax, according to Corbett, did one unforgivable thing — it created class warfare, pitting the poor against the wealthy; by keeping the duty, the government played favorites with the impoverished over the affluent.[2] Senator George Williams of Oregon also spoke out against the income tax. "I have been of the opinion from the beginning that our true policy was to drop this income tax," he simply said. "I shall vote now to strike out these other sections imposing the income tax."[3]

Cornelius Cole offered his opinion on the tax again. As an avid anti-income tax Republican, Cole held that the tax was no longer needed and had to be removed because of the original date set for its expiration — 1870. He explained,

> The people throughout the United States, particularly those upon whom the tax bears so heavily, have constantly expected that they were to be relieved from this onerous tax at the expiration of this year, that being included in the operation of the tax, and they have waited patiently for the time to come when they would be relieved from this great and unequal burden.

To Cole, not only did the tax function incorrectly, but also the expiration of tax could not allow the Congress to continue it without breaking a pledge to those who paid it. The United States had to keep its word in this matter.[4]

Missouri Senator Charles Drake, however, countered Corbett's statement. He contended that the Grand Old Party

> cannot face before the people of the United States the continuance upon the statue-book of taxes which touch every man and woman in the United States, in order to get rid of a tax which only touches two hundred and sixty thousand people in this country... we have been the champions of the downcast and the oppressed, and of the many against the few; and

---

[1] Ibid., 4759-4760.
[2] Ibid., 4811.
[3] Ibid., 4809.
[4] Ibid., 4761-4762.

now we change front to make ourselves in our taxation the champions of the few against the great multitude of this nation.

Drake wanted the wealthy in the United States to "bear their portion of the burdens of this country," and, since these individuals have the income to pay the tax, they "are the men who at the end of the year have the means to pay the tax. Why should they not pay it?" The rich had to "bear their proportion of the burdens of this country. Let them bear it upon their income. Let them bear it upon what they have realized." Drake railed against the taxes that fell upon the poor class, calling it a ridiculous concept to make them shoulder the expenses of the government. "You tax the poor man upon what he tries to realize every day, and at the end of the year not one cent has he left upon this broad earth," he uttered.[1]

Coming to the aid of Drake was Justin Morrill, now the senator from Vermont. Morrill wished for the Congress to create a flat tax, as he had proposed many times in the past while a member of the House of Representatives, but did not care to see the income tax eradicated.[2] Morton, as he stated before on the Senate floor, was opposed to its repeal because he wanted rather to reduce taxes on articles of consumption, such as sugar and tea. When the income tax was struck out of the bill, however, he knew that the Congress had no choice but to raise the taxes on items of necessity. These consumption taxes "must be restored, because we have concluded to take off entirely this small tax upon the superfluities of the rich." Morrill had not heard any reasonable arguments in favor of eradicating the income tax, instead choosing to support its preservation for the time being. He added, "The arguments against the repeal it seems to me are overwhelming."[3]

William Kellogg, a veteran of the war and a carpetbagger in his state of Louisiana, took to the Senate floor on June 27 to criticize the income tax as "unjust, inquisitorial, illegal, and anti-republican."[4] Illinois Senator Richard Yates, as well, recognized that the tax not only was no longer vital for the revenue of the country, but also was a mechanism that caused people to be angered and avoid paying their share in taxes. He explained that his objection of the income tax "now is that the cloud has passed away. The storm-cloud of war is no longer visible." The Congress made a guarantee to remove the tax by 1870, and Yates planned to keep his word on this matter. He proudly proclaimed,

---

[1] Ibid., 4810-4811.
[2] Ibid., 4808-4809.
[3] Ibid., 4894.
[4] Ibid., 4892.

I am glad to stand up here against the income tax now, because I know
that we had these men on our side when the rebellion was subdued and
we had not the money with which to do it. There had been no such tax
ever levied before our late war... Men of means came forward and offered
their means, to the utmost of their ability, to raise regiments and clothe
them and support them. They stood by the country and paid this tax,
under the solemn promise of the Government, under its covenant, under,
to use a stronger term, its word — for, I repeat, the word of a great nation
must be kept — that this tax should exist only until 1870, and no longer.

Yates, as well, hated the idea that rich people were singled out to pay the
debts of the country. He condemned the concept, stating, "do not select the men
who by their enterprise, their vigor, their intelligence, their firmness of purpose
— men who, unaided by fortune, poor in early life, have reached this prize — do
not select them out, and say that they shall be the victims of taxation." Since
the tax had elapsed in usefulness and excessively taxed the rich to benefit other
economic classes in American society, Yates believed, "this income tax law, with
its frauds, its inquisitorial character, its cheats, its deceptions, by which the
honest men pay and the dishonest escape, should be blotted from the American
statue-books."[1]

That same day, on the other hand, several Republicans stood up in favor of
maintaining the income tax in the United States. Former Vice President under
Abraham Lincoln, Hannibal Hamlin of Maine, voiced his support "to retain the
tax upon incomes. In reviewing the whole matter I believed it to be wise and
proper to do so."[2] Timothy Howe of Wisconsin described it as the best form of
taxation due to its unequivocal equality. "It is just as manifest that the burdens
of that tax are equal among all those upon whom it falls, as that the exemptions
are equal," Howe argued. "Who shall complain of that? The burdens of the tax
are equal, exactly equal; the exemptions of the tax are exactly equal to all who
are visited by the tax." Portraying it as a tax "so little felt, so absolutely unfelt
in the payment of it," he justified it retention because only "possessors of the
great fortunes" paid any of it. In addition, he noted, "the business of the Government is to protect persons and property. The more property the individual has
to protect the larger share he has in the benefits of the Government." Basically,
Howe believed if a person had more property that the federal government had to

---

[1] Ibid., 4894-4897.
[2] Ibid., 4892.

protect, the more in taxes to uphold the government the person was responsible to pay. Calling the income tax "the only tax which can be paid without real inconvenience and real feeling," Howe repeatedly touched on the fact that the tax was so miniscule and affected such a small minority in the nation that there was no pressing urgency to get rid of it; this was his main reasoning for retaining it.[1]

On July 1, in an attempt to reach a compromise, Henry Wilson, an income tax opponent, presented an amendment that would increase exemptions up to two thousand dollars and place a two and one-half percent tax on incomes over that amount. The income tax would stay in effect until 1872, when it would finally expire. Wilson acknowledged his hatred for the income tax, saying "I voted for the repeal of the income tax in hope that we could do it and at the same time reduce the rates on tea, coffee and sugar;" he found out "on careful examination, that this cannot be done." Wilson presumed that it was better to tax incomes now when money was needed for Reconstruction rather than raising consumption tax rates. "I am against the income tax; but I am also in favor of reducing the tax on tea, coffee, and sugar," explained Wilson. "Therefore, I am willing to vote to retain the income tax at two and a half per cent for the years 1871 and 1872, and 'no longer.'" Wilson also cautioned the other senators from listening to the wrong groups when coming to a conclusion on whether or not to remove the income tax. Admitting how unpopular the income tax was with certain individuals and factions, Wilson added, "Senators must remember that the men of wealth and the large presses of the country, the great corporations of the country, not always the best representatives of public opinion." These rationales motivated Wilson to propose his amendment as a middle ground solution to the income tax dilemma.[2]

Pro-income tax Republicans began to support his proposition. Frederick Sawyer of South Carolina, a former teacher, called the tax on incomes, "a tax which it seemed to me involved a great many inequalities, and one which it was very desirable to get rid of." Although he detested the income tax, Sawyer backed Wilson's proposal "as a choice of evils."[3] Veteran Benjamin Rice, Senator from Arkansas, simply put it, "I am in favor of taxing incomes from whatever source derived."[4] Aaron Cragin of New Hampshire, too, wanted to keep the income tax and supported Wilson's amendment. He stated,

[1] Ibid., 4887.
[2] Ibid., 5085-5086.
[3] Ibid., 5085.
[4] Ibid., 5079.

I am very anxious to vote for it... I am fully convinced that the greatest mistake this Senate has made this session — or it will be so if this vote is to stand — was the vote striking out the provisions in favor of the income tax. I believe myself that it is one of the most just taxes imposed by the Government... In my judgment it is of the highest importance that this tax should be retained in some shape.[1]

Dartmouth alumnus and New Hampshire Senator James Patterson insisted,

the people in the cities, who are making the money that is made in this country, are paying the income tax, that is no reason why we should take off the income tax... The great mass of the voters and tax-payers of this country will not approve of our striking out the income tax, and leaving other taxes resting upon the people and upon those who are less able to bear the taxes of the country. I believe that this would be wrong in itself, and that we should find that it would meet the disapprobation of the people of the country... Let those pay the taxes who are best able to pay the taxes, and let the great mass of the people of the country who feel the burden of taxes, and whose industries are crippled by taxes, be first relieved.[2]

James Howell of Iowa argued that the income tax "can be easily borne, and which can be collected without oppression upon any class of the community."[3] William Sprague of Rhode Island, a participant in the First Battle of Bull Run, trusted "that the tax will be retained," because the wealthy, in his view, were the only ones really affected by this tax; they were not, however, affected much on consumption taxes that bore more heavily upon the middle and lower classes.[4] Drake, as well, believed that removal of this tax would manifestly place the tax burden upon the laborers and working people in the United States. "Voting away the income tax is voting a tax off the shoulders of every one of us and putting it in other matters upon the shoulders of the great mass of the people," he affirmed. Drake wished to always maintain the arduous taxes on those with greater wealth "and keep down the taxes upon the masses of the people."[5]

Wilson's amendment, however, still persuaded none of those Republicans who worked to see the income tax eradicated from the pocketbooks of citizens.

---

[1] Ibid., 5085.
[2] Ibid., 5086.
[3] Ibid., 5086.
[4] Ibid., 5085.
[5] Ibid., 5085-5086.

"We have all heard of the annoyance that this is to the tax payers generally, it being in the character of an inquisition upon everybody, whether he pays the tax, or is liable to pay it, or not," remarked Cole. "I shall vote against it is that if the tax is stricken off entirely... and this will reduce very much the expenses of the Government, besides at the same time relieving the country from a very great annoyance."[1] Sumner, who utilized the slogan, "Down with the taxes," in order to gain popular support in Massachusetts for his cause, expressed doubts that the tax could be altered to correct its inequities and oppressive features.[2] He contended that "if this new form of income tax is adopted you have the same system of inquisition, the same offensive proceeding, the same espionage — those same odious things which have justly made the existing income tax so offensive." Convinced that the income tax could, in no way, be justified as a fair and proportionate tax, Sumner concluded that there was "not an argument which can be brought against this milder substitute. Milder in some respects it is, but then essentially the same principle, and obnoxious to every one of the arguments brought against the other."[3]

In the same way, the author of the Fifteenth Amendment, William Stewart, considered the tax in any form to be oppressive. Regarding it "as a tax upon enterprise," the Nevada senator argued the United States needed to get rid of the tax as soon as possible. He had "heard more complaint about this income tax than all other taxes together... I think it is the most offensive tax we have... I believe it is a most offensive tax to the American people. I hope it will not be retained in any shape."[4] Corbett, as well, commended his fellow senators for deleting the section in the bill dealing with the income tax, telling them that it had caused "general satisfaction throughout the country." "We free the people from this inquisitorial tax," he said, "it reaches every portion of the community, and it has created more dissatisfaction than any other tax levied by this Government."[5]

Wilson's amendment was voted down in the Senate, and the anti-tax Republicans presented an alternative proposal — complete removal as a revenue source. The measure passed with the help of some Democrats who also wanted to end the income tax. The final tally for the Republicans was sixteen yeas (42%) and

---

[1] Ibid., 5085.

[2] David Herbert Donald, *Charles Sumner Part II: Charles Sumner and the Rights of Man* (New York: Da Capo Press, 1996), 416.

[3] *Congressional Globe, 41st Congress, 2nd Session*, 5085.

[4] Ibid., 5085.

[5] Ibid., 5085.

twenty-two nays (58%). One of the more intriguing votes was that of Hiram Revels, the first black US senator, from the state of Mississippi; Revels voted to kill the income tax.[1]

A few days after the vote, Wilson reoffered his amendment of a two-thousand-dollar exemption and a two and one-half percent tax above that. The Senate voted twenty-six to twenty-five to reconsider the amendment. Naturally, many Republicans were none to pleased. "To my mind it is a bloody tax, and I wish to have it cease," exclaimed Sumner. It had an "inequitable character," and functioned "unjustly, taxing the proceeds of labor, of industry, of professional service." For this rationale, Sumner realized the income tax was "grossly unjust."[2] Corbett, always an opponent, added, "I believe this tax to be the most obnoxious tax that has ever been levied upon the American people during a time of peace... I am opposed to levying a tax upon incomes of two and a half per cent, or to renewing the income tax." He informed other Republicans that if they chose to begin again collecting the income tax, it would lead to a horrible disaster for the party in future election cycles.[3]

Henry Anthony of Rhode Island regarded other taxes, such as excise taxes and tariffs, to be a superior form than the income tax. He deemed that it was "better that the railroads and express companies and other great corporations should pay a tax than that every man should pay a tax on his income ascertained by a most inquisitorial, disagreeable, and offensive process."[4] George Edmunds, the famed politician who fought polygamy in the state of Utah, made an analogous proclamation. "I preferred," noted the Vermont Senator, "to continue the tax upon railway companies and monopolies and theaters, and to get rid of this tax upon industry and income... I have not defended the income tax; I have been opposed to it as an evil that ought to be redressed."[5] Tennessee Republican Senator Joseph Fowler simply believed the tax on incomes should not "be assessed and collected from the people any longer." These Grand Old Party members wanted a return to the way taxes were originally collected, as Alexander Hamilton had proposed, before the Civil War, which, most likely to them, appeared to have worked since the nation's founding.[6]

---

[1] Ibid., 5090.
[2] Ibid., 5100.
[3] Ibid., 5100.
[4] Ibid., 5095.
[5] Ibid., 5101.
[6] Ibid., 5101.

Howell made one final appeal on behalf of those Republicans who wanted Wilson's amendment (keeping the income tax intact) to become law. Using common man rhetoric, he derided the Northern capitalists as the culprits behind the calls to end the tax, recognizing that it was "shameful... to place these great capitalists here and try to excite sympathy in their favor, while you still grind down the poor by taxes which they find difficult to pay, and which are burdensome upon them."[1]

Wilson's amendment ultimately passed with twenty-two Republicans voting yes (67%), and only eleven voting no (33%). On July 5, Samuel Pomeroy of Kansas, given one more attempt, offered an amendment to strike out the income tax altogether; once more, the hostility within the Republican Party over the issue boiled over in the debate. "Men argue against an income tax," deplored Morton, "a tax upon clear income, clear profit which falls... upon those who are able to bear it and scarcely feel it."[2] Cragin, like Morton, pleaded with his G.O.P. associates not to abandon the income tax and force harsher taxes on the majority of citizens. He said,

> I have voted uniformly to retain this income tax, because I believed it to be just, because I believed it to be good party policy, and that the most suicidal policy that could be adopted would be to repeal or abandon it... If you choose to tax the people of this country for the tea and coffee that they drink and the sugar that they use, and abolish this income tax upon wealth, upon net receipts, then I wash my hands of that business.[3]

Opponents of the income tax, additionally, in giving their final appeals, did not argue on the basis of who was best able to pay the tax, but on the principle with which the tax was collected. They worried that the perception on inequality in the tax system was of greater importance, because, in their opinion, the government had no option but to treat each person no different than another, including the wealthy and poor. "I vote against the income tax because, while I admit that theoretically it is a perfect way of getting revenue, yet in its practical operation it lays a tax upon conscience," explained Matthew Carpenter.[4] The greatest voice against its retention, Sumner, labeled it as "burdensome" and be-

---

[1] Ibid., 5097-5098.
[2] Ibid., 5235.
[3] Ibid., 5236.
[4] Ibid., 5236.

rated the income tax since "it operates unequitably," while also maintaining that the "income tax is pecuniary unjust."[1]

The final vote in the Senate on Pomeroy's amendment was a tie with each side exactly twenty-six yeas and nays apiece. Sixteen Republicans voted affirmative (42%) while twenty-two voted against the measure (58%), which meant the proposal was rejected. The entire Schenck bill, with Wilson's amendment, passed the Senate; the only Republican opposing it was John Harris of Louisiana.[2]

In both chambers, the Republican Party, as noted before, was divided, as the New England and Western congressional members, for the most part, consistently attacked the income tax, while the Southern and Midwesterners typically supported it. Among the Northeastern and Western wing, fifty-four voted yes (72%), while twenty-one voted no (28%); with the Midwestern and Southern congressmen, thirty-seven voted in favor (35%), sixty-nine opposed it (65%). The reason for this division was apparent — the New England and Western states paid almost seventy percent of the revenue taken from the income tax, and the Southern and Midwestern states and New Hampshire only paid eleven percent of that revenue.[3]

The debate over the income tax became somewhat volatile in 1870. From the commencement of the Civil War, Republicans united in supporting the tax to pay for the victory of the Union, though some had reservations about its implementation. Now that the war had ended, a noticeable split emerged as the needs of the government had slowly dissipated. Each time a tax bill came to the floor of Congress, the voices who opposed the income tax became louder and more persistent. The income tax was still in place by the end of 1870, but the anti-tax forces within the Party of Lincoln would not go down quietly as they made one last attempt to repeal it before its 1872 expiration.

---

[1] Ibid., 5236.

[2] Ibid., 5237.

[3] Steven R. Wesiman, *The Great Tax Wars Lincoln to Wilson: The Fierce Battles Over Money and Power that Transformed the Nation* (New York: Simon and Schuster, 2002), 70.

Chapter 8. One Last Try: 1871

"The tax is unjust, unequal, inquisitorial, and unconstitutional." — Senator John
  Scott (Republican — Pennsylvania)
"I believe that the tax is doing us great injury." — Senator Henry Corbett
  (Republican — Oregon)

The income tax problem appeared to be solved in 1870, with agreement that a small percentage rate would remain until the cessation year of 1872. Despite the passage of Schenck's bill the previous year, a number of Northeastern Republicans were still upset that the income tax had not been absolutely deleted. In fact, they refused to remain silent on the matter; adversaries fashioned a new bill to hopefully annul the income tax before its deadline for extinction.

Various groups throughout the country protested the tax, though most were well-financed by wealthy organizations intent on destroying the income tax. The Anti-Income Tax Association of New York City published an article in several of the leading newspapers in 1871 demanding that the people back their effort to repeal the tax forever. "A tax unpopular among all classes, in direct violation of the provisions of the Constitution, has been laid by the Congress upon the people," the statement read. "Let the people assert their rights and no longer consent to be oppressed by an unjust law." Indeed, those who paid the income tax were now pushing back at the federal government for implementing something they regarded unreasonably targeted their property at the expense of the working class. Groups like the Anti-Income Tax Association of New York City, of course, were not alone in hatred for the income tax.[1]

By this time, the newspapers in the United States almost unanimously clamored for the repeal of the income tax, and not many displayed any nominal support for it; only a handful of newspapers, like *Pomeroy's Democrat*, liked the idea of keeping the tax in place.[2] The most blatant example of anti-income tax bias in the media was from *The New York Times*. For most of the Civil War and Reconstruction, the paper defended the tax as a necessary, albeit burdensome; by 1871, the *Times* had altered its tune. "The income tax has been unpopular from the moment of its enactment," declared the paper. "We have reached the time when the income tax can be no further defended. The people demand its repeal with one voice, and repealed it should be."[3] Concurring with the *Times* was the *Trenton State Gazette*, which noted, "This was one of the most unpopular, inquisitive and oppressive modes of raising tax that our citizens have ever been called upon to submit to."[4] Contending that the tax was an "odious impost," the *New Hampshire Sentinel* argued that the public was eagerly anticipating that "the measure shall be swept away altogether, and we trust that their feeling has made itself so well understood that it will be heeded promptly by Congress."[5] A fellow New Hampshire newspaper, the *Patriot*, said,

> There are three very good reasons for abolishing this tax; first, because it is unjust, unequal and burdensome in its operation; second, because it is universally odious and its abolition is generally desired by the people, and third, because in all but the city districts, the tax does not pay the expense of assessing and collecting.[6]

In the same manner, *The Sun* of Baltimore attacked it, portraying the tax as "odious, unjust as well as unconstitutional,"[7] and that its only relevant purpose was to "line the pockets of officeholders."[8] *Eastern Argus* yearned for the tax "to be repealed without hesitation,"[9] and the *Times Picayune* in New Orleans merely

---

[1] "Anti-Income Tax, Address to the People of the United States," *San Francisco Bulletin*, 22 April 1871.

[2] "The Income Tax," *Pomeroy's Democrat*, 8 February 1871.

[3] "The Income Tax," *New York Times*, 19 January 1871.

[4] "Abolition of the Income Tax," *Trenton State Gazette*, 25 June 1870.

[5] "The Income Tax," *New Hampshire Sentinel*, 15 December 1870.

[6] "The Income Tax," *New Hampshire Patriot*, 28 December 1870.

[7] "The Income Tax," *The Sun*, 23 January 1871.

[8] "The Income Tax," *The Sun*, 4 January 1872.

[9] "The Income Tax," *Eastern Argus*, 26 January 1871.

stated, "get rid of the odious tax."[1] Additionally, the *Philadelphia Inquirer* saw the "only satisfaction which the public has in reviewing this unpleasant business is that we are rid of it, we hope, forever."[2] *The Macon Weekly Telegraph* decreed the tax to be "unconstitutional beyond all reasonable doubt;"[3] taking a similar viewpoint was the *Weekly Arizona Miner* that also labeled the income tax unconstitutional.[4]

There was a strong resentment to the income tax, and the newspapers reflected the views of many of its readers. Several Republicans in Congress, as well, were listening to these reactions, and they were prepared to try one last time to remove the income tax forever, even though it was due to terminate in one year.

On January 25, 1871, Senator John Scott submitted a bill, H.R. 1083, to revoke the income tax immediately. As in the other debates, pro- and anti-tax Republicans wrestled with the issue, with each side strongly defending its point of view. Since he introduced the measure, Scott was given first shot to criticize the tax. "There have been such loud and frequent complaints against this tax, there have been so many demands for its repeal, that decisive action should be taken now," he uttered. *The Pennsylvania Native* also condemned it as "unjust, unequal, inquisitorial, and unconstitutional" and reasoned that "the security of that Government which does not treat rich and poor alike, both in its rights and its exactions, is fast disappearing." To him, the wealthy and the impoverished had to be handled equally, and he disliked the fact that people had to turn over their documents indicating their true wealth to the government. Scott reiterated the point that

> in view of the fact that many of the best men in the country feel keenly the injustice of the inquisition which is made annually into their private affairs, and in view of the fact that in the most patriotic districts of the country there is more discontent arising from this inquisition than there is from the amount of the tax — in view of all these facts, that the Senate will now at once remove this cause of irritation, wipe off the income tax, wipe off as rapidly as we can all internal taxes.

Scott utilized the same arguments that so many anti-tax Republicans employed over the past few years: unjust, discriminatory and pried into the private affairs of American citizens. He most definitely delved into the same playbook

[1] "The Income Tax: The Argument before the Committee of Ways and Means," *Times Picayune*, 1 February 1872.
[2] "The Income Tax," *Philadelphia Inquirer*, 5 December 1872.
[3] "Income Tax," *Macon Weekly Telegraph*, 25 April 1871.
[4] "New feature in the Income Tax," *Weekly Arizona Miner*, 17 June 1871.

that won so many Northern Republicans favor with their more prosperous constituents.[1]

A longtime fighter for the continuation of the income tax, John Sherman, took to the Senate floor that same day to elucidate why the tax had to be kept. He sensed that to rid the nation of the income tax at this point was "wrong, both in policy and justice." Sherman recognized, "I never knew a tax that was not odious and unpopular with the people who paid it," but ultimately discerned that "it would be act of folly to repeal the income tax or any other tax levied; that the income tax ought not be singled out from among the masses of taxes levied on our people." He wanted it "to be borne by the wealthy people of our country a little while longer." Insisting that nobody could legitimately "single out a single tax like this, the only tax that bears upon property as against consumption, the only tax that bears upon sixty thousand people rather than upon thirty or forty millions," the Ohio Senator felt he had a moral obligation to retain the income tax rather than forcing higher rates on the laboring class. He explained that he was "impelled by a sense of duty, in the interest of the whole people, I feel bound, without any regard either to my own personal interest or the interest of my State, to maintain this and all other taxes until I can see daylight ahead and a better time to repeal them." Sherman, for most of his career, deduced that the United States government ought to have a small tax on income as part of its overall revenue sources.[2] "I then believed, and I now believe that a moderate income tax... should be levied," he later wrote in his autobiography.[3]

The debate picked up again the next day and, as was custom, anti-tax Republicans used the same arguments: unequal, unjust, and an unnecessary burden. William Buckingham conceded, "It is true that no system of taxation has yet been devised which will bear equally upon all," but "that does not justify us in maintaining an objectionable system if we can adopt one that is more in harmony with the principles of justice." He also opposed the income tax "not because it exempts from its provisions men of moderate means, but because it does not reach out its hand and compel those who are able to fill its obligations." To Buckingham, the correct action to take "when there is such doubt in regard to equity, justice, and constitutionality of this act, when it bears so unjustly and so heavily

---

[1] *The Congressional Globe: Official Proceedings of Congress, 41st Congress, 3rd Session* (Washington, D.C.: John C. Rives, 1871), 720-723.

[2] Ibid., Appendix 58-64.

[3] John Sherman, *John Sherman's Recollections of Forty Years in the House, Senate and Cabinet: An Autobiography*, vol. I (Chicago: The Werner Company, 1895), 81.

upon the people, to give the people the benefit of the doubt." In his view, he had a responsibility to respond to the voices of voters "and in doing I shall vote for the repeal of this tax." There was no need, in his view, to continue enforcing the income tax because it was simply an unequal measure instituted by the United States government.[1]

After Buckingham, Cornelius Cole took to the Senate floor to restate his conviction on the subject, identifying the income tax as "an outgrowth of the war" and insisting that it "was imposed to meet and extraordinary emergency, and was intended only as a measure of temporary relief. By the terms of the law it would have expired with the year 1870." He reiterated a complaint that he claimed to have heard from his voters in California of worry that the United States was paying off the national debt too quickly by remarking,

> the only way to prevent its too rapid payment is to dispense with some of the sources of revenue, and if any is to be dispensed with everybody will agree it should be 'the odious income tax... There has never been such a universal demand for the repeal of a tax as there has been for the repeal of this. The importunity upon the subject has almost reached the magnitude of a public clamor, and few of us will have the temerity to meet our constituents if it is left upon the statue-books... The income tax is odious, because it is inquisitorial, and this is the reason it needs to be abolished. It has often proved ruinous to business reputation. It has in many instances destroyed the credit of persons and firms and broken up their occupations... The people of the United States ought not to be subject to any such inconvenience, and their virtue ought not to be put to such a strain... It is mischievous, and the sooner we destroy its expensive and cumbrous machinery the better it will be for the Republic... The people regard it as more odious than any other description of taxation whatever; and not the least objectionable feature of it is its inequality... Equality and uniformity are the redeeming features of taxation, and while these are conspicuous the people will be content under it, however burdensome; but divest it of these features and it becomes, as the tax really is, odious and repulsive to the last degree... The people undoubtedly desire the abolition of the income tax, and this alone is a sufficient reason why it should be abolished.

Recapping the remarks of a number of his colleagues, Cole believed that the government had to be impartial to every citizen. They had somewhat succeeded in this goal with the race issue through not only a war, but also legislation during

---

[1] *Congressional Globe, 41st Congress, 3rd Session*, 746.

Reconstruction. Since they were now regarding African Americans and whites as equals, Cole and many Republicans argued that the same standard should extend to American citizens when it came to the issue of income level. The income tax, in their eyes, did the exact opposite — it discriminated against the wealthy class — and, therefore, had to be repealed. Corbett stated, as he had on several occasions, that the income tax harmed citizens who had to pay it; to him, the tax must cease so that people would be able to fully enjoy the fruits of their labor without government interference. "I believe that the tax is doing us great injury... The effect of the tax upon the people has been bad. It is very objectionable indeed, and they cry out against it," Corbett added.[1]

Other anti-income tax Republicans were more concise in their estimations. For instance, James Flanagan of Texas judged that "certainly the continuance of this tax is not favored by the country."[2] In a rare show of support, a Midwestern Republican, Matthew Carpenter of Wisconsin, joined the cries to end the tax. Thinking that the income tax was "unconstitutional," Carpenter also depicted the tax as "the most vexatious, and oppressive, and unjust of all taxes levied by the Government."[3]

Leading the charge for preserving the tax was Justin Morrill. Although he had championed a low, flat tax rate in the mid-1860s and had not shown enthusiasm for a tax on incomes, he never expressed a desire to completely remove it from the nation. The Senator from Vermont explained he had "no particular affection for it. I take it as I would a medicine, not with an appetite, but because it seems necessary for health." Reasoning that "an income tax, to be properly levied, ought to be levied upon the incomes of all persons," Morrill hoped there would always be "an exemption of the average amount that all men earn by the labor of their hands. All above that... should be subjected to the tax." He, nonetheless, conceded that, if there were a tax upon incomes, people would find ways to avoid paying it. "I know that an income tax is not equal, and that rogues escape, but no more in our country than in any other, if as much," he said. "Taxes, in any form, are ever odious, and yet may be necessary."[4]

James Howell of Iowa argued that it was fair and just for the wealthy to bear the burdens of the country and not the lower class. Howell opened his oration by saying,

[1] Ibid., 746-747.
[2] Ibid., 753.
[3] Ibid., 755.
[4] Ibid., 750-751.

> I deny that the people are impressed with the idea that this is an un-
> just tax or an odious tax... I deny that the masses of the people have been
> affected by it. I deny that there is any public sentiment of the masses of
> the people anywhere throughout this broad land in favor of the repeal of
> this income tax.

He perceived that the only real opposition came from the wealthy and industrial classed in the United States, who, in his estimation, should be shouldering
the burden of the income tax. Knowing that the business and the communities
of affluence were pushing for the cancelling of the income tax, Howell advocated
the idea, and "that the property of the country should bear the burdens of the
taxation of the country," since the "property of the country is that which is supported and defended by the Government of the country." Therefore, given that
the government protected and provided the freedom of men to accumulate property and wealth, he thought that the citizenry had to share some of its prosperity
with it. Without question, he reasoned that there would be a more just outcome
if the wealthy paid an income tax rather than removing it and raising rates on
taxes that affect the poor, such as property and consumption taxes. "I believe,"
Howell asserted, "that the rich who are able to pay should pay, rather than that
this burden should be taken off them and put upon the poor who are not able to
pay, and whose necessities demand that they must consume."[1]

Several Republicans held this same view. Willard Warner of Alabama pleaded with his Republican colleagues not only to support the continuance of the income tax, but also to not be chastised as the party of the privileged. He observed,

> There can be no doubt as to the voice of the people in this matter...
> There is a clamor, a loud clamor, from the men who pay this tax for its
> repeal... but the great masses of the people who pay taxes upon the neces-
> sities of life, such as sugar, tea and coffee, do not come here, and they are
> not heard here. But they will be heard when we go home.

Warner did not want the G.O.P. to be seen as the party who alleviates "the
rich while we are leaving the taxes upon the poor." Summing up his position, he
said, "Until we are ready to relieve the poor, I am not willing to vote for the repeal
of the tax, the taking off of which is specially for the relief of the rich." Warner
understood the notion that since the income tax fell mostly on the property of
the wealthy, it would be political suicide to remove the tax altogether; by doing

---

[1] Ibid., 752.

this, Republican opponents could successfully demonize them as hating the impoverished and helping the privileged.[1]

Corresponding to this statement, Aaron Cragin expressed a willingness to vote against the income tax when "all internal taxes can be abolished properly, and we maintain the Government," but not before accomplishing that feat. Admitting that it "is inconvenient to pay taxes," he noted that "all taxes are burdensome; and, for one, I should be glad to be rid of taxes." He felt that if any taxes were to remain, the very last one that should be eliminated was the tax on incomes. Cragin knew the complaints came "simply from the men who pay this tax — from the wealthy men" and believed the income tax was "the most just and proper tax collected under this system, and it will be the last that I shall vote to abolish."[2]

Thomas Tipton, a minister and senator from Nebraska, pointed out that his "constituents certainly do not desire the repeal of this tax." He defended the income tax while offering how he would deal with the tax if he were a business owner or wealthy individual. "If I were a capitalist," Tipton said, "I would pay without carrying the case to the United States Supreme Court. Hence, I shall vote against the repeal of the income tax." Pay the tax without complaint was the basic advice from Tipton; in his opinion, these affluent individuals should be glad that they had the means to live luxurious lifestyles and not grumble for having to hand over a small portion of their wealth to support the government.[3]

The debate on the removal of the income tax did not last long due to the fact that they had already debated this issue several times in the past. On this occasion, however, the legislation passed the Senate by a one-vote margin, twenty-six to twenty-five; among the Republicans, twenty voted for passage (48%), and twenty-two voted against it (52%). The bill was sent to the House of Representatives, but it was killed on a technicality since the United States Constitution declared, "All bills for raising revenue shall originate in the House of Representatives." Essentially, the House must initiate bills dealing with finances for the government, including repealing of taxes, so the actions of the Senate were unconstitutional. Though defeated this time, the anti-tax Republicans tried once more to get rid of the income tax.[4]

---

[1] Ibid., 754.
[2] Ibid., 754.
[3] Ibid., 753.
[4] Ibid., 755.

On February 7, 1871, Samuel Hooper of Massachusetts offered bill H.R. 2994 in the House of Representatives to repeal the income tax before 1872. The discussion on Hooper's bill was minimal as most everything that could have been said on the subject had already been said; debate commenced two days afterwards with James Negley, a participant in the Battle of Chickamauga during the Civil War, leading the charge to rescind the tax. He told his Senate elected officials,

> The wishes of my constituents, as far as known to me, are clearly in favor of the repeal of the income tax, and all my observations tell me that this tax is more obnoxious and offensive to the American people than any other forced upon us by the late civil war... I do maintain that it is an unequal tax, making an unjust discrimination between the rich and the poor... If the poor man has an unquestionable right of the equality with the rich under and before the law, so the latter has the same right of equality with the former, unless we abandon republican principles and reenact federal distinctions of classes, pairing off heavier duties with larger immunities.

He unequivocally voiced his opposition to the income tax, declaring his intention to "vote for the immediate repeal of the act authorizing its assessment and collection." Negley highlighted the same points that many Republicans had done in the debates over the income tax, citing its discriminatory features and the need of Congress to recognize every citizen as equal under the law; this included not treating people differently based upon economic class.[1]

The supporters of the income tax countered Negley's arguments. "We have, I venture to say, no law on our statue-books for the collection of revenue so fair, so equitable, and in all respects so unobjectionable as the one we are now asked to repeal," said John Beatty of Ohio, a fellow veteran with Negley. He condemned several people in his own party for listening to the rich and not the majority of citizens throughout the nation. He saw the

> disposition on the part of many members to succumb to the persistent clamor of a few selfish men, regardless of the welfare and wishes of the great body of people... It discloses the fact that a determined and immediate effort will be made to legislate still further in the interest of capital and the capitalist, and against productive industry and the laboring masses of the country, by shifting... the burden of taxation from those who are well able to bear it to the shoulders of those who are least able to do so.

---

[1] Ibid., Appendix 103-104.

Challenging the principle that the rich were not "entitled to any exemption from taxation at the expense of the less fortunate citizen," Beatty summarized his conviction that there was "no tax more just, equal, and reasonable than this. It bears lightly upon those who pay it." Needless to say, Beatty threw his support behind keeping the tax in practice because it only affected a small number of people, whereas most in the country did not have to pay it.[1]

In the same way, the creator of the Justice Department, William Lawrence, commented that the income tax "for the present at least ought to be retained. If men who have incomes of $2,000 and over, after paying their taxes, charges for insurance, repairs, &c., cannot pay a tax upon their incomes, who can pay taxes?" After the many years of debate, amendments and bills, Lawrence would be the last Republican to make a statement on the Civil War income tax.[2]

Hooper asked for the House of Representatives to suspend the rules and vote on his bill to revoke the income tax. The bill went down to defeat as ninety-one members voted yes while one hundred and seventeen voted against the measure. Of the G.O.P. congressional representatives, fifty-five voted in favor (37%), and ninety-five voted no (63%). At the time, there were two African American members of the House, Joseph Rainey, the South Carolina representative and first black to be elected to Congress, and Jefferson Long of Georgia; Long voted for the repeal of the tax, and Rainey wanted it to be kept as a revenue source.[3] Hooper withdrew his bill immediately upon its rejection by the House of Representatives, and the Civil War income tax quietly expired in 1872 without any attempts to retain it.[4]

Once again, the division was apparent among the different sections of the Republican Party. Between the two bills of 1871, fifty members from Northeastern and Western states, who paid the majority of the bill, voted to eliminate the income tax (64%), while twenty-eight voted to keep it (36%). Midwestern and Southern congressmen overwhelming supported retaining the income tax, as eighty-nine voted in favor of it (78%), and twenty-five rejected it (22%).

The income tax debate was a real turning point for the Grand Old Party, as the issue did not end at that moment. Throughout the discussions, a noticeable split emerged between the Northeastern and Western Republicans, who,

---

[1] Ibid., 1242-1243.

[2] Ibid., 1247.

[3] Ibid., 1851.

[4] Edwin Robert Anderson Seligman, *The Income Tax Part 2* (New York: The Macmillan Company, 1911), 467.

for the most part, aimed at destroying the income tax, and the Midwestern and Southern Republicans, who fought to keep it intact (as was shown through their voting records). Despite failing to eliminate the income tax in 1871, the anti-tax Republicans could later claim a victory. For the next one hundred and forty years, it was obvious that their ideology took control of the party and fashioned the direction of the G.O.P. on economic issues. The principles of lowering or eliminating taxes, especially on incomes, became the identity of the party; indeed, Republicans from every part of the United States normally express revulsion when it comes to the idea of raising any tax on the voters, and, in almost all elections, promise to keep taxes low. The anti-tax philosophy has even rubbed off on all sections of their party, as even Midwestern and Southern Republicans now typically take the same approach to their economic policies and politics.

CHAPTER 9. REPUBLICANS AND THE INCOME TAX SINCE 1872

"Taxation should be only with the consent of the taxed, through their own representatives, is a cardinal principle of all free government." — William Fessenden.[1]

Since 1872, there has been a strong faction of the Republican Party that consistently opposes either raising the rates of the income tax or wiping it clean from the law books of the United States. A small minority, such as Theodore Roosevelt, Robert LaFollette, Fiorella LaGuardia and Lincoln Chafee, wanted the income tax to remain a vital entity of United States law. For the most part, however, the Grand Old Party always finds some fault with the income tax code, and they continually berate it as unfair, unjust, confiscatory, or simply communistic; this anti-income tax wing has maintained constant control over the party for more than a century. Whatever the charge, they display a hatred for the income tax since its inception during the Civil War, as the anti-tax wing has become the base of the party, fashioning its economic philosophy based on this principle. This chapter will be divided into three sections: late nineteenth and early twentieth century, mid-twentieth century, and late twentieth century to present day. Each section will show, in a limited way, how the Republican Party over time became known as the party of hating taxes.

---

[1] Francis Fessenden, *The Life and Public Services of William Pitt Fessenden: United States Senator From Maine 1854-1864; Secretary of the Treasury 1864-1865; United States Senator From Maine 1865-1869*, vol. II (Boston: Houghton, Mifflin and Company, 1907), 78.

Before the passage of the Sixteenth Amendment, which allowed the federal government to collect an income tax from citizens, some members of the Party of Lincoln viewed the income tax, especially its progressive rates, as the stepping-stone to communism in the United States. When debate on a progressive federal income tax appeared in 1894, John Sherman, the same man who argued for the retention of flat income tax in the 1860s and 1870s, now was starkly opposed to it. "In a republic like ours," he stated, "where all men are equal, this attempt to array the rich against the poor or the poor against the rich is socialism, communism, devilism."[1] Sherman, once a defender of the income tax, completely believed in the destructive nature of progressive income tax rates. Being from the industrial state of Ohio, he did not wish to see his nation turned into a socialist economy.

Former President James Garfield took a similar position as Sherman. He had served in Congress for many years after he fought for the Union and had participated in the debates over keeping the income tax in the law books; in his diary, Garfield wrote how he despised the progressive tax rates and railed against their unfair treatment of certain classes in society. He believed them to be "unconstitutional and communistic as well."[2] In a rather simplistic and blunt manner, Garfield expressed his perspective on the controversial manner; to him, progressive tax rates were nothing less than a way to convert the nation to a Marxian society.

After the Sixteenth Amendment of the Constitution was established, many Republicans began to call for a reduction in tax rates. Since removing an amendment from the Constitution is a fairly difficult task, party members decided the best course of action would be to basically demand tax cuts rather than a total change in the tax system. One of the first Republicans to do so was President Warren G. Harding. Elected in 1920, the Ohio native asked the members of Congress to reduce the heavy taxes placed on the country during World War I. "I know of no more pressing problem at home than to restrict our national expenditures," Harding remarked, "and at the same time measurably lift the burdens of war taxation from the shoulders of the American people."[3]

In the same way, Harding's successor, Calvin Coolidge, understood the problems that arise from having too many taxes on people and businesses. "Realizing

---

[1] *The Congressional Record Containing the Proceedings and Debates of the 53rd Congress, 3rd Session Volume 26* (Washington, D.C.: John C. Rives, 1894), 6695.

[2] Henry James Brown and Frederick D. Williams, eds., *The Diary of James Garfield: Volume IV 1878-1881* (East Lansing: Michigan State University Press, 1981), 52.

[3] Jerold L. Waltman, *Political Origins of the U.S. Income Tax* (Oxford: University Press of Mississippi, 1985), 87.

the power to tax is the power to destroy," he said, "and that the power to take a certain amount of property or of income is only another way of saying that for a certain proportion of his time a citizen must work for the government, the authority to impose a tax upon the people must be carefully guarded...It condemns the citizen to servitude."[1] With his words, Coolidge referred to Chief Justice John Marshall's contention that the power to tax is the power to destroy in the Supreme Court's decision of *McCulloch v. Maryland*. Coolidge alluded to the idea that workers are in service to the government for periods of the year to pay their share of the federal income tax. In essence, citizens of the United States are slaves, and the slave owner is the ever-growing bureaucracy that confiscates their hard-earned money.

Cabinet members at this same time were also arguing for decreased tax rates, as they deemed that it hurt the economy and the consumer. Elihu Root, a stalwart Republican of the late nineteenth and early twentieth century, stated that the income tax amounts to nothing more than legal confiscation by the government of a person's private property. He observed, "What these people want to do is to take away the money of the rich, classifying as rich all who have over four thousand dollars a year, and then to pass laws distributing it among their people at home."[2] Indeed, Root felt that certain politicians, in order to bring money back to their own states and win support among their electorate, used the income tax as a political ploy; these politicians stole money from the wealthy to benefit them in the end.

The Secretary of the Treasury under Coolidge and Hoover, Andrew Mellon, offered a massive tax cut plan in the late 1920s to continue the boom that had been taking place on Wall Street. Mellon wanted most of the tax cut to benefit the wealthy, whom he judged to be the ones to best invest the money and drive the economy forward. "The income tax in this country has become a class rather than national tax," he said.[3] Mellon, who later would be blamed for causing the Great Depression through disastrous economic policies, thought that the income tax was unjustly skewed to hurt the rich, and it was his goal to make it equal.

In Congress in the early twentieth century, several Republicans voiced their opposition to high taxes on the people. Massachusetts Senator Henry Cabot

---

[1] Robert Sobel, *Coolidge: An American Enigma* (Washington, D.C.: Regnery Publishing, 1998), 312.
[2] Richard W. Leopold, *Elihu Root and the Conservative Tradition* (Boston: Little, Brown and Company, 1954), 92.
[3] David Cannadine, *Mellon: An American Life* (New York: Alfred A Knopf, 2006), 318.

Lodge, Sr., whose grandson would run an unsuccessful bid for the Vice Presidency with Richard Nixon in 1960, viewed taxes as the "pillage of a class."[1] Lodge reviled taxes, and he claimed that they were piracy by the government on targeted economic classes in the nation, especially among the affluent.

Similarly, George Norris noted in his book, *Fighting Liberal: The Autobiography of George W. Norris*, that during World War I, the government utilized high taxes to pay for the debt of the United States. Norris referred to them as a "stupendous burden of taxation" and expressed his disdain for those high taxes on the population.[2]

Additionally, the Republican Party platforms of this time conveyed the principle of tax reduction throughout the country. The 1920 platform was first time any anti-tax language appeared at a Republican National Convention. The 1920 platform stated,

> But sound policy equally demands the early accomplishment of that real reduction of the tax burden which may be achieved by substituting simple for complex tax laws and procedure, prompt and certain determination of the tax liability for delay and uncertainty tax laws which do not for tax laws which do excessively mulct the consumer or needlessly repress enterprise and thrift.[3]

Four years later, the 1924 platform for the Republican Party argued that high tax rates led to government overspending, usually on futile things, rather than spending the revenue wisely. It also contended,

> The wisest of taxation rests most rightly on the individual and economic life of the country. The public demand for a sound tax policy is insistent. Progressive tax reduction should be accomplished through tax reorganization. It should not be confined to less than 4,000,000 of our citizens who pay direct taxes, but is the right of more than 100,000,000 who are daily paying their taxes through their living expenses. Congress has in the main confined its work to tax reduction. The matter of tax reform is still unsettled and is equally essential. We pledge ourselves to the progressive reduction of taxes of all the people as rapidly as may be done with due regard for the essential expenditures for the government

---

[1] Sheldon D. Pollack, *Refinancing America: The Republican Antitax Agenda* (New York: State University of New York Press, 2003), 28.

[2] George W. Norris, *Fighting Liberal: The Autobiography of George W. Norris* (New York: The Macmillan Company, 1945), 409.

[3] *Republican Party Platform*, 1920.

administered with rigid economy and to place our tax system on a sound peacetime basis.[1]

Sixteen years later, the 1940 platform complained that the "Public spending has trebled under the New Deal, while tax burdens have doubled," but acknowledged the fact that "Huge taxes are necessary to pay for New Deal waste and for neglected national defense." The party pledged to "revise the tax system and remove those practices which impede recovery and shall apply policies which stimulate enterprise."[2] In 1944, the G.O.P. nominated Thomas Dewey, Governor of New York, as their party's nominee for the presidency. Similar to previous years, the party claimed that, once World War II ended, "the present rates of taxation on individual incomes, on corporations, and on consumption should be reduced as far as is consistent with the payment of the normal expenditures of government in the postwar period."[3] The platforms clearly display a desire by the Grand Old Party to reduce the taxes, because, in their view, it helped the economy of the nation flourish and relieved individuals of a strenuous liability.

The late-nineteenth and early twentieth century witnessed the reemergence of the anti-tax Republicans into the party. Although the faction had been there since the Civil War, the income tax was not part of the revenue stream for the federal government since its expiration in 1872; therefore, it was not mentioned much by Republicans until the ratification of the Sixteenth Amendment. Once the income tax became part of the Constitution, the anti-tax bloc of the G.O.P. started to express their desire to reduce or eliminate it, and this faction grew stronger and stronger through the progression of the century.

As the twentieth century moved forward, the Republican Party became increasingly more antagonistic towards taxes. By the 1950s and 1960s, the G.O.P constructed its image as the party of cutting taxes and keeping them as low as possible, and its presidential leaders slowly but surely embraced this vision. The hero of the D-Day Invasion, Dwight Eisenhower, won the presidency in 1952 and 1956, and made the observation, "Long continued taxes that are only a little below the confiscatory level will destroy free government."[4] He recognized the possible dilemma high tax rates would place on the ability of people to remain not only economically free, but also free on the individual level. In his opinion, people can-

---

[1] *Republican Party Platform, 1924.*
[2] *Republican Party Plaform, 1940.*
[3] *Republican Party Platform, 1944.*
[4] Elsie Gollagher, ed., *The Quotable Dwight D. Eisenhower* (New York: Droke House, 1967), 198.

not be free to do as they please if the finances to do so are being snatched away by the government.

Richard Nixon, Eisenhower's Vice President, lost the election of 1960 to John Kennedy, yet was able to make a comeback and claim victory in 1968; he, unfortunately, left office in disgrace due to his possible involvement in the Watergate Scandal. Throughout his political career, Nixon advocated cutting taxes for the people, saying, "I believe that where the choice is between massive new public works spending...and a tax cut, I personally favor a tax cut."[1] He also stated his belief in his acceptance speech for the Republican nomination for president in 1972,

> Our Administration, as you know, has provided the biggest tax cut in history, but taxes are still too high. That is why one of the goals of our next Administration is to reduce the property tax which is such an unfair and heavy burden on the poor, the elderly, the wage earner, the farmer, and those on fixed incomes.[2]

When Nixon resigned from the presidency in 1974, Vice President Gerald Ford assumed the office. He was able to secure his party's nomination two years later and reminded voters in his speech to the Republican National Convention that he had "called for a permanent tax cut."[3] As president, Eisenhower, Nixon and Ford shaped the direction of the Grand Old Party when it came to taxes as they clearly stood in favor of a discount to taxpayers, and a wave formed in all levels of elected officials within the party.

Republican Congressional leaders and governors took charge of stimulating voters by utilizing anti-tax rhetoric and cutting taxes while in office. For instance, the 1964 Republican Presidential Nominee, Barry Goldwater, stated in his famous book, *The Conscience of a Conservative*, "The graduated tax is a confiscation tax. Its effect, and to a large extent its aim, is to bring down all men to a common level."[4] The Senator from Arizona believed that the tax seized money from people to achieve the objective of eliminating class warfare by making every citizen economically equal. Stating parallel ideas as Thaddeus Stevens and Justin Morrill, Goldwater realized the excessive nature of graduated rates and the inherent unfairness of them on certain individuals in society; his position on the

---

[1] Perry D. Hall, *The Quotable Richard M. Nixon* (New York: Droke House, 1967), 163.

[2] Richard Nixon, *Speech to the 1972 Republican National Convention*, 23 August 1972.

[3] Gerald R. Ford, *Speech to the 1976 Republican National Convention*, 19 August 1976.

[4] Barry M. Goldwater, *The Conscience of a Conservative* (New York: McFadden Books, 1960), 64.

issue certainly benefited him when he won the party nomination for president in 1964.

Ohio Senator Robert Taft took a strongly conservative position on income taxes. As the son of former President and Chief Justice of the United States Supreme Court William Howard Taft, Robert Taft followed in his father's political footsteps, serving in Congress and as Governor of Ohio. He, like Garfield and Sherman in the late 1800s, considered progressive income taxes to be the stepping-stones that would lead the nation to socialism or communism. "There is," he said, "some point at which high taxes must lead directly to socialism." Without question, Taft thought the idea of high taxes to be a principle of Karl Marx and not the capitalistic, free market system promoted throughout the existence of the United States. Contending that large tax burdens were "an evil in itself," Taft called tax cuts "essential to the welfare of the country."[1] Promoting a longstanding tradition of the Republican Party, Taft noted that tax cuts were more beneficial to the economy and society as whole than a heavy tax burden, while also keeping the nation from moving towards socialism.

Earl Warren had a vast political career before joining the Supreme Court as Chief Justice in 1954. He was chosen as Thomas Dewey's running mate in the 1948 presidential election and had served as the Republican Governor of California in the 1940s. During his tenure as governor, he displayed an utter disdain for taxes. "I dislike raising the tax load on our people," Warren said. "I have never done it. We have always lived within our means and have reduced taxes whenever possible."[2]

Nelson Rockefeller, the former governor of New York and Vice President under Gerald Ford, made a promise to voters of New York when he ran to lead the state. "There won't be any tax increases. I won't let you down," he said. Later in his term as governor, Rockefeller bragged to the public that he was "proud to say that in the past 11 years there has not been a single new business tax in New York State."[3]

In *Maverick: A Life in Politics*, Lowell Weicker, Jr. reflected on his time as governor of Connecticut, pointing out the success of his administration for opposing

---

[1] James T. Patterson, *Mr. Republican: A Biography of Robert A. Taft* (Boston: Houghton Mifflin Company, 1972), 373.

[2] Leo Katcher, *Earl Warren: A Political Biography* (New York: McGraw-Hill, 1967), 297.

[3] Michael Kramer and Sam Roberts, "I Never Wanted to be Vice-President of Anything!:" An Investigative Biography of Nelson Rockefeller (New York: Basic Books, 1976), 238, 336.

raising taxes on his constituents. When Connecticut attempted to pass a state income tax, Weicker strongly condemned the measure. "I myself opposed a state income tax," he wrote in the book. He also trusted the principle that if "taxes are increased too much, economic growth will be stifled."[1]

In addition, former Minnesota Governor Elmer Andersen noted in his book, *A Man's Reach*, "I wanted lower property taxes for farmers, homeowners, and small business owners. I wanted to eliminate the highly unpopular personal property tax. I wanted complete tax reform that would bring to fore some incentives for business growth."[2]

Walter Kohler, Jr., a governor of Wisconsin in the mid-1950s, felt a sense a pride for being a champion for lower taxes, especially when he abolished the income tax surcharge in his state. He was content with the measure, telling members of his administration that he had been "looking forward to this day;" he knew that it would bring benefits to Wisconsin both among its citizens and in business.[3]

In 1968, Michigan Governor George Romney sought the Republican Party nomination for president, eventually losing to Nixon. He noted in his campaign pamphlet that he had successfully balanced the state budget without resorting to increasing the tax burden.[4] Indeed, these governors considered raising taxes as a political and economic disaster, preferring instead to give their people and the business community incentives to spend money and create jobs in their respective states. They took hold of the Republican image as an anti-tax party willing to give back to taxpayers more of the fruits of their hard labor.

As was the case in the early portion of the twentieth century, the Republican Party platforms contributed to the perception of the party supporting cutting taxes for every American. With the nomination of Eisenhower in 1956, the party endorsed "further reductions in taxes with particular consideration for low and middle income families. Initiation of a sound policy of tax reductions which will encourage small independent businesses to modernize and progress."[5] Likewise, the 1964 Republican National Convention, which nominated Goldwa-

---

[1] Lowell P. Weicker, Jr., with Barry Sussman, *Maverick: A Life in Politics* (Boston: Little, Brown and Company, 1995), 9, 185.

[2] Elmer L. Andersen, *A Man's Reach* (Minneapolis: University of Minnesota Press, 2000), 187.

[3] Gregory A. Fossedal, *Kohler: A Political Biography of Walter J. Kohler, Jr.* (New Brunswick: Transaction Publishers, 2003), 37.

[4] *George Romney For President 1968*, Campaign Brochure.

[5] *Republican Party Platform, 1956.*

ter, affirmed that the party wanted "complete reform of the tax structure, to include simplification as well as lower rates to strengthen individual and business incentives."[1] In 1968, the party declared its intention "to reduce the heavy tax burden,"[2] whereas the 1976 platform added,

> The Republican Party advocates a legislative policy to obtain a balanced federal budget and reduced tax rates. While the best tax reform is tax reduction, we recognize the need for structural tax adjustments to help the working men and women of our nation. To that end, we recommend tax credits for college tuition, postsecondary technical training and child care expenses incurred by working parents.[3]

These platforms merely reflected the concept that the Republicans were returning to their roots of despising internal taxation, most notably the income tax. The Republican presidents, many members of Congress and governors, through their words, appeared to agree that raising the tax burden was a poor idea for not only the economic success of the nation, but also the economic success of the individual. When the United States moved into the era of Reagan, there was no longer any doubt that the Republican Party stood firmly behind the notion of combating high rates of taxation.

Over the last thirty years, the Republicans thoroughly accepted their position as the party of lower taxes; it is the one issue that seems to unite them as a party during election cycles. Members may disagree on issues such as abortion or the environment, but cutting taxes is the one topic that they will agree almost unanimously. Throughout his successful political career, former president Ronald Reagan without fail showed a preference to slash taxes to help stimulate economic growth. He noted in his memoirs, *An American Life*, that "you reduce tax rates and allow the people to spend or save more of what they earn, they'll be more industrious; they'll have more incentive to work hard."[4] Similarly, at the 1980 Republican Convention, Reagan espoused his conviction of reducing taxes for every citizen. He told the delegates.

> The American people are carrying the heaviest peacetime tax burden in our nation's history--and it will grow even heavier, under present law, next January. We are taxing ourselves into economic exhaustion and stagnation, crushing our ability and incentive to save, invest and produce.

---

[1] *Republican Party Platform, 1964.*
[2] *Republican Party Platform, 1968.*
[3] *Republican Party Platform, 1976.*
[4] Ronald Reagan, *An American Life* (New York: Simon and Schuster, 1990), 232.

This must stop. We must halt this fiscal self-destruction and restore sanity to our economic system. I have long advocated a 30 percent reduction in income tax rates over a period of three years. This phased tax reduction would begin with a 10 percent "down payment" tax cut in 1981, which the Republicans and Congress and I have already proposed. A phased reduction of tax rates would go a long way toward easing the heavy burden on the American people.[1]

When Reagan left the White House in 1989 after two terms as president, his Vice President, George Herbert Walker Bush, received the nomination for the presidency by the Republican Party. Always a backer of lower taxes, Bush made one the most famous remarks to the members of the Republican National Convention dealing with the tax issue. He told them, "The Congress will push me to raise taxes, and I'll say no, and they'll push, and I'll say no, and they'll push again, and I'll say to them, 'Read my lips: no new taxes.'"[2] His words, however, would forever haunt his tenure in office as he raised taxes to stave off high budget deficits.

In addition, Bush's son, George W. Bush, was a proponent of cutting taxes across-the-board for all United States citizens. In his book, *A Charge to Keep*, which he wrote one year before running for the presidency, Bush claimed that the country "will be prosperous if we cut taxes. Reducing marginal tax rates will increase economic growth." He also aimed to make the tax code to be more just. "The current tax structure makes it difficult for people to move from near poverty to the middle class, and we should remove that barrier," he added.[3] Bush, unlike his father, kept his promise and lowered income tax rates in 2001 and 2003.

The last three Republican presidents maintained their commitment to reducing the taxes, albeit sometimes having to go back on their word; Reagan and the Bushes promoted it through their rhetoric, and, in most cases, through their actions as president. They, nonetheless, would be only a small portion of Grand Old Party members to express a longing to eradicate taxes in the past few decades of American history.

The role of the vice president is not only to take over for the president in case of a national emergency or his or her death, but also to be supportive of his or her policies for the country. That has mainly been the case for the last few Re-

---

[1] Ronald Reagan, *Speech to the 1980 Republican National Convention*, 17 July 1980.

[2] George H.W. Bush, *Speech to the 1988 Republican National Convention*, 18 August 1988.

[3] George W. Bush, *A Charge to Keep* (New York: William Morrow and Company, Inc., 1999), 237-238.

publican vice presidents, as they have typically backed their bosses' initiatives to cut taxes; one, however, would be placed in the unfortunate position of having to encourage a policy that he totally disagreed with implementing. When George H.W. Bush decided to raise taxes, Vice president Dan Quayle, an ardent guardian of low taxes, was forced to explain the rationale behind the President's decision, even though he opposed it. In *Standing Firm: A Vice Presidential Memoir*, Quayle regretted that time during his term and for allowing Bush to go against the promise he made to the public in his 1988 acceptance speech. "I knew we were buying into bad politics and bad economics," he recalled, "the economy is going to slide — because that's what happens when taxes are raised."[1] Quayle was none to pleased, but, like a good soldier, he stood shoulder-to-shoulder with Bush despite his better judgment.

On the other hand, Dick Cheney, who served in the position from 2001-2009, did not need to worry as President George W. Bush kept his pledge to cut tax rates and never repealed them. At the 2000 Republican National Convention, the former Secretary of Defense and Congressman from Wyoming articulated his philosophy that reducing taxes benefited the economy as well as families. He and Bush had a plan to "reform the tax code, so that families can keep more of what they earn, more dollars that they can spend on what they value, rather than on what the government thinks is important."[2] Without question, these former vice presidents continued the legacy of the G.O.P. as the party of tax-haters through their words. Regrettably, when Bush decided to raise taxes to prevent further federal deficits, Quayle was placed in a peculiar predicament for which there was no way for him to win.

Recent members of the Grand Old Party's presidential tickets have continually touted the notion that if the nominees were elected, their first order of business would be the dropping of tax rates. "And I say, let the people be free. Free to keep. Let the people be free to keep as much of what they earn as the government can strain with all its might not to take," proclaimed Robert Dole at his 1996 acceptance speech for the party's nomination. He boasted that once he won the White House, it would be his administration "who will reduce taxes 15 percent across-the-board for every taxpayer in America." Dole's ultimate goal was to "end the IRS as we know it."[3] Additionally, Dole's running mate, Jack Kemp of New

---

[1] Dan Quayle, *Standing Firm: A Vice Presidential Memoir* (New York: Harpercollins Publishers, 1994), 194.

[2] Dick Cheney, *Speech to the 2000 Republican National Convention*, 2 August 2000.

[3] Robert Dole, *Speech to the 1996 Republican National Convention*, 15 August 1996.

York, gave an impassioned speech on the need to cut taxes for every American. The former football player-turned-politician stated at the same convention, "The American people can use their money more wisely than can the government. It's time they had more of a chance, and we will give them that chance."[1]

During the 2008 race for the Republican Party nomination, almost every candidate appealed to the anti-tax sentiments of party loyalists throughout the campaign. George Romney's son, Mitt, who had served as governor of Massachusetts, said, "It's high time to lower taxes."[2]

Kansas Senator Sam Brownback supported "an optional flat tax, that lets the people choose to pay one low, flat rate between 15 to 20 percent,"[3] whereas Mike Huckabee, the former Arkansas governor, touted a national sales tax proposal and looked forward to "nailing the 'going out of business' sign on the front door of the IRS."[4]

The eventual nominee, John McCain of Arizona, had had an unbalanced record on the issue of tax cuts; in some instances, he supported tax cuts, and in others, he was willing to maintain the rates that were currently in place at that moment. For the duration of the campaign, McCain communicated his aspiration that the tax cuts signed into law by President George W. Bush would be made permanent, and that he had "never voted for a tax increase in 24 years."[5] At the 2008 convention, McCain conveyed to the Republican Party delegates that, if elected, he "will keep taxes low and cut them where I can."[6]

Likewise, at the same convention, Alaska Governor Sarah Palin plainly uttered that the taxes were "too high," and needed to be reformed.[7] Once again, Republicans understood their anti-tax base and allured them in order to gain their confidence and assistance, like McCain, who has displayed vacillating views on the subject all through his political career.

In 1994, the Republican Party took control of both chambers of Congress for the first time in more than forty years. Successful due to offering the famous "Contract with America," which stated many conservative goals, they attempted to pass many of them over the next ten years; one of those goals, naturally, was

---

[1] Jack Kemp, *Speech to the 1996 Republican National Convention*, 14 August 1996.

[2] Mitt Romney, *Speech to the Conservative Political Action Committee*, 7 February 2008.

[3] Sam Brownback, *Speech at the Ames Straw Poll*, 10 August 2007.

[4] Mike Huckabee, *Super Tuesday Speech*, 5 February 2008.

[5] Cliff Schecter, *The Real McCain: Why Conservatives Don't Trust Him and Why Independents Shouldn't* (Sausalito: Polipoint Press, 2008), 129.

[6] John McCain, *Speech to the 2008 Republican National Convention*, 4 September 2008.

[7] Sarah Palin, *Speech to the 2008 Republican National Convention*, 3 September 2008.

to reduce tax rates. "Working people," said Representative J.C. Watts of Oklahoma in his book, *What Color is a Conservative?: My Life and My Politics*, "deserve lower taxes...When it comes to tax relief, the only color that matters is green."[1]

Similarly, in *Lessons Learned the Hard Way: A Personal Report*, former Speaker of the House Newt Gingrich believed that tax cuts were "right in itself."[2] Another former Speaker, Dennis Hastert, proclaimed in his work, *Speaker: Lessons from Forty Years in Coaching and Politics*, that he wanted to "give money back to the people who earned it anyway."[3]

In *The Freedom Revolution*, Dick Armey, a former economics teacher and leader of the Republicans in the House of Representatives, held that the best solution for the United States was to create a flat tax. "We should scrap our entire tax code and replace it with one flat rate that applies to all Americans," he wrote.[4] Echoing the sentiments of Stevens and Morrill, Armey contended that the flat rate was the only fair way to collect taxes. Another former Republican majority leader, Tom Delay of Texas, called for removing the current income tax structure and replacing it with either a flat tax rate or a national sales tax. "The people should not be forced to pay more than 10 percent of their income to support their government," he wrote in his book, *No Retreat, No Surrender: One American's Fight*.[5] Undoubtedly, Delay, along with other Republicans who signed on to the "Contract with America," believed not only that the money collected by the government belonged to the American people, but also that progressive rates were inherently unequal to those who make more income. In essence, they wanted every citizen to be treated equally in the tax code, regardless if he or she makes more money in a year.

Current and former Republican Party members, as well, have overwhelmingly been in favor of tax reduction, and their harsh words towards taxes supports this concept. Some advocate, or have advocated, just simply cutting taxes. Current Alabama Senator Richard Shelby desires for the government "to lower the

---

[1] Watts, Jr., J.C. with Chris Winston, *What Color is a Conservative?: My Life and My Politics* (New York: Harpercollins Publishers, 2002), 49-50.

[2] Newt Gingrich, *Lessons Learned the Hard Way: A Personal Report* (New York: Harpercollins Publishers, 1998), 25.

[3] Denny Hastert, *Speaker: Lessons from Forty Years in Coaching and Politics* (Washington, D.C.: Regnery Publishing, 2004), 193.

[4] Dick Armey, *The Freedom Revolution: The New Republican House Majority Leader Tells Why Big Government Failed, Why Freedom Works, and How We Will Rebuild America* (Washington, D.C.: Regnery Publishing, 1995), 150.

[5] Tom Delay with Stephen Mansfield, *No Retreat, No Surrender: One American's Fight* (New York: Sentinel, 2007), 172.

massive tax burden that the American people currently labor under," because the current progressive rates punish "individuals and families by penalizing their economic success."[1] In *Power, Pasta and Politics: The World According to Senator Al D'Amato*, the former New York Senator pointed out that he always defended "cutting taxes and scaling back government."[2] One of Nixon's speechwriters and former Republican candidate for president, Patrick J. Buchanan, stated in his work, *Right From the Beginning*, "tax cuts that expand the wealth of the people ought not be surrendered."[3] Orrin Hatch, a longtime senator from the state of Utah, expressed pride in the fact that he was a fervent sponsor of George W. Bush's tax cuts in 2001 and 2003. "Lower taxes," he commented, "mean more money in the pockets of Utahans, who know how to spend their money much better than the federal government. I will continue to support tax cuts for all Americans."[4] Gary Franks, one of only three black Republicans to be elected to Congress since 1934, as well, wrote in his book, *Searching for the Promised Land: An African American's Optimistic Odyssey*, that he believed lower taxes were of the most benefit to the nation, and that the economy would never accomplish any new wealth "through raising taxes."[5] Former Republican-turned-Independent Jim Jeffords of Vermont thought when the federal government runs a surplus, the best solution for it is to give the money back to the taxpayers through cutting their tax rates.[6] In addition, James Baker III, Roger Wicker, Robert Bennett, Kit Bond, Mike Crapo, Mike Enzi, Mike Johanns, John Thune, Bob Corker, Jim Sensenbrenner, David Vitter, Bobby Jindal, Jim Bunning, Jim DeMint, Trent Lott, Mike Pence, and former Republican Arlen Specter all believe that the best fiscal policy is relieving United States citizens

[1] Richard Shelby, "Taxes," 17 August 2009, http://shelby.senate.gov/public/index.cfm?FuseAction=IssueStatements.View&Issue_id=cf510ea2-e2c1-516c-80ce5b99fbaa35d3&CFID=15586717&CFTOKEN=82348717.

[2] Al D'Amato, *Power, Pasta and Politics: The World According to Senator Al D'Amato* (New York: Hyperion, 1995), 129-130.

[3] Patrick J. Buchanan, *Right From the Beginning* (Boston: Little, Brown and Company, 1988), 347.

[4] Orrin Hatch, "Economy and Taxes," 22 July 2009, http://hatch.senate.gov/public/index.cfm?FuseAction=IssuePositions.View&IssuePosition_id=76682398-3614-40b4-a9a4-ac81e05c1a6b.

[5] Congressman Gary Franks, *Searching for the Promised Land: An African American's Optimistic Odyssey* (New York: Regan Books, 1996), 173-177.

[6] Senator Jim Jefford with Yvonne Daley, *An Independent Man: Adventures of a Political Servant* (New York: Simon and Schuster, 2003), 255.

from heavy burdens of taxation, which would place more money in the hands of businesses and consumers and jumpstart economic activity and growth.[1]

Several Republicans have pushed the ideas of flat income tax rates, or scraping the entire tax code for a national sales tax. In *Flat Tax Revolution: Using a Postcard to Abolish the IRS*, former Republican Candidate for President Steve Forbes complained that the "complexity and confusion of the current code corrupts our behavior and values and is ruining the quality of life for us as individuals and as a society."[2] The late Senator Jesse Helms of North Carolina stated that "higher taxes had never boosted production," and the solution to the country's

---

[1] Robert Bennett, "Economy and Taxes," 17 August 2009, http://bennett.senate.gov/public/index.cfm?p=EconomyTaxes.; "Bond Comments on Tax Day & Promotes the Fair and Simple Tax Act," 17 August 2009, http://bond.senate.gov/public/index.cfm?FuseAction=PressRoom.FloorStatements&ContentRecord_id=57ed9c75-bb71-de92-43c3 204bde0ea03b&Region_id=&Issue_id=153dae89-3b23-4667-aa11-2865ed6f2090.; Jim Bunning, "Taxes," 17 August 2009, http://bunning.senate.gov/public/index.cfm?FuseAction=IssueStatements.View&Issue_id=eaa83d9f-9117-439a-aacf-9a0a41e29c83&CFID=15585394&CFTOKEN=72812793.; Bob Corker, "Fiscal Responsibility," 17 August 2009, http://corker.senate.gov/public/index.cfm?FuseAction=IssueStatements.View&Issue_id=b3744ca7-b5a8-a5eb-fc67-c52717b9f5cb&CFID=15585884&CFTOKEN=19972755.; Mike ,Crapo "Taxes," 17 August 2009, http://crapo.senate.gov/issues/taxes/tax.cfm.; Mike Enzi, "Budget/Taxes," 17 August 2009, http://enzi.senate.gov/public/index.cfm?FuseAction=IssueStatements.View&Issue_id=d69335e2-bd22-28ee-4b26-ebc301978ad1&CFID=15586192&CFTOKEN=91275372.; Mike Johanns, "Economy and Jobs," 17 August 2009, http://johanns.senate.gov/public/?p=EconomyJobs.; John Thune, "Taxes," 17 August 2009, http://thune.senate.gov/public/index.cfm?FuseAction=Issues.Detail&Issue_id=b55256c0-c910-4c2a-8251-a232df22bb92.; David Vitter, "Taxes," 17 August 2009, http://vitter.senate.gov/public/index.cfm?FuseAction=IssueStatements.View&Issue_id=3d9080b5-ab31-4070-b94d6b6efda4e2ec&CFID=15586870&CFTOKEN=81461959.; Roger Wicker, "Taxes," 17 August 2009, http://wicker.senate.gov/public/index.cfm?FuseAction=IssueStatements.View&Issue_id=e429918e-f67e-8ef5-74a9d b6b3529f718&CFID=15586934&CFTOKEN=46795966.; Mike Pence, "Economy," 17 August 2009, http://mikepence.house.gov/index.php?option=com_content&view=article&id=1250%3Aeconomy&catid=51%3Aissue-center&Itemid=56.; Jim Sensenbrenner, "Economy," 17 August 2009, http://sensenbrenner.house.gov/Issues/Issue/?IssueID=5089.; Bobby Jindal, "A Trillion Here, a Trillion There," *Politico.com*, 20 July 2009, Accessed 22 July 2009, http://www.politico.com/news/stories/0709/25136.html.; Sen. Trent Lott, "From Theory to Fact," *GulfCoastNews.com*, 12 May 2006, Accessed 22 July 2009, http://gulfcoastnews.com/GCNopEdLottTaxes.htm.; Jim Demint, "Economic Growth," 22 July 2009, http://demint.senate.gov/public/index.cfm?FuseAction=Issues.Detail&Issue_id=95633845-4058-4bc9-b441-a3f638044696.; Senator Arlen Specter with Charles Robbins, *Passion for Truth: From Finding JFK's Single Bullet to Questioning Anita Hill to Impeaching Bill Clinton* (New York: William Morrow, 2000), 422; James A. Baker III With Steve Fiffer, "Work Hard, Study...and Keep Out of Politics!"*Adventures and Lessons from an Unexpected Public Life* (New York: G.P. Putnam's Sons, 2006), 217.

[2] Steve Forbes, *Flat Tax Revolution: Using a Postcard to Abolish the IRS* (Washington, D.C.: Regnery Publishing, Inc., 2005), 35.

---

tax problems was "a simple flat tax rate."[1] Georgia Senator Saxby Chambliss has strong faith not in a flat tax rate, but a national sales tax that would be based on consumption,[2] and Tom Coburn concurred. Coburn said that a national sales tax "would repeal the burdensome income tax."[3]

Lowering taxes has also played a prominent role in the campaigns and administrations of G.O.P. governors and mayors. "I am a strong supporter of tax cuts," former New Jersey Governor Christine Todd Whitman penned in her book, *It's My Party Too: The Battle for the Heart of the GOP and the Future of America.*[4] During her tenure as governor, Whitman instituted a tax cut program to "give families more control over the money that they earn."[5]

In a related fashion, George Pataki set for a goal that New York would be "number one in cutting taxes instead of in tax burden." Outraged at the state's "oppressive taxes," Pataki put forth the argument "that high levels of taxation invite fraud, a disincentive to work harder... I will always try to reduce the tax burden on the taxpayers."[6] A fellow New Yorker, Rudy Giuliani, cut taxes for the Big Apple because he consistently maintained, "Tax cuts are important."[7]

When he ran for governor of California in 2003, Arnold Schwarzenegger appealed to those voters who were growing weary over the state's many types of taxes, from sales to income. He said,

---

[1] Senator Jesse Helms, *Here's Where I Stand: A Memoir* (New York: Random House, 2005), 259.

[2] "Chambliss, Linder, Price Promote Fairtax At Atlanta Press Conference," 3 April 2007, Accessed 17 August 2009. http://www.chambliss.senate.gov/public/index.cfm?p=PressR eleases&ContentRecord_id=b926ce03-802a-23ad-42a4 85493ba76a86&ContentType_ id=757b7bb6-a540-4ca5-b4ee-9040fba13700&cla81bb1-3e33-4e40-8d06- 5402ec195049&0f375d20-f53a-40ec-be62-076b5b6ca521&0a9faa4e-93c0-4ea7- 8789f3a1af6a4b91&946091a3-c04f-730a-033e-84400d85f615&ef1e98ff-a083-451e- ba7999661067032c&070d7e2c-edf9-4220-a1fb-b964a76176d2&5c81ba67-be20-4229- a615-966ecb0ccad6&9a28c5ad-6654-46f4-afb8e502885aa68a&Group_id=a2539167- 571a-43e6-8f3f-c129d2b1fbfe.

[3] Tom Coburn, "Tax Reform," 17 August 2009, http://coburn.senate.gov/public/index. cfm?FuseAction=Issues.View&Issue_id=d5d76b2e-7f31-4b2e-af8c 44c99728f428&CFI D=15585718&CFTOKEN=94738946.

[4] Christine Todd Whitman, *It's My Party Too: The Battle for the Heart of the GOP and the Future of America* (New York: The Penguin Press, 2005), 233.

[5] Patricia Beard, *Growing Up Republican Christie Whitman: The Politics of Character* (New York: Harpercollins Publishers, 1996), 209.

[6] George E. Pataki with Daniel Paisner, *Pataki: An Autobiography* (New York: Viking, 1998), 67, 147.

[7] Fred Siegel with Harry Siegel, *The Prince of the City: Giuliani, New York and the Genius of American Life* (San Francisco: Encounter Books, 2005), 266; Andrew Kirtzman, *Rudy Giuliani: Emperor of the City* (New York: William Morrow, 2000), 40.

The people of California have been punished enough. From the time they get up in the morning and flush the toilet, they're taxed. Then they go and get coffee, they're taxed. They get into their car. They're taxed. They go to the gas station. They're taxed. They go to lunch. They're taxed... Even when they go to bed, you can go to bed in fear that you may get taxed while you're sleeping. There's a sleeping tax.[1]

There is no doubt that in the last thirty years, the Republican Party has been the home for those who fight taxes in all shapes and forms. Republican candidates are keenly aware of their most prominent constituency, and they know that they must appeal to them through anti-tax rhetoric and actions. It is for that reason that the Grand Old Party and its members continually attack raising taxes on the people.

At the Republican National Convention in 1988, the party, in the midst of a successful period with Reagan and Bush, crafted a platform that stated the ideals of supply-side economics and lower taxes. "We oppose any attempts to increase taxes," read the party platform. "Tax increases harm the economic expansion and reverse the trend to restoring control of the economy to individual Americans. We reject calls for higher taxes from all quarters."[2]

In 1996, the party presented its most scathing assail on taxes, especially the increases put into place by Democratic President Bill Clinton in 1993. The platform asserted,

> These proposals making the current tax code fairer and less burdensome should be viewed as an interim step towards comprehensive tax reform. The current tax code is ridiculously complex and unfair. It is also an unnecessary drag on the economy. At a time when business investment plans are greatly diminished and savings rates are unacceptably low, we must reform our tax system to remove existing artificial, government-induced bias against saving and investment. To that end, we firmly commit to a tax code for the 21st century that will raise revenue sufficient for a smaller, more effective and less wasteful government without increasing the national debt. That new tax system must be flatter, fairer, and simpler, with a minimum of exclusions from its coverage, and one set of rules applying to all... It must expand the economy and increase opportunity by rewarding initiative and hard work. It must foster job creation and end

---

[1] Joe Mathews, *The People's Machine: Arnold Schwarzenegger and the Rise of Blockbuster Democracy* (New York: Public Affairs, 2006), 155.

[2] *Republican Party Platform, 1988.*

bias against saving. It must promote personal freedom and innovation. It must do all this in order to boost wages and raise living standards for all of America's working families.... To protect the American people from those who would undo their forthcoming victory over big government, we support legislation requiring a super-majority vote in both houses of Congress to raise taxes.[1]

The most recent platform of 2008 expressed the need to make President George W. Bush's tax cuts permanent and reduce taxes whenever it is necessary. It read,

Sound tax policy alone may not ensure economic success, but terrible tax policy does guarantee economic failure. Along with making the 2001 and 2003 tax cuts permanent so American families will not face a large tax hike, Republicans will advance tax policies to support American families, promote savings and innovation, and put us on a path to fundamental tax reform.[2]

These are but a few examples, but it has been a common theme for the party to promote either maintaining or lowering the tax burden. This ideal has been true for Republicans for a very long period of time. Every Republican Party platform since 1920, with the exception of 1932 and 1936 when the United States was in the midst of the Great Depression, has advocated a reduction in tax rates for the American citizens, and it appears that the trend will mostly likely continue with future party platforms.

When the first income tax was repealed in 1872, most Republicans originally attempted to prevent it from becoming law again. After the passage of the 16th Amendment in 1913, the goal of the party has been to keep the rates as low as possible and cut them at any possible opportunity. Republicans, for the most part, have favored dropping tax rates on the American public, but recently some have been pushing for a national sales tax to replace it. If they cannot remove the income tax from law, it is obvious that most of them would be satisfied, as an alternative, with a great reduction in the rates.

No one can understand the politics of today without knowledge of history, which is certainly the case with taxes and the Grand Old Party. For the past nine decades, most Republican politicians and platforms have been on a rampage to either reduce or eliminate taxes, especially ones on income. They view it as a threat to not only the economy, but also the individual freedom of Ameri-

---

[1] *Republican Party Platform, 1996.*
[2] *Republican Party Platform, 2008.*

cans. The question that is naturally asked is — Why? Well, it is because hatred for the internal taxes began with the ideas of Alexander Hamilton, and it later evolved into the economic philosophies of the Whig Party. Once the party dissolved in the 1850s, the former Whigs took their views into a new party called "Republican." The income tax, which had at one time been advocated by G.O.P. members during the Civil War, eventually morphed into a target for destruction by many Republicans in the Reconstruction era. Although a majority of Republicans wanted the tax to be retained, there were many in the party that fought for it to be repealed, including Hiram Revels, the first black senator. The examples presented in this chapter are but a few of the hundreds of Republicans over the last century who have insisted on slashing tax rates. It has been a longstanding tradition for Republicans to oppose the income tax, and they will most likely carry on the battle, just like they did during Reconstruction, as long as it remains an amendment in the Constitution.

This table shows how each member of Congress between 1861 and 1871 voted on the different tax bills introduced at that time. "Y" represents a "yes" vote; "N" represents a "no" vote, and "N/A" means that no vote was recorded for that individual on the bill. There are several reasons why an "N/A" appears on the chart: the congressman did not vote on the bill, was no longer a member at the time of the bill, or was a member of the opposite chamber and the bill did not pass (for example, in for H.R. 2994, the bill was killed by the House of Representatives, so the Senate never had the opportunity to vote on it).

TABLE 1: VOTES BY CONGRESSMEN ON THE TAX BILLS, 1861–187

Name	State	H.R.71 (1861)	H.R.312 (1862)	H.R.405 (1864)	H.R.744 (1865)	H.R.513 (1866)	H.R.1161 (1867)	H.R.2045 (1870)	H.R.1083 (1871)	H.R.2994 (1871)
Abbott	NC	N/A	N/A	N/A	N/A	N/A	N/A	N/A	N	N/A
Adams	MA	N/A	N/A	N/A	N/A	N/A	N/A	N/A	N/A	N/A
Aldrich	MN	N	Y	N/A	N/A	N/A	N/A	N/A	N/A	N/A
Alley	MA	Y	Y	Y	N/A	N/A	N/A	N/A	N/A	N/A
Allison	IA	N/A	N/A	Y	Y	Y	N/A	Y	N/A	N
Ambler	OH	N/A	N/A	N/A	N/A	N/A	N/A	N	N/A	Y
Ames, A	MS	N/A	N/A	N/A	N/A	N/A	N/A	N/A	N/A	N/A
Ames, O	MA	N/A	N/A	Y	Y	Y	N/A	Y	N/A	Y

Anderson, G	MO	N/A	N/A	N/A	N/A	N/A	N/A	N/A	N/A	N/A
Anthony	RI	Y	Y	Y	N/A	N/A	N/A	N	Y	N/A
Armstrong	PA	N/A	N/A	N/A	N/A	N/A	N/A	Y	N/A	Y
Arnell	TN	N/A	N/A	N/A	N/A	N/A	N/A	N	N/A	N
Arnold, I	IL	N	Y	Y	Y	N/A	N/A	N/A	N/A	N/A
Arnold, S	RI	N/A	N/A	N/A	N/A	N/A	N/A	N/A	N/A	N/A
Ashley, D	NV	N/A	N/A	N/A	N/A	N/A	N/A	N/A	N/A	N/A
Ashley, J	OH	Y	Y	N/A	Y	N/A	N/A	N/A	N/A	N/A
Asper	MO	N/A	N/A	N/A	N/A	N/A	N/A	N	N/A	N
Atwood	WI	N/A	N/A	N/A	N/A	N/A	N/A	N	N/A	N
Ayer	VA	N/A	N/A	N/A	N/A	N/A	N/A	Y	N/A	Y
Babbitt	PA	Y	Y	N/A	N/A	N/A	N/A	N/A	N/A	N/A
Bailey, A	NY	N/A	N/A	N/A	N/A	N/A	N/A	N	N/A	N/A
Bailey, G	MA	Y	N/A	N/A	N/A	N/A	N/A	N/A	N/A	N/A
Baker, E	OR	Y	Y	N/A	N/A	N/A	N/A	N/A	N/A	N/A
Baker, J	IL	N/A	N/A	N/A	N/A	Y	N/A	N/A	N/A	N/A
Baldwin	MA	N/A	N/A	Y	Y	Y	N/A	N/A	N/A	N/A
Banks, N	MA	N/A	N/A	N/A	N/A	Y	N/A	Y	N/A	Y
Barker	PA	N/A	N/A	N/A	N/A	N/A	N/A	N/A	N/A	N/A
Barry	MS	N/A	N/A	N/A	N/A	N/A	N/A	Y	N/A	N
Baxter	VT	Y	Y	Y	Y	Y	N/A	N/A	N/A	N/A
Beaman	MI	N	Y	Y	Y	Y	N/A	N	N/A	N
Beatty	OH	N/A	N/A	N/A	N/A	N/A	N/A	N	N/A	N
Benjamin	MO	N/A	N/A	N/A	N/A	N/A	N/A	N	N/A	N/A
Bennett	NY	N/A	N/A	N/A	N/A	N/A	N/A	Y	N/A	Y
Benton	NH	N/A	N/A	N/A	N/A	N/A	N/A	N	N/A	N
Bethune	GA	N/A	N/A	N/A	N/A	N/A	N/A	N/A	N/A	Y
Bidwell	CA	N/A	N/A	N/A	N/A	Y	N/A	N/A	N/A	N/A
Bingham, J	OH	Y	Y	N/A	N/A	N/A	N/A	Y	N/A	Y
Bingham, K	MI	Y	N/A	N/A	N/A	N/A	N/A	N/A	N/A	N/A
Blaine	ME	N/A	N/A	Y	Y	Y	N/A	N/A	N/A	N/A
Blair, A	MI	N/A	N/A	N/A	N/A	N/A	N/A	N	N/A	N
Blair, F	MO	N	Y	N/A	N/A	N/A	N/A	N/A	N/A	N/A
Blair, S	PA	Y	Y	N/A	N/A	N/A	N/A	N/A	N/A	N/A
Blake	OH	Y	Y	N/A	N/A	N/A	N/A	N/A	N/A	N/A
Blow	MO	N/A	N/A	Y	Y	N/A	N/A	N/A	N/A	N/A

Boles	AR	N/A	N/A	N/A	N/A	N/A	N/A	N	N/A	N
Boreman	WV	N/A	N/A	N/A	N/A	N/A	N/A	N	N	N/A
Boutwell	MA	N/A	N/A	Y	Y	N/A	N/A	N/A	N/A	N/A
Bowen	SC	N/A	N/A	N/A	N/A	N/A	N/A	Y	N/A	Y
Boyd, S	MO	N/A	N/A	Y	Y	N/A	N/A	N	N/A	N/A
Bradford	CO	N/A	N/A	N/A	N/A	N/A	N/A	N/A	N/A	N/A
Brandegee	CT	N/A	N/A	Y	Y	N/A	N/A	N/A	N/A	N/A
Bromwell	IL	N/A	N/A	N/A	N/A	Y	N/A	N/A	N/A	N/A
Brooks	MA	N/A	N/A	N/A	N/A	N/A	N/A	Y	N/A	Y
Broomall	PA	N/A	N/A	Y	Y	N/A	N/A	N/A	N/A	N/A
Brown, B	MO	N/A	N/A	Y	N/A	N/A	N/A	N/A	N/A	N/A
Browning	IL	Y	Y	N/A	N/A	N/A	N/A	N/A	N/A	N/A
Brownlow	TN	N/A	N/A	N/A	N/A	N/A	N/A	N/A	N	N/A
Buffinton	MA	N	N	N/A	N/A	N/A	N/A	Y	N/A	Y
Buck	AL	N/A	N/A	N/A	N/A	N/A	N/A	N/A	N/A	N/A
Buckingham	CT	N/A	N/A	N/A	N/A	N/A	N/A	N/A	Y	N/A
Buckland	OH	N/A	N/A	N/A	N/A	Y	N/A	N/A	N/A	N/A
Buckley	AL	N/A	N/A	N/A	N/A	N/A	N/A	N/A	N/A	N
Bundy	OH	N/A	N/A	N/A	N/A	N/A	N/A	N/A	N/A	N/A
Burchard	IL	N/A	N/A	N/A	N/A	N/A	N/A	N	N/A	N
Burdett	MO	N/A	N/A	N/A	N/A	N/A	N/A	N	N/A	N
Burleigh	DK	N/A	N/A	N/A	N/A	N/A	N/A	N/A	N/A	N/A
Burnham	CT	N/A	N/A	N/A	N/A	N/A	N/A	N/A	N/A	N/A
Butler, B	MA	N/A	N/A	N/A	N/A	N/A	N/A	N	N/A	N/A
Butler, R	TN	N/A	N/A	N/A	N/A	N/A	N/A	N	N/A	N
Cake	PA	N/A	N/A	N/A	N/A	N/A	N/A	N/A	N/A	N/A
Cameron	PA	N/A	N/A	N/A	N/A	N/A	N/A	N/A	Y	N/A
Campbell	PA	Y	Y	N/A	N/A	N/A	N/A	N/A	N/A	N/A
Carpenter	WI	N/A	N/A	N/A	N/A	N/A	N/A	Y	Y	N/A
Cattell	NJ	N/A	N/A	N/A	N/A	N/A	N/A	N/A	N/A	N/A
Cessna	PA	N/A	N/A	N/A	N/A	N/A	N/A	N/A	N/A	Y
Chamberlain	NY	Y	Y	N/A	N/A	N/A	N/A	N/A	N/A	N/A
Chandler	MI	Y	Y	N/A	N/A	N/A	N/A	N	N/A	N/A
Chaves	NM	N/A	N/A	N/A	N/A	N/A	N/A	N/A	N/A	N/A
Churchill	NY	N/A	N/A	N/A	N/A	N/A	N/A	N/A	N/A	Y
Clark, A	NY	Y	Y	N/A	Y	N/A	N/A	N/A	N/A	N/A

Clark, D	NH	Y	Y	Y	N/A	N/A	N/A	N/A	N/A	N/A
Clark, W	TX	N/A	N/A	N/A	N/A	N/A	N/A	N	N/A	N
Clarke, F	NY	N/A	N/A	Y	Y	N/A	N/A	N/A	N/A	N/A
Clarke, R	OH	N/A	N/A	N/A	N/A	Y	N/A	N/A	N/A	N/A
Clarke, S	KS	N/A	N/A	N/A	N/A	Y	N/A	Y	N/A	N
Cobb, A	WI	N/A	N/A	Y	Y	Y	N/A	N	N/A	N
Cobb, C	NC	N/A	N/A	N/A	N/A	N/A	N/A	N/A	N/A	N/A
Coburn	IN	N/A	N/A	N/A	N/A	N/A	N/A	N	N/A	N
Cole, C	CA	N/A	N/A	Y	Y	N/A	N/A	Y	Y	N/A
Colfax	IN	N	Y	N/A	N/A	N/A	N/A	N/A	N/A	N/A
Collamer	VT	Y	Y	Y	N/A	N/A	N/A	N/A	N/A	N/A
Conger	MI	N/A	N/A	N/A	N/A	N/A	N/A	N	N/A	N
Conkling, F	NY	Y	Y	N/A	N/A	N/A	N/A	N/A	N/A	N/A
Conkling, R	NY	Y	Y	N/A	N/A	Y	N/A	Y	Y	N/A
Conness	CA	N/A	N/A	N/A	N/A	N/A	N/A	N/A	N/A	N/A
Conway	KS	Y	N/A	N/A	N/A	N/A	N/A	N/A	N/A	N/A
Cook, B	IL	N/A	N/A	N/A	N/A	Y	N/A	N	N/A	N
Corbett	OR	N/A	N/A	N/A	N/A	N/A	N/A	Y	Y	N/A
Corwin	OH	N/A	N/A	N/A	N/A	N/A	N/A	N/A	N/A	N/A
Covode	PA	Y	Y	N/A	N/A	N/A	N/A	Y	N/A	N/A
Cowan	PA	Y	Y	N/A	N/A	N/A	N/A	N/A	N/A	N/A
Cowles	NY	N/A	N/A	N/A	N/A	N/A	N/A	Y	N/A	N
Cragin	NH	N/A	N/A	N/A	N/A	N/A	N/A	N	N	N/A
Creswell	CT	N/A	N/A	Y	Y	N/A	N/A	N/A	N/A	N/A
Cullom	IL	N/A	N/A	N/A	N/A	Y	N/A	N	N/A	N
Culver	PA	N/A	N/A	N/A	N/A	N/A	N/A	N/A	N/A	N/A
Curtis	IA	N/A	N/A	N/A	N/A	N/A	N/A	N/A	N/A	N/A
Cutler	OH	Y	N/A	N/A	N/A	N/A	N/A	N/A	N/A	N/A
Daily	NE	N/A	N/A	N/A	N/A	N/A	N/A	N/A	N/A	N/A
Darling	NY	N/A	N/A	N/A	N/A	Y	N/A	N/A	N/A	N/A
Darrall	LA	N/A	N/A	N/A	N/A	N/A	N/A	N/A	N/A	Y
Davis, N	NY	N/A	N/A	N/A	N/A	N/A	N/A	Y	N/A	N/A
Davis, T	NY	N/A	N/A	N/A	Y	Y	N/A	N/A	N/A	N/A
Davis, W	PA	Y	Y	N/A	N/A	N/A	N/A	N/A	N/A	N/A
Dawes	MA	Y	Y	Y	Y	Y	N/A	Y	N/A	Y
Defrees	IN	N/A	N/A	N/A	N/A	Y	N/A	N/A	N/A	N/A

Degener	TX	N/A	N/A	N/A	N/A	N/A	N/A	Y	N/A	N
Delano, Ch	MA	Y	Y	N/A	N/A	N/A	N/A	N/A	N/A	N/A
Delano, Co	OH	N/A	N/A	N/A	N/A	Y	N/A	N/A	N/A	N/A
Deming	CT	N/A	N/A	Y	Y	N/A	N/A	N/A	N/A	N/A
Denny	WA	N/A	N/A	N/A	N/A	N/A	N/A	N/A	N/A	N/A
Deweese	NC	N/A	N/A	N/A	N/A	N/A	N/A	N/A	N/A	N/A
Dickey	PA	N/A	N/A	N/A	N/A	N/A	N/A	N/A	N/A	N/A
Diven	NY	Y	Y	N/A	N/A	N/A	N/A	N/A	N/A	N
Dixon, J	CT	Y	Y	N/A	N/A	N/A	N/A	N/A	N/A	N/A
Dixon, N	RI	N/A	N/A	Y	Y	Y	N/A	N/A	N/A	Y
Dockery	NC	N/A	N/A	N/A	N/A	N/A	N/A	N	N/A	N
Dodge	NY	N/A	N/A	N/A	N/A	Y	N/A	N/A	N/A	N/A
Doolittle	WI	Y	Y	Y	N/A	N/A	N/A	N/A	N/A	N/A
Donley	PA	N/A	N/A	N/A	N/A	N/A	N/A	Y	N/A	N
Donnelly	MN	N/A	N/A	Y	N/A	Y	N/A	N/A	N/A	N/A
Drake	MO	N/A	N/A	N/A	N/A	N/A	N/A	N	N/A	N/A
Driggs	MI	N/A	N/A	Y	Y	N/A	N/A	N/A	N/A	N/A
Duell	NY	N/A	Y	N/A	N/A	N/A	N/A	N/A	N/A	N/A
Dumont	IN	N/A	N/A	N/A	N/A	Y	N/A	N/A	N/A	N/A
Dunn	IN	N/A	Y	N/A	N/A	N/A	N/A	N/A	N/A	N/A
Duval	WV	N/A	N/A	N/A	N/A	N/A	N/A	Y	N/A	N
Dyer	MO	N/A	N/A	N/A	N/A	N/A	N/A	N/A	N/A	N/A
Eckley	OH	N/A	N/A	Y	Y	Y	N/A	N/A	N/A	N/A
Edgerton	OH	N	Y	N/A	N/A	N/A	N/A	N/A	N/A	N/A
Edmunds	VT	N/A	N/A	N/A	N/A	N/A	N/A	N	N/A	N/A
Edwards, T	NH	Y	Y	N/A	N/A	N/A	N/A	N/A	N/A	N/A
Eggleston	OH	N/A	N/A	N/A	N/A	Y	N/A	N/A	N/A	N/A
Ela	NH	N/A	N/A	N/A	N/A	N/A	N/A	N	N/A	N
Eliot	MA	Y	Y	Y	Y	N/A	N/A	N/A	N/A	N/A
Ely	NY	N/A	N/A	N/A	N/A	N/A	N/A	N/A	N/A	N/A
Farnsworth	IL	N/A	N/A	Y	N/A	Y	N/A	N	N/A	N
Farquhar	IN	N/A	N/A	N/A	N/A	Y	N/A	N/A	N/A	N/A
Farwell	ME	N/A	N/A	N/A	N/A	N/A	N/A	N/A	N/A	N/A
Fenton	NY	N/A	N/A	Y	N/A	N/A	N/A	Y	Y	N/A
Ferriss	NY	N/A	N/A	N/A	N/A	N/A	N/A	Y	N/A	N
Ferry, O	CT	N/A	N/A	N/A	N/A	N/A	N/A	N/A	N/A	N/A

Ferry, T	MI	N/A	N/A	N/A	N/A	Y	N/A	N/A	N/A	N
Fessenden, S	ME	N/A	N/A	N/A	N/A	N/A	N/A	N/A	N/A	N/A
Fessenden, T	ME	Y	Y	N/A	N/A	N/A	N/A	N/A	N/A	N/A
Fessenden, W	ME	Y	Y	Y	N/A	N/A	N/A	N/A	N/A	N/A
Field	NJ	N/A	N/A	N/A	N/A	N/A	N/A	N/A	N/A	N/A
Finkelnburg	MO	N/A	N/A	N/A	N/A	N/A	N/A	Y	N/A	N
Fisher	NY	N/A	N/A	N/A	N/A	N/A	N/A	Y	N/A	N
Fitch	NV	N/A	N/A	N/A	N/A	N/A	N/A	Y	N/A	Y
Flanagan	TX	N/A	N/A	N/A	N/A	N/A	N/A	N/A	Y	N/A
Fogg	NH	N/A	N/A	N/A	N/A	N/A	N/A	N/A	N/A	N/A
Foot	VT	Y	Y	N/A	N/A	N/A	N/A	N/A	N/A	N/A
Foster	CT	Y	Y	Y	N/A	N/A	N/A	N/A	N/A	N/A
Fowler	TN	N/A	N/A	N/A	N/A	N/A	N/A	Y	Y	N/A
Franchot	NY	Y	N/A	N/A	N/A	N/A	N/A	N/A	N/A	N/A
Frank	NY	Y	Y	N/A	Y	N/A	N/A	N/A	N/A	N/A
Frelinghuysen	NJ	N/A	N/A	N/A	N/A	N/A	N/A	N/A	N/A	N/A
Garfield	OH	N/A	N/A	Y	Y	Y	N/A	N	N/A	Y
Garfielde	LA	N/A	N/A	N/A	N/A	N/A	N/A	N/A	N/A	N/A
Gilbert	FL	N/A	N/A	N/A	N/A	N/A	N/A	Y	N/A	N/A
Gilfillan	PA	N/A	N/A	N/A	N/A	N/A	N/A	Y	N/A	Y
Gooch	MA	Y	Y	N/A	N/A	N/A	N/A	N/A	N/A	N/A
Goodwin	ME	Y	N/A	N/A	N/A	N/A	N/A	N/A	N/A	N/A
Granger	MI	Y	Y	N/A	N/A	N/A	N/A	N/A	N/A	N/A
Grimes	IA	Y	Y	Y	N/A	N/A	N/A	N/A	N/A	N/A
Grinnell	IA	N/A	N/A	Y	Y	N/A	N/A	N/A	N/A	N/A
Griswold	NY	N/A	N/A	Y	Y	N/A	N/A	N/A	N/A	N/A
Grow	PA	N/A	N/A	N/A	N/A	N/A	N/A	N/A	N/A	N/A
Gurley	OH	Y	Y	N/A	N/A	N/A	N/A	N/A	N/A	N/A
Hale, E	ME	N/A	N/A	N/A	N/A	N/A	N/A	N	N/A	N
Hale, James	PA	N	Y	N/A	N/A	N/A	N/A	N/A	N/A	N/A
Hale, John	NH	Y	Y	N/A	N/A	N/A	N/A	N/A	N/A	N/A
Hale, R	NY	N/A	N/A	N/A	N/A	Y	N/A	N/A	N/A	N/A
Hamilton, C	FL	N/A	N/A	N/A	N/A	N/A	N/A	Y	N/A	N
Hamilton, M	TX	N/A	N/A	N/A	N/A	N/A	N/A	N	Y	N/A
Hamlin	ME	N/A	N/A	N/A	N/A	N/A	N/A	N	N	N/A
Hanchett	WI	N	Y	N/A	N/A	N/A	N/A	N/A	N/A	N/A

Harding	IL	N/A	N/A	N/A	N/A	Y	N/A	N/A	N/A	N/A
Harlan	IA	Y	Y	Y	N/A	N/A	N/A	N	N	N/A
Harris, G	MS	N/A	N/A	N/A	N/A	N/A	N/A	Y	N/A	Y
Harris, I	NY	Y	Y	Y	N/A	N/A	N/A	N/A	N/A	N/A
Harris, J	LA	N/A	N/A	N/A	N/A	N/A	N/A	Y	N/A	N/A
Hart	NY	N/A	N/A	N/A	N/A	Y	N/A	N/A	N/A	N/A
Hawkins	TN	N/A	N/A	N/A	N/A	N/A	N/A	N	N/A	N
Hawley	IL	N/A	N/A	N/A	N/A	N/A	N/A	N	N/A	N
Hay	IL	N/A	N/A	N/A	N/A	N/A	N/A	N	N/A	N
Hayes, R	OH	N/A	N/A	N/A	N/A	N/A	N/A	N/A	N/A	N/A
Hays	AL	N/A	N/A	N/A	N/A	N/A	N/A	N	N/A	N
Heaton	NC	N/A	N/A	N/A	N/A	N/A	N/A	N/A	N/A	N/A
Heflin	AL	N/A	N/A	N/A	N/A	N/A	N/A	Y	N/A	N
Henderson, Ja	OR	N/A	N/A	N/A	N/A	Y	N/A	N/A	N/A	N/A
Henderson, Jo	MO	N/A	N/A	Y	N/A	N/A	N/A	N/A	N/A	N/A
Hickman	PA	N/A	Y	N/A	N/A	N/A	N/A	N/A	N/A	N/A
Hill, John	NJ	N/A	N/A	N/A	N/A	N/A	N/A	Y	N/A	Y
Hill, Joshua	GA	N/A	N/A	N/A	N/A	N/A	N/A	N/A	N/A	N/A
Hill, R	IN	N/A	N/A	N/A	N/A	N/A	N/A	N/A	N/A	N/A
Higby	CA	N/A	N/A	Y	Y	N/A	N/A	N/A	N/A	N/A
Hitchcock	NE	N/A	N/A	N/A	N/A	N/A	N/A	N/A	N/A	N/A
Hoar	MA	N/A	N/A	N/A	N/A	N/A	N/A	Y	N/A	N
Hoge	SC	N/A	N/A	N/A	N/A	N/A	N/A	N/A	N/A	Y
Holmes	NY	N/A	N/A	N/A	N/A	Y	N/A	N/A	N/A	Y
Hooper	MA	N/A	Y	Y	Y	Y	N/A	Y	N/A	Y
Hopkins	WI	N/A	N/A	N/A	N/A	N/A	N/A	N/A	N/A	N/A
Horton	OH	Y	Y	N/A	N/A	N/A	N/A	N/A	N/A	N/A
Hotchkiss	NY	N/A	N/A	Y	Y	Y	N/A	Y	N/A	N
Howard	MI	N/A	Y	Y	N/A	N/A	N/A	N/A	N	N/A
Howe	WI	Y	Y	Y	N/A	N/A	N/A	N	N	N/A
Howell	IA	N/A	N/A	N/A	N/A	N/A	N/A	N	N	N/A
Hubbard, A	IA	N/A	N/A	Y	Y	Y	N/A	N/A	N/A	N/A
Hubbard, C	WV	N/A	N/A	N/A	N/A	Y	N/A	N/A	N/A	N/A
Hubbard, D	NY	N/A	N/A	N/A	N/A	Y	N/A	N/A	N/A	N/A
Hubbard, J	CT	N/A	N/A	Y	Y	Y	N/A	N/A	N/A	N/A
Hubbell	OH	N/A	N/A	N/A	N/A	Y	N/A	N/A	N/A	N/A

Hulburd	NY	N/A	N/A	N/A	N	Y	N/A	N/A	N/A	N/A
Humphrey	NY	N/A	N/A	N/A	N/A	Y	N/A	N/A	N/A	N/A
Hutchins	OH	Y	Y	N/A	N/A	N/A	N/A	N/A	N/A	N/A
Ingersoll	NY	N/A	N/A	N/A	Y	Y	N/A	N	N/A	N
Jenckes	RI	N/A	N/A	Y	Y	N/A	N/A	Y	N/A	Y
Jewett	MO	N/A	N/A	N/A	N/A	N/A	N/A	N/A	N/A	N/A
Jones, A	NC	N/A	N/A	N/A	N/A	N/A	N/A	N	N/A	N/A
Judd	IL	N/A	N/A	N/A	N/A	N/A	N/A	Y	N/A	N/A
Julian	IN	Y	Y	Y	N/A	Y	N/A	N/A	N/A	N
Kasson	IA	N/A	N/A	Y	Y	N/A	N/A	N/A	N/A	N/A
Kelley, W	PA	Y	Y	Y	Y	Y	N/A	Y	N/A	Y
Kellogg, F	MI	N	Y	Y	Y	N/A	N/A	N/A	N/A	N/A
Kellogg, O	NY	N/A	N/A	Y	Y	N/A	N/A	N/A	N/A	N/A
Kellogg, S	CT	N/A	N/A	N/A	N/A	N/A	N/A	Y	N/A	Y
Kellogg, W	IL	Y	N/A	N/A	N/A	N/A	N/A	N/A	N/A	N/A
Kellogg, W.P.	LA	N/A	N/A	N/A	N/A	N/A	N/A	Y	N/A	N/A
Kelsey	NY	N/A	N/A	N/A	N/A	N/A	N/A	N	N/A	N
Ketcham	NY	N/A	N/A	N/A	N/A	Y	N/A	Y	N/A	Y
Killinger	PA	N/A	Y	N/A	N/A	N/A	N/A	N/A	N/A	N/A
King, P	NY	Y	Y	N/A	N/A	N/A	N/A	N/A	N/A	N/A
Kirkwood	IA	N/A	N/A	N/A	N/A	N/A	N/A	N/A	N/A	N/A
Knapp	NY	N/A	N/A	N/A	N/A	N/A	N/A	Y	N/A	Y
Koontz	PA	N/A	N/A	N/A	N/A	N/A	N/A	N/A	N/A	N/A
Kuykendall	IL	N/A	N/A	N/A	N/A	Y	N/A	N/A	N/A	N/A
Laflin	NY	N/A	N/A	N/A	N/A	N/A	N/A	Y	N/A	Y
Lane, H	IN	Y	Y	N/A	N/A	N/A	N/A	N/A	N/A	N/A
Lane, J	KS	N/A	N/A	N/A	N/A	N/A	N/A	N/A	N/A	N/A
Lansing	NY	Y	Y	N/A	N/A	N/A	N/A	N/A	N/A	N/A
Lash	NC	N/A	N/A	N/A	N/A	N/A	N/A	N	N/A	N
Lawrence, G	PA	N/A	N/A	N/A	N/A	Y	N/A	N/A	N/A	N/A
Lawrence, W	OH	N/A	N/A	N/A	N/A	Y	N/A	Y	N/A	N
Lewis	VA	N/A	N/A	N/A	N/A	N/A	N/A	N/A	N/A	N
Littlejohn	NY	N/A	N/A	N/A	N	N/A	N/A	N/A	N/A	N/A
Loan	MO	N/A	N/A	Y	Y	Y	N/A	N/A	N/A	N/A
Logan	IL	N/A	N/A	N/A	N/A	N/A	N/A	N	N/A	Y
Long, J	GA	N/A	N/A	N/A	N/A	N/A	N/A	N/A	N/A	Y

Longyear	MI	N/A	N/A	Y	Y	Y	N/A	N/A	N/A	N/A
Loomis	CT	Y	Y	N/A	N/A	N/A	N/A	N/A	N/A	N/A
Loughridge	IA	N/A	N/A	N/A	N/A	N/A	N/A	N	N/A	N
Lovejoy	IL	N	Y	N/A	N/A	N/A	N/A	N/A	N/A	N/A
Low	CA	N/A	N/A	N/A	N/A	N/A	N/A	N/A	N/A	N/A
Lynch	ME	N/A	N/A	N/A	N/A	Y	N/A	Y	N/A	Y
Marquette	NE	N/A	N/A	N/A	N/A	N/A	N/A	N/A	N/A	N/A
Marston	NH	N/A	N/A	N/A	N/A	Y	N/A	N/A	N/A	N/A
Marvin	NY	N/A	N/A	Y	Y	Y	N/A	N/A	N/A	N/A
Maynard	TN	N/A	N/A	N/A	N/A	N/A	N/A	N	N/A	N
McBride	OR	N/A	N/A	Y	Y	N/A	N/A	N/A	N/A	N/A
McCarthy	NY	N/A	N/A	N/A	N/A	N/A	N/A	Y	N/A	Y
McClurg	MO	N/A	N/A	Y	Y	Y	N/A	N/A	N/A	N/A
McCrary	IA	N/A	N/A	N/A	N/A	N/A	N/A	N	N/A	N
McDonald	AR	N/A	N/A	N/A	N/A	N/A	N/A	Y	Y	N/A
McGrew	WV	N/A	N/A	N/A	N/A	N/A	N/A	Y	N/A	N
McIndoe	WI	N/A	N/A	Y	N/A	N/A	N/A	N/A	N/A	N/A
McKean	NY	Y	N/A	N/A	N/A	N/A	N/A	N/A	N/A	N/A
McKee	KY	N/A	N/A	N/A	N/A	Y	N/A	N/A	N/A	N
McKnight	PA	Y	Y	N/A	N/A	N/A	N/A	N/A	N/A	N/A
McPherson	PA	Y	Y	N/A	N/A	N/A	N/A	N/A	N/A	N/A
McRuer	CA	N/A	N/A	N/A	N/A	Y	N/A	N/A	N/A	N/A
Mercur	PA	N/A	N/A	N/A	N/A	Y	N/A	N	N/A	N
Miller, G	PA	N/A	N/A	N/A	N/A	N/A	N/A	N/A	N/A	N/A
Miller, S	NY	N/A	N/A	Y	Y	N/A	N/A	N/A	N/A	N/A
Mitchell, W	IN	Y	Y	N/A	N/A	N/A	N/A	N/A	N/A	N/A
Moore, E	OH	N/A	N/A	N/A	N/A	N/A	N/A	N	N/A	N
Moore, J	IL	N/A	N/A	N/A	N/A	N/A	N/A	N	N/A	N
Moore, W	NJ	N/A	N/A	N/A	N/A	N/A	N/A	Y	N/A	Y
Moorhead	PA	Y	Y	Y	Y	Y	N/A	N/A	N/A	N/A
Morey	LA	N/A	N/A	N/A	N/A	N/A	N/A	N/A	N/A	Y
Morgan, E	NY	N/A	N/A	N/A	N/A	N/A	N/A	N/A	N/A	N/A
Morphis	MS	N/A	N/A	N/A	N/A	N/A	N/A	N	N/A	N
Morrell	PA	N/A	N/A	N/A	N/A	N/A	N/A	Y	N/A	Y
Morrill, A	ME	Y	Y	N/A	N/A	N/A	N/A	N/A	N/A	N/A
Morrill, J	VT	Y	Y	Y	Y	Y	N/A	N	N	N/A

Name	State									
Morrill, L	ME	Y	Y	N/A	N/A	N/A	N/A	N/A	N/A	N/A
Morrill, S	ME	N/A	N/A	N/A	N/A	N/A	N/A	N	N/A	N
Morris, D	NY	N/A	N/A	Y	Y	Y	N/A	N/A	N/A	N/A
Morris, E	PA	N	N/A	N/A	N/A	N/A	N/A	N/A	N/A	N/A
Morton	IN	N/A	N/A	N/A	N/A	N/A	N/A	N	N/A	N/A
Mott	NV	N/A	N/A	N/A	N/A	N/A	N/A	N/A	N/A	N/A
Moulton	IL	N/A	N/A	N/A	N/A	N/A	N/A	N/A	N/A	N/A
Myers, A	PA	N/A	N/A	Y	Y	N/A	N/A	N/A	N/A	N/A
Myers, L	PA	N/A	N/A	Y	Y	N/A	N/A	Y	N/A	Y
Negley	PA	N/A	N/A	N/A	N/A	N/A	N/A	Y	N/A	Y
Newell	NJ	N/A	N/A	N/A	N/A	N/A	N/A	N/A	N/A	N/A
Newsham	LA	N/A	N/A	N/A	N/A	N/A	N/A	Y	N/A	N/A
Nixon	NJ	N/A	Y	N/A	N/A	N/A	N/A	N/A	N/A	N/A
Noell	MO	N/A	N/A	N/A	N/A	N/A	N/A	N/A	N/A	N/A
Norton, D	MN	N/A	N/A	N/A	N/A	N/A	N/A	N/A	N/A	N/A
Norton, J	IL	N/A	N/A	Y	Y	N/A	N/A	N/A	N/A	N/A
Nye	NV	N/A	N/A	N/A	N/A	N/A	N/A	N	N/A	N/A
Olin	NY	N/A	Y	N/A	N/A	N/A	N/A	N/A	N/A	N/A
O'Neill	PA	N/A	N/A	Y	Y	Y	N/A	Y	N/A	Y
Orth	IN	N/A	N/A	Y	Y	Y	N/A	Y	N/A	N/A
Osborn	FL	N/A	N/A	N/A	N/A	N/A	N/A	N/A	Y	N/A
Packard	PA	N/A	N/A	N/A	N/A	N/A	N/A	N	N/A	N
Packer	PA	N/A	N/A	N/A	N/A	N/A	N/A	Y	N/A	N
Paine	WI	N/A	N/A	N/A	N/A	Y	N/A	N	N/A	N
Palmer	IA	N/A	N/A	N/A	N/A	N/A	N/A	N/A	N/A	N
Patterson	NH	N/A	N/A	Y	N/A	Y	N/A	N	N	N/A
Patton	PA	N/A	Y	N/A	N/A	N/A	N/A	N/A	N/A	N/A
Peck	OH	N/A	N/A	N/A	N/A	N/A	N/A	N	N/A	N
Perce	MS	N/A	N/A	N/A	N/A	N/A	N/A	Y	N/A	N
Perea	NM	N/A	N/A	N/A	N/A	N/A	N/A	N/A	N/A	N/A
Perham	ME	N/A	N/A	Y	Y	Y	N/A	N/A	N/A	N/A
Peters	ME	N/A	N/A	N/A	N/A	N/A	N/A	Y	N/A	N/A
Phelps, D	PA	N/A	N/A	N/A	N/A	N/A	N/A	N	N/A	N
Phelps, T	CA	N/A	Y	N/A	N/A	N/A	N/A	N/A	N/A	N/A
Pike	ME	N/A	Y	Y	Y	Y	N/A	N/A	N/A	N/A
Plants	OH	N/A	N/A	N/A	N/A	N/A	N/A	N/A	N/A	N/A

Platt	VA	N/A	N/A	N/A	N/A	N/A	N/A	N/A	N/A	N
Poland	VT	N/A	N/A	N/A	N/A	N/A	N/A	N/A	N/A	N
Pomeroy, C	IA	N/A	N/A	N/A	N/A	N/A	N/A	N	N/A	N
Pomeroy, S	KS	N/A	Y	Y	N/A	N/A	N/A	Y	Y	N/A
Pomeroy, T	NY	Y	Y	Y	Y	N/A	N/A	N/A	N/A	N/A
Pool	NC	N/A	N/A	N/A	N/A	N/A	N/A	N	N/A	N/A
Porter, A	IN	N	Y	N/A	N/A	N/A	N/A	N/A	N/A	N/A
Poston	AZ	N/A	N/A	N/A	N/A	N/A	N/A	N/A	N/A	N/A
Potter	WI	Y	Y	N/A	N/A	N/A	N/A	N/A	N/A	N/A
Porter, C	VA	N/A	N/A	N/A	N/A	N/A	N/A	Y	N/A	N
Pratt	IN	N/A	N/A	N/A	N/A	N/A	N/A	N/A	N	N/A
Price	IA	N/A	N/A	Y	Y	Y	N/A	N/A	N/A	N
Prosser	TN	N/A	N/A	N/A	N/A	N/A	N/A	Y	N/A	N
Rainey	SC	N/A	N/A	N/A	N/A	N/A	N/A	N/A	N/A	N
Ramsey	MN	N/A	N/A	Y	N/A	N/A	N/A	N	N	N/A
Raymond	NY	N/A	N/A	N/A	N/A	N/A	N/A	N/A	N/A	N/A
Revels	MS	N/A	N/A	N/A	N/A	N/A	N/A	Y	N/A	N/A
Rice, A	MA	Y	Y	Y	Y	Y	N/A	N/A	N/A	N/A
Rice, B	AR	N/A	N/A	N/A	N/A	N/A	N/A	N	Y	N/A
Rice, J	ME	Y	Y	Y	Y	Y	N/A	N/A	N/A	N/A
Riddle	OH	Y	Y	N/A	N/A	N/A	N/A	N/A	N/A	N/A
Robertson	SC	N/A	N/A	N/A	N/A	N/A	N/A	Y	N/A	N/A
Rollins	NH	Y	Y	Y	Y	Y	N/A	N/A	N/A	N/A
Roots	AR	N/A	N/A	N/A	N/A	N/A	N/A	N	N/A	N
Ross, E	KS	N/A	N/A	N/A	N/A	N/A	N/A	N	N/A	N/A
Sanford	NY	N/A	N/A	N/A	N/A	N/A	N/A	N/A	N/A	Y
Sargent	CA	N/A	Y	N/A	N/A	N/A	N/A	Y	N/A	Y
Sawyer, F	SC	N/A	N/A	N/A	N/A	N/A	N/A	N	N	N/A
Sawyer, P	WI	N/A	N/A	N/A	N/A	Y	N/A	Y	N/A	N
Schenck	OH	N/A	N/A	Y	Y	Y	N/A	N	N/A	N/A
Schurz	MO	N/A	N/A	N/A	N/A	N/A	N/A	N	N/A	N/A
Scofield	PA	N/A	N/A	Y	N/A	Y	N/A	Y	N/A	N/A
Scott	PA	N/A	N/A	N/A	N/A	N/A	N/A	Y	Y	N/A
Scranton	PA	N/A	N/A	N/A	N/A	N/A	N/A	N/A	N/A	N/A
Sedgwick	NY	Y	N/A	N/A	N/A	N/A	N/A	N/A	N/A	N/A
Shanks	IN	N	Y	N/A	N/A	N/A	N/A	N/A	N/A	N

Shannon	CA	N/A	N/A	Y	Y	N/A	N/A	N/A	N/A	N/A
Sheffield	RI	Y	Y	N/A	N/A	N/A	N/A	N/A	N/A	N/A
Sheldon, L	LA	N/A	N/A	N/A	N/A	N/A	N/A	N	N/A	Y
Sheldon, P	NY	N/A	N/A	N/A	N/A	N/A	N/A	Y	N/A	N
Shellabarger	OH	Y	Y	N/A	N/A	Y	N/A	N/A	N/A	N/A
Sherman, J	OH	Y	N/A	N/A	N/A	N/A	N/A	N	N	N/A
Sherman, S	NY	Y	Y	N/A	N/A	N/A	N/A	N/A	N/A	N/A
Simmons, J	RI	Y	Y	N/A	N/A	N/A	N/A	N/A	N/A	N/A
Sloan	WI	N/A	Y	Y	Y	N/A	N/A	N/A	N/A	N/A
Smith, J	OH	N/A	N/A	N/A	N/A	N/A	N/A	N	N/A	N
Smith, Wi	IA	N/A	N/A	N/A	N/A	N/A	N/A	N	N/A	N
Smith, Wo	VT	N/A	N/A	N/A	N/A	N/A	N/A	Y	N/A	Y
Smithers	DE	N/A	N/A	N/A	Y	N/A	N/A	N/A	N/A	N/A
Smyth	IA	N/A	N/A	N/A	N/A	N/A	N/A	N	N/A	N/A
Spalding	OH	N/A	N/A	Y	Y	Y	N/A	N/A	N/A	N/A
Spaulding	NY	Y	Y	N/A	N/A	N/A	N/A	N/A	N/A	N/A
Spencer	AL	N/A	N/A	N/A	N/A	N/A	N/A	N	N	N/A
Spink	DK	N/A	N/A	N/A	N/A	N/A	N/A	N/A	N/A	N/A
Sprague	RI	N/A	N/A	N/A	N/A	N/A	N/A	N/A	N	N/A
Starkweather	CT	N/A	N/A	N/A	N/A	N/A	N/A	Y	N/A	Y
Starr	NJ	N/A	N/A	N/A	N/A	N/A	N/A	N/A	N/A	N/A
Stearns	MN	N/A	N/A	N/A	N/A	N/A	N/A	N/A	N	N/A
Stevens, A	NH	N/A	N/A	N/A	N/A	N/A	N/A	N/A	N/A	N
Stevens, T	PA	Y	Y	Y	Y	Y	N/A	N/A	N/A	N/A
Stevenson	OH	N/A	N/A	N/A	N/A	N/A	N/A	Y	N/A	Y
Stewart	NV	N/A	N/A	N/A	N/A	N/A	N/A	Y	Y	N/A
Stilwell	IN	N/A	N/A	N/A	N/A	Y	N/A	N/A	N/A	N/A
Stokes	TN	N/A	N/A	N/A	N/A	N/A	N/A	N	N/A	N
Stoughton	MI	N/A	N/A	N/A	N/A	N/A	N/A	N	N/A	N
Stratton	NJ	Y	Y	N/A	N/A	N/A	N/A	N/A	N/A	N/A
Strickland	MI	N/A	N/A	N/A	N/A	N/A	N/A	N	N/A	N
Strong	CT	N/A	N/A	N/A	N/A	N/A	N/A	Y	N/A	Y
Sumner	MA	Y	Y	Y	N/A	N/A	N/A	Y	Y	N/A
Sypher	LA	N/A	N/A	N/A	N/A	N/A	N/A	N/A	N/A	N/A
Taffe	NE	N/A	N/A	N/A	N/A	N/A	N/A	N/A	N/A	N
Tanner	NY	N/A	N/A	N/A	N/A	N/A	N/A	Y	N/A	N

Taylor	PA	N/A	N/A	N/A	N/A	N/A	N/A	Y	N/A	Y
Ten Eyck	NJ	Y	Y	Y	N/A	N/A	N/A	N/A	N/A	N/A
Thayer, J	NE	N/A	N/A	N/A	N/A	Y	N/A	N/A	N/A	N/A
Thayer, M	PA	N/A	N/A	Y	Y	N/A	N/A	N/A	N/A	N/A
Thomas, F	MD	N/A	Y	Y	Y	N/A	N/A	N/A	N/A	N/A
Tillman	TN	N/A	N/A	N/A	N/A	N/A	N/A	N	N/A	N
Tipton	NE	N/A	N/A	N/A	N/A	N/A	N/A	N/A	N	N/A
Townsend	PA	N/A	N/A	N/A	N/A	N/A	N/A	Y	N/A	N
Tracy	PA	N/A	N/A	N/A	Y	N/A	N/A	N/A	N/A	N/A
Train	MA	Y	Y	N/A	N/A	N/A	N/A	N/A	N/A	N/A
Trimble	OH	N/A	N/A	N/A	N/A	N/A	N/A	N/A	N/A	N/A
Trowbridge	MI	N	Y	N/A	N/A	Y	N/A	N/A	N/A	N/A
Twichell	MA	N/A	N/A	N/A	N/A	N/A	N/A	Y	N/A	Y
Tyner	IN	N/A	N/A	N/A	N/A	N/A	N/A	N	N/A	N
Upson, C	MI	N/A	N/A	Y	Y	Y	N/A	N/A	N/A	N/A
Upson, W	OH	N/A	N/A	N/A	N/A	N/A	N/A	Y	N/A	Y
Van Aernam	NY	N/A	N/A	N/A	N/A	Y	N/A	N/A	N/A	N/A
Van Horn, B	NY	Y	Y	N/A	N/A	Y	N/A	N/A	N/A	N/A
Van Horn, R	MO	N/A	N/A	N/A	N/A	N/A	N/A	N	N/A	N/A
Van Valkenburgh	NY	N/A	Y	N/A	Y	N/A	N/A	N/A	N/A	N/A
Van Winkle	WV	N/A	N/A	Y	N/A	N/A	N/A	N/A	N/A	N/A
Van Wyck	NY	Y	N/A	N/A	N/A	N/A	N/A	N/A	N/A	Y
Vandever	IA	N	N/A	N/A	N/A	N/A	N/A	N/A	N/A	N/A
Verree	PA	N/A	Y	N/A	N/A	N/A	N/A	N/A	N/A	N/A
Wade	OH	Y	Y	N/A	N/A	N/A	N/A	N/A	N/A	N/A
Wadsworth	KY	N	Y	N/A	N/A	N/A	N/A	N/A	N/A	N/A
Walker	MA	N/A	N/A	N/A	N/A	N/A	N/A	N/A	N/A	N/A
Wall	NY	Y	N/A	N/A	N/A	N/A	N/A	N/A	N/A	N/A
Wallace, A	SC	N/A	N/A	N/A	N/A	N/A	N/A	N	N/A	N
Wallace, J	PA	Y	Y	N/A	N/A	N/A	N/A	N/A	N/A	N/A
Wallace, W	WA	N/A	N/A	N/A	N/A	N/A	N/A	N/A	N/A	N/A
Wallace, William	ID	N/A	N/A	N/A	N/A	N/A	N/A	N/A	N/A	N/A
Walton, C	ME	N	N/A	N/A	N/A	N/A	N/A	N/A	N/A	N/A
Walton, E	VT	Y	Y	N/A	N/A	N/A	N/A	N/A	N/A	N/A
Ward, H	NY	N/A	N/A	N/A	N/A	Y	N/A	N	N/A	N/A

Warner, S	CT	N/A	N/A	N/A	N/A	N/A	N/A	N/A	N/A	N/A
Warner, W	AL	N/A	N/A	N/A	N/A	N/A	N/A	N	N	N/A
Washburn, C	WI	N/A	N/A	N/A	N/A	N/A	N/A	N/A	N/A	N
Washburn, W	MA	N/A	N/A	Y	Y	Y	N/A	Y	N/A	Y
Washburne	IL	Y	N/A	Y	Y	Y	N/A	N/A	N/A	N/A
Watts	NM	N/A	N/A	N/A	N/A	N/A	N/A	N/A	N/A	N/A
Welker	OH	N/A	N/A	N/A	N/A	Y	N/A	Y	N/A	N
Wentworth	IL	N/A	N/A	N/A	N/A	N/A	N/A	N/A	N/A	N/A
Whaley	WV	N/A	N/A	N/A	Y	N/A	N/A	N/A	N/A	N/A
Wheeler	NY	Y	Y	N/A	N/A	N/A	N/A	Y	N/A	Y
White, A	IN	Y	Y	N/A	N/A	N/A	N/A	N/A	N/A	N/A
Whiteley	GA	N/A	N/A	N/A	N/A	N/A	N/A	N/A	N/A	N/A
Whitmore	TX	N/A	N/A	N/A	N/A	N/A	N/A	N/A	N/A	N
Whittemore	SC	N/A	N/A	N/A	N/A	N/A	N/A	N/A	N/A	N/A
Wilder	KS	N/A	N/A	Y	Y	N/A	N/A	N/A	N/A	N/A
Wilkinson	MN	Y	N/A	N/A	N/A	N/A	N/A	N	N/A	N/A
Willard	VT	N/A	N/A	N/A	N/A	N/A	N/A	N	N/A	N
Willey	WV	N/A	N/A	Y	N/A	N/A	N/A	N	N	N/A
Williams, G	OR	N/A	N/A	N/A	N/A	N/A	N/A	N	N	N/A
Williams, T	PA	N/A	N/A	Y	Y	Y	N/A	N/A	N/A	N/A
Williams, W	IN	N/A	N/A	N/A	N/A	N/A	N/A	N	N/A	N
Wilmot	PA	Y	Y	N/A	N/A	N/A	N/A	N/A	N/A	N/A
Wilson, H	MA	Y	Y	Y	N/A	N/A	N/A	Y	N	N/A
Wilson, Ja	IA	N/A	Y	Y	Y	Y	N/A	N/A	N/A	N/A
Wilson, Jo	OH	N/A	N/A	N/A	N/A	N/A	N/A	Y	N/A	N
Wilson, S	PA	N/A	N/A	N/A	N/A	N/A	N/A	N/A	N/A	N/A
Winans	OH	N/A	N/A	N/A	N/A	N/A	N/A	Y	N/A	Y
Windom	MN	N	Y	Y	Y	Y	N/A	N/A	N/A	N/A
Witcher	WV	N/A	N/A	N/A	N/A	N/A	N/A	N	N/A	N
Wolf	IA	N/A	N/A	N/A	N/A	N/A	N/A	N/A	N/A	N
Woodbridge	VT	N/A	N/A	N/A	N	Y	N/A	N/A	N/A	N/A
Worcester	OH	Y	Y	N/A	N/A	N/A	N/A	N/A	N/A	N/A
Worthington	NV	N/A	N/A	N/A	Y	N/A	N/A	N/A	N/A	N/A
Yates	IL	N/A	N/A	N/A	N/A	N/A	N/A	N/A	Y	N/A

TABLE 2: YEAS AND NAYS OF REPUBLICANS ON EACH TAX BILL

Bill	Yeas	Yeas %	Nays	Nays %
H.R.71 (1861)	94	82	20	18
H.R.312 (1862)	114	99	1^	1
H.R.405 (1864)	98	100	0	0
H.R.744 (1865)	80	96	3	4
H.R.513 (1866)	95	100	0	0
H.R.1161 (1867)	*	*	*	*
H.R.2045 (1870)	91	50	90	50
H.R.1083 (1871)	20	48	22	52
H.R.2994 (1871)	55	37	95	63

TABLE 3: H.R. 71 (1861): STATISTICS BY REGION

Region	Yeas	Yeas %	Nays	Nays %
Northeast	65	94	4	6
Midwest	29	69	13	21
South	0	0	2	100
West	0	0	1	100

TABLE 4: H.R. 312 (1862): STATISTICS BY REGION

Region	Yeas	Yeas %	Nays	Nays %
Northeast	69	99	1^	1
Midwest	39	100	0	0
South	3	100	0	0
West	3	100	0	0

TABLE 5: H.R. 405 (1864): STATISTICS BY REGION

Region	Yeas	Yeas %	Nays	Nays %
Northeast	51	100	0	0
Midwest	36	100	0	0
South	7	100	0	0
West	4	100	0	0

TABLE 6: H.R. 744 (1865): STATISTICS BY REGION

Region	Yeas	Yeas %	Nays	Nays %
Northeast	45	94	3	6
Midwest	25	100	0	0
South	5	100	0	0
West	5	100	0	0

TABLE 7: H.R. 513 (1866): STATISTICS BY REGION

Region	Yeas	Yeas %	Nays	Nays %
Northeast	46	100	0	0
Midwest	43	100	0	0
South	3	100	0	0
West	3	100	0	0

TABLE 8: H.R. 2045 (1870): STATISTICS BY REGION

Region	Yeas	Yeas %	Nays	Nays %
Northeast	49	72	19	28
Midwest	15	27	41	73
South	22	44	28	56
West	5	71	2	29

TABLE 9: H.R. 1083 (1871): STATISTICS BY REGTION

Region	Yeas	Yeas %	Nays	Nays %
Northeast	7	54	6	46
Midwest	3	21	11	79
South	6	55	5	45
West	4	100	0	0

TABLE 10: H.R. 2994 (1871): STATISTICS BY REGION

Region	Yeas	Yeas %	Nays	Nays %
Northeast	37	63	22	37
Midwest	7	14	43	86
South	9	23	30	77
West	2	100	0	0

*No votes were recorded in the Congressional Globe, only that the bill was passed.
^Only no vote was Buffinton (MA)

Bibliography

Primary Sources - Books

Andersen, Elmer L. *A Man's Reach*. Minneapolis: University of Minnesota Press, 2000.

Armey, Dick. *The Freedom Revolution: The New Republican House Majority Leader Tells Why Big Government Failed, Why Freedom Works, and How We Will Rebuild America*. Washington, D.C.: Regnery Publishing, 1995.

Baker, James A. III. With Steve Fiffer. "Work Hard, Study...and Keep Out of Politics!" *Adventures and Lessons from an Unexpected Public Life*. New York: G.P. Putnam's Sons, 2006.

Basler, Roy P. ed. *The Collected Works of Abraham Lincoln*. Eight volumes. New Brunswick: Rutgers University Press, 1953.

Brooks, Preston. "In Defense of His Attack on Sumner." 22 August 2009, http://www.bartleby. com / 268/9/15.html.

Brown, Henry James and Frederick D. Williams. eds. *The Diary of James Garfield: Volume IV*. East Lansing: Michigan State University Press, 1981.

Brownback, Sam. *Speech at the Ames Straw Poll*. 10 August 2007.

Buchanan, Patrick J. *Right From the Beginning*. Boston: Little, Brown and Company, 1988.

Bush, George H.W. Speech to the 1988 Republican National Convention. 18 August 1988.

Bush, George W. *A Charge to Keep*. New York: William Morrow and Company, 1999.

Cheney, Dick. Speech to the 2000 Republican National Convention. 2 August 2000.

D'Amato, Al. *Power, Pasta and Politics: The World According to Senator Al D'Amato*. New York: Hyperion, 1995.

Davis, Jefferson. *1st Inaugural Address*. 18 February 1861.

Delay, Tom with Stephen Mansfield. *No Retreat, No Surrender: One American's Fight*. New York: Sentinel, 2007.

Dole, Robert. Speech to the 1996 Republican National Convention. 15 August 1996.

Fessenden, Francis. *The Life and Public Services of William Pitt Fessenden: United States Senator From Maine 1854-1864; Secretary of the Treasury 1864-1865; United States Senator From Maine 1865-1869*. vol. II. Boston: Houghton, Mifflin and Company, 1907.

Ford, Gerald R. Speech to the 1976 Republican National Convention. 19 August 1976.

Franks, Congressmen Gary. *Searching for the Promised Land: An African American's Optimistic Odyssey*. New York: Regan Books, 1996.

Giddings, Joshua and Salmon P. Chase. *Appeal of the Independent Democrats in Congress to the People of the United States*. 15 January 1854.

Gingrich, Newt. *Lessons Learned the Hard Way: A Personal Report*. New York: Harper-Collins Publishers, 1998.

Goldwater, Barry M. *The Conscience of a Conservative*. New York: McFadden Books, 1960.

Gollagher, Elsie. ed. *The Quotable Dwight D. Eisenhower*. New York: Droke House, 1967.

Grant, Ulysses S. Report of Major General U.S. Grant on the Battle of Shiloh. 9 April 1862.

Hall, Perry D. *The Quotable Richard M. Nixon*. New York: Droke House, 1967.

Hamilton, Alexander, James Madison and John Jay. *The Federalist Papers*. Cutchogue: Buccaneer Books, 1992.

Hastert, Denny. Speaker: Lessons From Forty Years in Coaching and Politics. Washington, D.C.: Regnery Publishing, 2004.

Helms, Senator Jesse. *Here's Where I Stand: A Memoir*. New York: Random House, 2005.

Huckabee, Mike. *Super Tuesday Speech*. 5 February 2008.

Jeffords, Senator Jim with Yvonne Daley and Howard Coffin. *An Independent Man: Adventures of a Public Servant*. New York: Simon and Schuster, 2003.

Kemp, Jack. Speech to the 1996 Republican National Convention. 14 August 1996.

Lee, Robert E. *Farewell Address*. 10 April 1865.

Lincoln, Abraham. *1st Inaugural Address*. 4 March 1861.

———. *2nd Inaugural Address*. 4 March 1861.

_____. *Emancipation Proclamation.* 1 January, 1863.

_____. *Gettysburg Address.* 19 November 1863.

McCain, John. Speech to the 2008 Republican National Convention. 4 September 2008.

Niven, John. ed. The Salmon P. Chase Papers, Volume 3: Correspondence, 1858-March 1863. Kent: Kent State University Press, 1996.

_____. The Salmon P. Chase Papers, Volume 4: Correspondence 1863-1864. Kent: Kent State University Press, 1997.

Nixon, Richard. Speech to the 1972 Republican National Convention. 23 August 1972.

Norris, George W. Fighting Liberal: The Autobiography of George W. Norris. New York: The MacMillan Company, 1945.

Palin, Sarah. Speech to the 2008 Republican National Convention. 3 September 2008.

Palmer, Beverly Wilson and Holly Byers Ochoa. *The Selected Papers of Thaddeus Stevens, Volume 1: January 1814-March 1865.* Pittsburgh: University of Pittsburgh Press, 1997.

Pataki, George E. with Daniel Paisner. *Pataki: An Autobiography.* New York: Viking, 1998.

Quayle, Dan. Standing Firm: A Vice Presidential Memoir. New York: HarperCollins Publishers, 1994.

Reagan, Ronald. *An American Life.* New York: Simon & Schuster, 1990.

_____. Speech to the 1980 Republican National Convention. 17 July 1980.

Romney, Mitt. Speech to the Conservative Political Action Committee. 7 February 2008.

Seward, William. "Higher Law." 22 August 2009. http://history.furman.edu/-benson/docs/seward.htm.

Sherman, John. John Sherman's Recollections of Forty Years in the House, Senate and Cabinet: *An Autobiography. Vol. 1.* Chicago: The Werner Company, 1895.

Specter, Senator Arlen with Charles Robbins. *Passion for Truth: From Finding JFK's Single Bullet to Questioning Anita Hill to Impeaching Bill Clinton.* New York: William Morrow, 2000.

Watts, J.C., Jr. with Chris Winston. *What Color is a Conservative?: My Life and My Politics.* New York: HarperCollins Publishing, 2002.

Weicker, Lowell Jr. with Barry Sussman. *Maverick: A Life in Politics.* Boston: Little, Brown and Company, 1995.

Whitman, Christine Todd. *It's My Party Too: The Battle for the Heart of the GOP and the Future of America*. New York: The Penguin Press, 2005.

Wilste, Charles M. and Alan R. Berolzheimer. eds. *The Papers of Daniel Webster: Speeches and Formal Writings, Volume 2 1834-1852*. Hanover: University Press of New England, 1988.

Documents

Free Soil Party Platform, 1852.

George Romney for President 1968. Campaign Brochure.

Report of the Commissioner of Internal Revenue for 1864. Washington, D.C.: 1865.

Report of the Commissioner of Internal Revenue for the Year Ending June 30, 1869. Washington, D.C.: 1869.

Report of the Secretary of Treasury for the Year 1861. Washington, D.C.: 1861.

Republican Party Platform, 1860.

Republican Party Platform, 1920.

Republican Party Platform, 1924.

Republican Party Platform, 1940.

Republican Party Platform, 1944.

Republican Party Platform, 1956.

Republican Party Platform, 1964.

Republican Party Platform, 1968.

Republican Party Platform, 1976.

Republican Party Platform, 1988.

Republican Party Platform, 1996.

Republican Party Platform, 2008.

South Carolina Ordinance of Secession. 20 December 1860.

The Congressional Globe: Official Proceedings of Congress, 31st Congress, 1st Session. Washington, D.C.: John C. Rives, 1850.

The Congressional Globe: Official Proceedings of Congress, 37th Congress, 1st Session. Washington, D.C.: John C. Rives, 1861.

The Congressional Globe: Official Proceedings of Congress, 37th Congress, 2nd Session. Washington, D.C.: John C. Rives, 1862.

The Congressional Globe: Official Proceedings of Congress, 38th Congress, 1st Session. Washington, D.C.: John C. Rives, 1864.

The Congressional Globe: Official Proceedings of Congress, 38th Congress, 2nd Session. Washington, D.C.: John C. Rives, 1865.

The Congressional Globe: Official Proceedings of Congress, 39th Congress, 1st Session. Washington, D.C.: John C. Rives, 1866.

The Congressional Globe: Official Proceedings of Congress, 39th Congress, 2nd Session. Washington, D.C.: John C. Rives, 1867.

The Congressional Globe: Official Proceedings of Congress, 41st Congress, 2nd Session. Washington, D.C.: John C. Rives, 1870.

The Congressional Globe: Official Proceedings of Congress, 41st Congress, 3rd Session. Washington, D.C.: John C. Rives, 1871.

The Congressional Record Containing the Proceedings and Debates of the 53rd Congress, 3rd Session. Vol. 26. Washington, D.C.: John C. Rives, 1894.

ARTICLES

"Abolish the Income Tax." *Pittsfield Sun*, 31 January 1867.

"Abolition of the Income Tax." *Trenton State Gazette*, 25 June 1870.

"Anti-Income Tax, Address to the People of the United States." *San Francisco Bulletin*, 22 April 1871.

"Congress and the Income Tax." *New York Times*, 27 January 1870.

"Down with the Taxes; Formation of an Anti-income Tax Association, Organization and Address to the Public." *New York Times*, 30 March 1871.

"The Financial Question." *The Sun*, 1 March 1865.

"Income Tax." *Galveston News*, 21 January 1870.

"Income Tax." *Macon Weekly Telegraph*, 25 April 1871.

"Income Tax." *The Crisis*, 10 September 1862.

"Inequality of the Income Tax." *Daily Iowa State Register*, 7 January 1868.

"Invalidity of the Income Tax Law." *Salt Lake Daily Telegraph*, 28 May 1868.

"Laus Deo!" *Weekly Journal Miner*, 16 July 1870.

"New feature in the Income Tax." *Weekly Arizona Miner*, 17 June 1871.

"Reduction of Income Tax." *San Francisco Bulletin*, 27 February 1867.

"Report of the Secretary of Treasury." *New York Times*, 7 December 1864.

"Republican, Radical." *Columbus Daily Enquirer*, 26 February 1870.

"Some Suggestions in Regard to Direct Taxation-An Income Tax." *New York Times*, 26 July 1861.

"Tax and Revenue." *Trenton State Gazette*, 3 December 1869.

"Taxation in Rebeldom." *Philadelphia Inquirer*, 17 March 1865.

"The Coming Era of Taxation." *San Francisco Bulletin*, 31 May 1862.

"The Income Tax." *Eastern Argus*, 26 January 1871.

"The Income Tax." *Flake's Bulletin*, 1 December 1869.

"The Income Tax." *Flake's Bulletin*, 4 May 1870.

"The Income Tax." *Houston Daily Union*, 16 April 1870.

"The Income Tax." *Idaho Statesman*, 17 February 1870.

"The Income Tax." *Idaho Statesman*, 30 April 1870.

"The Income Tax." *Macon Weekly Telegraph*, 30 July 1869.

"The Income Tax." *Morning Republican*, 8 February 1870.

"The Income Tax." *New Hampshire Patriot*, 28 December 1870.

"The Income Tax." *New Hampshire Sentinel*, 15 December 1870.

"The Income Tax." *New York Times*, 19 January 1871.

"The Income Tax." *Owyhee Avalanche*, 27 January 1870.

"The Income Tax." *Pomeroy's Democrat*, 8 February 1871.

"The Income Tax." *Philadelphia Inquirer*, 3 December 1869.

"The Income Tax," *Philadelphia Inquirer*, 13 December 1869.

"The Income Tax." *Philadelphia Inquirer*, 5 December 1872.

"The Income Tax." *San Francisco Bulletin*, 25 March 1870.

"The Income Tax." *The Sun*, 13 April 1868.

"The Income Tax," *The Sun*, 16 December 1869.

"The Income Tax." *The Sun*, 23 January 1871.

"The Income Tax." *The Sun*, 4 January 1872.

"The Income Tax." *The Weekly Patriot and Union*, 14 May 1863.

"The Income Tax." *Weekly Patriot and Union*, 16 December 1869.

"The Income Tax and Its Illegality." *Flake's Bulletin*, 15 May 1868.

"The Income Tax law Repealed." *New York Herald*, 9 March 1870.

"The Income Tax: The Argument before the Committee of Ways and Means." *Times Picayune*, 1 February 1872.

"The Income Tax — Why Not Abolish It?" *New York Herald*, 17 July 1869.

"The Internal Tax Bill." *New York Times*, 4 March 1862.

"The Rich Restive Under the Income Tax." *Minnesota Herald*, 7 May 1870.

"The Sun, the Income Tax." *Pittsfield Sun*, 2 September 1869.

"Thoughts on Taxation." *Barre Gazette*, 24 January 1862.

"Unconstitutional Legislation of Congress — Mr. Bartlett's Argument on the Income Tax." *New York Herald*, 9 April 1868.

"Unnecessary Taxes." *Weekly Patriot and Union*, 17 May 1866.

"Wasting Time." *Philadelphia Inquirer*, 9 March 1870.

SECONDARY SOURCES

Adams, Charles. *Those Dirty Rotten Taxes: The Tax Revolts that Built America.* New York: The Free Press, 1998.

Baxter, Maurice G. *Henry Clay and the American System.* Lexington: The University Press of Kentucky, 1995.

Beard, Patricia. *Growing Up Republican Christie Whitman: The Politics of Character.* New York: HarperCollins Publishers, 1996.

Blue, Frederick J. *Salmon P. Chase: A Life in Politics.* Kent: Kent State University Press, 1987.

Brownlee, W. Elliot. *Federal Taxation in America: A Short History.* New York: Cambridge University Press, 1996.

Buel, C.C. and R.U. Johnson. eds. *Battles and Leaders of the Civil War.* Vol. 2. New York: T. Yoseloff, 1956.

Cannadine, David. *Mellon: An American Life.* New York: Alfred A. Knopf, 2006.

Chernow, Ron. *Alexander Hamilton.* New York: The Penguin Press, 2004.

Oates, Stephen B. *To Purge This Land With Blood: A Biography of John Brown.* New York: HarperCollins, 1970.

Current, Richard N. *Daniel Webster and the Rise of National Conservatism.* Boston: Little, Brown and Company, 1955.

Donald, David Herbert. *Charles Sumner, Part I: Charles Sumner and the Coming of the Civil War.* New York: Da Capo Press, 1996

_____. *Charles Sumner, Part II: Charles Sumner and the Rights of Man.* New York: Da Capo Press, 1996.

_____. *Lincoln.* New York: Touchstone, 1996.

Ellis, Elmer. "Public Opinion and the Income Tax, 1860-1900." *The Mississippi Valley Historical Review* 27 no. 2 (September 1940): 225-242.

Fessenden, Francis. *The Life and Public Services of William Pitt Fessenden: United States Senator From Maine 1854-1864; Secretary of the Treasury 1864-1865; United States Senator From Maine 1865-1869.* Vol. II. Boston: Houghton, Mifflin and Company, 1907.

Forbes, Steve. *Flat Tax Revolution: Using a Postcard to Abolish the IRS.* Washington, D.C.: Regnery Publishing, Inc., 2005.

Fossedal, Gregory A. *Kohler: A Political Biography of Walter J. Kohler, Jr.* New Brunswick: Transaction Publishers, 2003.

Garner, James Wilford. *Reconstruction in Mississippi.* New York: The Macmillan Company, 1901.

Gould, Lewis L. *Grand Old Party: A History of the Republicans.* New York: Random House, 2003.

Guelzo, Allen C. *The Crisis of the American Republic: A History of the Civil War and Reconstruction Era.* New York: St. Martin's Press, 1995.

Harris, Alexander. *A Review of Political Conflict in America, From the Commencement of the Anti-Slavery Agitation to the Close of Southern Reconstruction: Comprising also a Resume of the Career of Thaddeus Stevens, Being a Survey of the Struggle of Parties, Which Destroyed the Republic and Virtually Monarchized Its Government.* New York: T. H. Pollock Publishers, 1876.

Hill, Joseph A. "The Civil War Income Tax." *The Quarterly Journal of Economics* 8 no. 4 (July 1894): 416-452.

Katcher, Leo. *Earl Warren: A Political Biography.* New York: McGraw-Hill, 1967.

Kirtzman, Andrew. *Rudy Giuliani: Emperor of the City.* New York: William Morrow, 2000.

Kramer, Michael and Sam Roberts. *"I Never Wanted to be Vice-President of Anything!" An Investigative Biography of Nelson Rockefeller.* New York: Basic Books, Inc., 1976.

Leopold, Richard W. *Elihu Root and the Conservative Tradition.* Boston: Little, Brown and Company, 1954.

Mathews, Joe. *The People's Machine: Arnold Schwarzenegger and the Rise of Blockbuster Democracy.* New York: Public Affairs, 2006.

Moyer, George H. *The Republican Party 1854-1964.* New York: Oxford University Press, 1964.

Moos, Malcolm. *The Republicans: A History of Their Party.* New York: Random House, 1956.

Myers, William S. *The Republican Party: A History.* New York: Johnson Reprint Corporation, 1968.

Nivens, Allan. *Hamilton Fish.* New York: Dodd Mead, 1936.

Patterson, James T. *Mr. Republican: A Biography of Robert A. Taft.* Boston: Houghton Mifflin Company, 1972.

Peterson, Merrill D. *The Great Triumvirate: Webster, Clay, and Calhoun.* New York: Oxford University Press, 1987.

Pollack, Sheldon D. *Refinancing America: The Republican Antitax Agenda.* New York: State University of New York Press, 2003.

Ratner, Sidney. *American Taxation: Its History as a Social Force in Democracy.* New York: W.W. Norton & Company, 1942.

Richardson, Heather Cox. *The Greatest Nation of the Earth: Republican Economic Policies During the Civil War*. Cambridge: Harvard University Press, 1997.

Roland, Charles P. *An American Iliad: The Story of the Civil War*. 2nd ed. Lexington: The University Press of Kentucky, 2002.

Schecter, Cliff. The Real McCain: Why Conservatives Don't Trust Him and Why Independents *Shouldn't*. Sausalito, California: PoliPoint Press, 2008.

Seligman, Edwin Robert Anderson. "The Income Tax." *Political Science Quarterly* 9 no. 4 (December 1894): 610-648.

_____. *The Income Tax Part 2*. New York: The Macmillan Company, 1911.

Siegel, Fred with Harry Siegel. The Prince of the City: Giuliani, New York and the Genius of *American Life*. San Francisco: Encounter Books, 2005.

Sobel, Robert. *Coolidge: An American Enigma*. Washington, D.C.: Regnery Publishing, 1998.

Stanley, Robert. Dimensions of Law in the Service of Order: Origins of the Federal Income Tax, *1860-1913*. New York: Oxford University Press, 1993.

Waltman, Jerold L. *Political Origins of the U.S. Income Tax*. Oxford: University Press of Mississippi, 1985.

Weisman, Steven R. *The Great Tax Wars Lincoln to Wilson: The Fierce Battles Over Money and Power that Transformed the Nation*. New York: Simon & Schuster, 2002.

Williams, T. Harry. "Thaddeus Stevens: An American Radical." *Commentary: A Jewish Review* 21 (1956): 578-583.

Witte, John F. *The Politics and Development of the Federal Income Tax*. Madison: The University of Wisconsin Press, 1985.

WEBSITES

Bennett, Robert. "Economy and Taxes." 17 August 2009. http://bennett.senate.gov/public/ index.cfm?p=EconomyTaxes.

Bunning, Jim. "Taxes." 17 August 2009. http://bunning.senate.gov/public/index.cfm? FuseAction=IssueStatements.View&Issue_id=eaa83d9f-9117-439a-aacf-9a0a41e29c83& CFID=15585394&CFTOKEN=72812793.

Coburn, Tom. "Tax Reform." 17 August 2009. http://coburn.senate.gov/public/ index.cfm? FuseAction=Issues.View&Issue_id=d5d76b2e-7f31-4b2e-af8c-44c99728f428&CFID= 15585718&CFTOKEN=94738946.

Corker, Bob. "Fiscal Responsibility." 17 August 2009. http://corker.senate.gov/public/index.cfm?FuseAction=IssueStatements.View&Issue_

id=b3744ca7-b5a8-a5eb-fc67-c52717b9f5cb&CFID=15585884&CFTOK
EN=19972755.

Crapo, Mike. "Taxes." 17 August 2009. http://crapo.senate.gov/issues/taxes/tax.
cfm.

Demint, Jim. "Economic Growth." 22 July 2009. http://demint.sen-
ate.gov/public/index.cfm?FuseAction=Issues.Detail&Issue
_id=95633845-4058-4bc9-b441-a3f638044696.

Enzi, Mike. "Budget/Taxes." 17 August 2009. http://enzi.senate.gov/pub-
lic/index.cfm?FuseAction=IssueStatements.View&Issue_id=d69335e2-
bd22-28ee-4b26-ebc301978ad1&CFID=15586192&CFTOK
EN=91275372.

Hatch, Orrin. "Economy and Taxes." 22 July 2009. http://hatch.
senate.gov/public/index.cfm?FuseAction=IssuePositions.
View&IssuePosition_id=76682398-3614-40b4-a9a4-ac8le05cla6b.

Jindal, Bobby. "A Trillion Here, a Trillion There." *Politico.com.* 20 July 2009. Accessed 22 July 2009. http://www.politico.com/news/stories/0709/25136.html.

Johanns, Mike. "Economy and Jobs." 17 August 2009. http://johanns.senate.gov/
public/?p=EconomyJobs.

Linder, Douglas O. "The Impeachment Trial of Andrew Johnson." 7 September
2009. http://www.law.umkc.edu/faculty/projects/ftrials/impeach/imp_ac-
count2.html.

Lott, Sen. Trent. "From Theory to Fact." *GulfCoastNews.com.* 12 May 2006. Accessed 22 July 2009. http://gulfcoastnews.com/GCNopEdLottTaxes.htm.

Pence, Mike. "Economy." 17 August 2009.http://mikepence.house.gov/index.
php?option=com_content&view=article&id=1250%3Aeconomy&catid=51%
3Aissue-center&Itemid=56.

Sensenbrenner, Jim. "Economy." 17 August 2009. http://sensenbrenner.house.
gov/Issues/Issue/?IssueID=5089.

Shelby, Richard. "Taxes." 17 August 2009. http://shelby.senate.gov/
public/index.cfm?FuseAction=IssueStatements.View&Issue_
id=cf510ea2-e2cl-516c-80ce-5b99fbaa35d3&CFID=15586717&CFTOK
EN=82348717.

Thune, John. "Taxes." 17 August 2009. http://thune.sen-
ate.gov/public/index.cfm?FuseAction=Issues.
Detail&Issue_id=b55256c0-c910-4c2a-8251-a232df22bb92.

Vitter, David. "Taxes." 17 August 2009. http://vitter.senate.gov/public/ index.cfm?FuseAction=IssueStatements.View&Issue_id=3d9080b5- ab31-4070-b94d-6b6efda4e2ec&CFID=15586870&CFTOK EN=81461959.

Wicker, Roger. "Taxes." 17 August 2009. http://wicker.senate.gov/public/index. cfm?FuseAction=IssueStatements.View&Issue_id=e429918e-f67e-8ef5- 74a9-db6b3529f718&CFID=15586934&CFTOKEN=46795966. "Bond Com- ments on Tax Day & Promotes the Fair and Simple Tax Act." 17 August 2009. http://bond.senate.gov/public/index.cfm?FuseAction=PressRoom. FloorStatements&ContentRecord_id=57ed9c75-bb71-de92-43c3 204bde0ea03b&Region_id=&Issue_id=153dae89-3b23-4667-aa11- 2865ed6f2090. "CHAMBLISS, LINDER, PRICE PROMOTE FAIRTAX AT ATLANTA PRESS CONFERENCE." 3 April 2007. 17 August 2009. http:// www.chambliss.senate.gov /public/index.cfm?p=PressReleases&Conte ntRecord_id=b926ce03-802a-23ad-42a4-85493ba76a86&ContentType_ id=757b7bb6-a540-4ca5-b4ee-9040fba13700&cla81bb1-3e33-4e40-8d06- 5402ec195049&0f375d20-f53a-40ec-be62-076b5b6ca521&0a9faa4e- 93c0-4ea7-8789-f3a1af6a4b91&946091a3-c04f-730a-033e- 84400d85f615&ef1e98ff-a083-451e-ba79-99661067032c&070d7e2c- edf9-4220-a1fb-b964a76176d2&5c81ba67-be20-4229-a615-966ecb0cc- ad6&9a28c5ad-6654-46f4-afb8e502885aa68a&Group_id=a2539167-571a- 43e6-8f3f-c129d2b1fbfe.

"George McClellan." 22 August 2009. http://en.wikipedia.org/wiki/ George_B._McClellan.

"John Wilkes Booth." 6 September 2009. http://en.wikipedia.org/wiki/ John_Wilkes_BoothKansas–Nebraska

INDEX

Printed in the United States
By Bookmasters